Praise for *War Fever*

"*War Fever* brilliantly weaves together the lives of three celebrities to tell the story of how the First World War reshaped America. Richly detailed and a pleasure to read."

—Michael S. Neiberg, author of *The Path to War: How the First World War Created Modern America*

"Roberts and Smith have written a fascinating and impressive book that sheds new light on the home front during World War I by examining the lives of three men and the city they loved. The fast-paced narrative is full of colorful characters, suspense, and intrigue. Although deeply researched and full of insight, the book reads more like a suspense novel than a work of history. Valuable for both history lovers and casual readers."

—Steven M. Gillon, author of *America's Reluctant Prince: The Life of John F. Kennedy*

WAR FEVER

WAR FEVER

Boston, Baseball, and America
in the Shadow of the Great War

**RANDY ROBERTS
AND JOHNNY SMITH**

BASIC BOOKS

New York

Basic Books
Hachette Book Group
1290 Avenue of the Americas, New York, NY 10104
www.basicbooks.com

Printed in the United States of America

First Edition: March 2020

Published by Basic Books, an imprint of Perseus Books, LLC, a subsidiary of Hachette Book Group, Inc. The Basic Books name and logo is a trademark of the Hachette Book Group.

The Hachette Speakers Bureau provides a wide range of authors for speaking events. To find out more, go to www.hachettespeakersbureau.com or call (866) 376-6591.

The publisher is not responsible for websites (or their content) that are not owned by the publisher.

Print book interior design by Jeff Williams.

Library of Congress Cataloging-in-Publication Data

Names: Roberts, Randy, author. | Smith, John Matthew, author.

Title: War fever: Boston, baseball, and America in the shadow of the Great War / Randy Roberts, and Johnny Smith. Other titles: Boston, baseball, and America in the shadow of the Great War

Description: First Edition. | New York: Basic Books, 2020. | Includes bibliographical references and index.

Identifiers: LCCN 2019045871 | ISBN 9781541672666 (hardcover) | ISBN 9781541672673 (ebook)

Subjects: LCSH: World War, 1914–1918—Massachusetts—Boston. | Boston (Mass.)—History—20th century. | World War, 1914–1918—Social aspects—United States. | Muck, Karl. | Ruth, Babe, 1895-1948. | Whittlesey, Charles White, 1884-1921. | Xenophobia—Massachusetts—Boston—History—20th century. | Baseball players—Massachusetts—Boston—Biography. | Germans—Massachusetts—Boston—Biography. | United States. Army. Division, 77th—History. | Boston (Mass.)—Biography.

Classification: LCC F73.25 .R63 2020 | DDC 974.4/6104—dc23

LC record available at https://lccn.loc.gov/2019045871

ISBNs: 978-1-5416-7266-6 (hardcover), 978-1-5416-7267-3 (ebook)

LSC-C

10 9 8 7 6 5 4 3 2 1

For the grandfather I never knew and the father
I knew too briefly, but loved dearly.

Charles Henry Roberts (1897–1929)
US Army, Mexican Expeditionary Force
American Expeditionary Force, France
Northern Russia Expeditionary Force

Clifford Edwin Roberts (1923–1963)
US Navy, World War II, Pacific
—RWR

For me, Boston means baseball and bonding with
family. And Fenway Park will forever be the place
where my sister McKenna and I celebrated the joys of
being together. This book is for her.
—JMS

Only the dead have seen the end of war.

—George Santayana, 1922

Contents

Contents

PART THREE. THE FLOOD

Preface

IN 1918, A FEVER GRIPPED BOSTON. NOT SINCE THE REVOLU-
tionary War had a passion this hot consumed the city. It lurked
palpably, appearing in various forms in every neighborhood. It was
present in the half-filled classrooms and quiet streets in Cambridge,
where students huddled in groups and discussed the conflict raging in France. Bostonians heard it in Symphony Hall, where careful listeners noticed a marked decline in the Boston Symphony
Orchestra's performances since its German conductor, Karl Muck,
had been accused of spying for Germany. And they saw it at Fenway
Park, where the Red Sox honored wounded soldiers and military
bands played "The Star-Spangled Banner." The draft had robbed
the team of much of its hitting talent, forcing Babe Ruth, a star left-
handed pitcher, to play the outfield and bat as a regular. Through
it all—as the feverish crowds cheered at ball games and decried invisible enemies—another fever, a deadly pandemic, was circling the
globe, moving toward Boston.

The events that year created and destroyed celebrities, a process
that reveals much about the values, desires, and fears of the country
during the war. In *War Fever* we explore the impact of the global
conflict on three men—how it changed their lives, how it gave

In 1917, Boston Common bustled with activity. While bands played military tunes, recruiters combed the crowds looking for potential soldiers, and signs called on citizens to "Protect America's Women: It Is a Patriotic Duty." *(Courtesy of the Leslie Jones Collection, Boston Public Library.)*

them purpose, and how it dictated their legacies. Like celebrities before and since, they were as complex and contradictory as the images they projected were elemental and flat. They were as much a product of the war as James Montgomery Flagg's propaganda poster of Uncle Sam declaring, "I Want You for U.S. Army."

The men we selected, each connected to Boston in some way—Charles Whittlesey, Karl Muck, and Babe Ruth—became, in 1918, the most famous war hero, war villain, and war athlete. Nearly everything they did was interpreted through the lens of the war. In that sense, they became a product of wartime propaganda, each serving a larger political purpose. Once they had been identified and cast in the Great War Production, they were all but powerless to undo it, pawns in the hands of proselytizers and the press.

AT THE BEGINNING OF 1918, Karl Muck reigned supreme as the world-renowned maestro of the Boston Symphony Orchestra, one of the most prestigious ensembles in the United States. With an imperious manner and unshakeable confidence, the acclaimed conductor, a friend of the Kaiser's, mesmerized wealthy elites in Boston and cities throughout the country. The year before, the Victor Talking Machine Company had recorded him and the BSO, and rushed out several 78 RPM records, including selections from Tchaikovsky and Wagner. By the spring, however, Muck's career had completely unraveled. Accused of espionage for the Imperial German government, exposed as a wanton libertine, he became a victim of the anti-German hysteria whipped up by the administration of Woodrow Wilson.[1]

The Justice Department first began investigating him in October 1917, after jingoists from Providence, Rhode Island, charged that he had refused to lead the orchestra in "The Star-Spangled Banner" during a concert at Infantry Hall. Many at the time were insisting that the anthem be played at every public occasion—during military parades, before sporting events, and certainly when symphony orchestras performed. Playing or singing the anthem not only demonstrated patriotism and loyalty, it also expressed a wartime consensus, the "Gospel of Americanism."[2]

During the hysteria over German spies and saboteurs, and under the cloud of suspicion cast by Muck's supposed refusal to conduct "The Star-Spangled Banner," the BSO's performances provoked violent protests in numerous cities. Patriotic groups demanded the maestro's expulsion from the country. In the darkness of war, the BSO—with about half of its musicians from Germany and Austria—came to be seen not just as a Teutonic institution but as a threat to "100% Americanism." Muck feared the rising current of anti-German extremism. He heard rumors about violent Boston thugs rounding up his countrymen and read stories about Germans who were publicly flogged or tarred and feathered. He could imagine a day when a mob would come knocking on his door.[3]

The mob never showed up at his home, but in late March 1918 federal agents did. Investigators questioned his associates and fellow musicians, and seized his private papers. From his correspondence, they learned that his closest friends included prominent German musicians, professors, and, most notably, Germany's chief of espionage, Count Johann von Bernstorff, who had ordered attacks on American supply depots during the war. Yet they could not tie the conductor to any nefarious activity against the United States. When federal agents arrested him on March 25, the public had no idea that the government's entire case rested on "obscene" letters between Muck and his young mistress—missives that divulged his deepest secrets and desires. Armed with what the government considered incriminating evidence, US Marshals delivered him to Fort Oglethorpe, Georgia, an internment camp for German prisoners.

WHILE MUCK LANGUISHED BEHIND A barbed-wire fence, George Herman "Babe" Ruth, the son of a German-American saloon-keeper, gave little consideration to how he could help win the war or how it might change his life. Baseball, booze, and brothels occupied his thoughts. For the irrepressible young ballplayer, the Great War was something happening somewhere else, and it involved other people. It was therefore of little interest to him. By the time the Red Sox completed spring training in 1918, Babe had discovered the thrill he felt—and the joy he brought spectators—swinging a bat. He found a new purpose entertaining crowds of soldiers with his mighty "war club," launching baseballs into the ether. In the past, pitching well had reliably brought him applause—but hitting home runs, he found, made the crowd roar.

It was the Great War that made possible his eventual transformation from the game's dominant left-handed pitcher to the sport's greatest slugger. Ruth filled a need for both the Red Sox and America. "The Colossus" redefined the dimensions of the game, displaying a kind of awesome power that portended a new era to come, one where the home run proved integral. After 1918, he was no longer just a ballplayer. With a bat in his hand, he became a showman unlike any other in the history of the sport.

In the context of America's deadly attacks on the Western Front, Ruth's power took on a new meaning. Where once informed spectators viewed baseball as a scientific game of slashing singles and strategic bunts, now the violent, full-bodied swings of Ruth's bat resonated with the country's glorification of unrestrained force. During the summer of 1918, as the Babe assailed American League fences, the American Expeditionary Force assaulted German positions in France. The US offensives at Cantigny, Château-Thierry, the Marne, and especially the Meuse-Argonne were artless frontal attacks, depending more on deadly straightforward drives in which lives were sacrificed for inches of ground than any sort of imaginative tactical planning.

In Boston, war fever turned Fenway Park, a stadium built for the masses, into a stage for "preparedness." During the sport's first significant political crisis, Major League Baseball became more than a diversion; it offered a template for Americanism. The national pastime took on a new meaning in the lives of citizens who viewed sports as critical to making good soldiers and promoting the nation's ideals. Babe Ruth and his teammates, wearing full baseball uniforms, substituted bats for rifles as they conducted military maneuvers under the instruction of a drill sergeant, a demonstration of patriotism that linked the national pastime to the country's war effort. Yet all the marching and posing was for show. Like the other owners in professional baseball, Harry Frazee understood the value of draping his squad in the American flag and did everything he could to convince the public that baseball was, in the words of columnist Hugh Fullerton, "the greatest single force for Americanization."[4]

In the summer of 1918, sportswriters hardly mentioned Ruth's German heritage. Writers, fans, and ballplayers called him "Babe" almost exclusively because "George Herman" sounded too German. During the last two years of the war, when any Teutonic-sounding name provoked suspicions of disloyalty, and the phrase "German-American" became a pejorative, "the Babe" served him well. It Americanized his last name and advertised his nonthreatening personality. Privately, he spoke German on occasion among friends or at his father's Baltimore saloon, but he never said anything publicly about his ancestors. Besides, he was not German-American. He was the Babe.

KARL MUCK AND BABE RUTH were the most visible personages of Boston's highbrow and popular cultures. Newspaper editors splashed their names across the city's papers, and Bostonians closely followed their exploits. Yet it was a Harvard Law graduate who would become the most widely publicized figure of the war. Before enlisting, Charles Whittlesey, a tall, gangling, bookish lawyer, attracted little notice. He seemed to have an aptitude for distinction, but not an iota of interest in fame. In truth, he desired a comfortable anonymity—he had no wife and no children, just a business partner and a few friends who did not know him very well.

Whittlesey and his younger brother Elisha, an idealistic, sickly undergraduate who also studied at Harvard, heard the bugle call early and immediately fell into line. They were products of an elite New England culture and an ethos of voluntarism that echoed throughout the halls of Harvard and other Ivy League institutions. The brothers lived by a code instilled in New England's sons to believe that defending their country was not only a sacred duty but also an ennobling one. Elisha drove camion trucks on the French Soissons front even before American troops went overseas, and Charles traveled across the Atlantic as an officer in the famed 77th "Statue of Liberty" Division, a melting pot of soldiers. In the language of the day, both men "did their part"—and then some. As the personification of the most noble ideals of the war, Charles captured the imagination of Americans when he led a strike force, dubbed the Lost Battalion, behind enemy lines and held it together against overwhelming numbers.

The "Lost Battalion"—a piece of inspired newspaper hyperbole—altered everything. A tiny part of an immense offensive became *the* story. Journalists transfigured Whittlesey into the Peter Pan of the Great War, the leader of a plucky flesh-and-blood band of Lost Boys—surrounded, battling against insurmountable odds, and refusing to surrender. The tale was truly compelling. Like a story about a child trapped in a well, it dripped human interest. Whittlesey's pedigree was spotless, and the fact that his second in command, millionaire George McMurtry, was a former Theodore Roosevelt Rough Rider added a soupçon of authenticity to the equation. It was as if overnight America decided that Whittlesey had to be saved, and though most early attempts bordered on suicidal, the rescue mission transfixed the nation.

Whittlesey and his men epitomized their country's iron resolve in the bloodiest campaign in American history. He returned to America determined to find meaning in all the bloodshed, but instead found himself locked in yet another conflict, fighting against intractable leaders and an apathetic public. The first Great War veteran to receive the Medal of Honor, he became an American hero. His name and face appeared on the front page of every major newspaper in the country. He had achieved the impossible, surviving the worst hell of battle and coming out with hardly a scratch. None that you could see anyway. Hollywood wanted to sell his story. Novelists wanted to write his story. And the government wanted to use his story—and him—for its own ends. Everyone wanted something from him, some piece, something that they could hold on to and share when they talked about all the men who never came home. But Whittlesey wanted none of it. All he wanted was peace. He could not bear living the war over and over again.

THIS IS THE STORY OF the disruptive forces of an epoch and a war that permanently altered Boston, America, and the lives of three public figures. In the turbulent year of 1918, Boston stood as a microcosm of America: a locus of urban strife, ethnic conflict, and fundamental, lasting change. The stories of Muck, Ruth, and Whittlesey reveal how a city and a nation confronted the havoc of a new world order, the struggle to endure the war and all its unforeseen consequences. Reading accounts from Boston's newspapers from that year, it's impossible to separate the war from popular culture. The citizens of Boston followed the war intently, reading stories about baseball players serving in Europe or evading the service; published accounts about accusations against the BSO's German conductor; tales about a heroic Harvard Law grad who refused to surrender in the Argonne Forest; and frightening reports about Boston's invisible enemy—the grippe—an unrelenting scourge that overwhelmed the city that summer and fall, killing thousands in the Hub and millions around the world.

The war's influence could be seen everywhere in Boston. The city became the military and naval headquarters for all of New England, and the main shipping port in the region. While workers at the Boston Navy Yard prepared war ships and cargo vessels, New England's men and women manufactured munitions, rifles, uniforms, boots, and supplies for the American and Allied armies. United in patriotism, every senator and congressman from New England voted in favor of the war, signaling the region's commitment to fighting the Germans no matter the cost.[5]

The Great War changed the lives of virtually every citizen in the Hub. Nowhere was that more evident than on the Boston Common. The vast green park became a theater of war, a battleground where anarchists, socialists, suffragists, soldiers, and sailors climbed onto soapboxes, proselytizing to crowds until their voices became hoarse. The tree-lined mall hummed with activity. One could hear the sharp notes of bugles, pounding drums, and the tramp of soldiers' boots drilling. The Salvation Army and the Knights of Columbus erected huts along Tremont Street while recruiting tents housed clean-shaven soldiers in olive drab and khaki uniforms. Conservationists planted Victory gardens and Red Cross volunteers trolled for donations. And police patrolmen interrogated anyone who seemed suspicious, especially men with dark features who looked stereotypically German, warning the public that the Kaiser's agents had infiltrated the city's factories and shipyards.[6]

That sense of fear pervaded the city and the country. The enemy seemed everywhere—prowling in submarines off the coast of Cape Cod, arriving on passenger ships at Boston Harbor, or disguised as the friend of workers, lecturing men at the munitions factories, saloons, and shipyards about the injustice of a sixty-hour workweek. Like a contagion, the pro-German conspirators, spies, and union radicals hiding in plain sight had to be contained, with force if necessary. Anyone who expressed dissent or un-American opinions could find himself jailed, beaten, or hanged. For the sake of victory, Americans tolerated suppression, censorship, and deprivation. In a nation at war with Germany—and itself—no sacrifice seemed too great.

PART ONE

GATHERING CLOUDS

1

"Something That I *Don't* Want To!"

CHARLES WHITE WHITTLESEY LIVED HIS LIFE IN SHADOWS, EVEN during those intense days and nights along the Charlevaux Brook. He was happy to speak on any subject except himself. Sometimes he entertained his friends with marvelous stories of school and camp life, featuring carefully imagined characters and preposterous scenes. Sitting among a group of friends at Williams College, or later at the Williams Club or the Harvard Club in New York City, he regaled listeners with his stories, drawing out his characters' accents and quirky mannerisms. Other times he tackled the big ideas—truth, beauty, duty. Weaving tales or discussing abstract ideas, he towered "like a cliff over a brook," a friend said. His soft but assured voice mesmerized. He was at his best then, for he "loved speculation and friendship; classic beauty; a jest; an argument; a convivial evening." Yet the stories, speculations, and arguments of the man his classmates called the Count seemed oddly impersonal, as if he lived separate from his words.[1]

There is a maddening paradox about his life. War correspondents and then journalists and historians have written so much about him, yet so little of what he wrote survives. A handful of battlefield messages, several after-action reports, a few frustratingly impersonal letters—that's about all. Only by digging into

At Williams College, classmates called Charles White Whittlesey "the Count" because of his precise, even stiff, manner of speaking and walking. Reserved yet well liked, he engaged in the world of the mind and seemed destined for a life behind a desk. *(Courtesy of Williams College Archives.)*

his years at Williams and Harvard can you glimpse the man who commanded the Lost Battalion, the leader who somehow held his unit together among the dead and dying, the stink and danger of a small hell they called the Pocket.

Although he had been born in Florence, Wisconsin, he was of *Mayflower* descent, and in 1894, at age ten, his father, Frank Russell Whittlesey, moved the family to Pittsfield, Massachusetts, because of a job transfer. Working as a production manager for the recently formed General Electric Corporation—in 1914 Pittsfield would soon earn the moniker High Voltage Capital of the World—Frank prospered, and his children enjoyed the advantages and responsibilities of his elevated position in the community. Charles inherited and further cultivated his father's *noblesse oblige*, which instilled in him a powerful faith in education, a belief in civic service, an acceptance of hard work, and a temperament that was steadfastly courteous, judicious, and moderate.

Always close to his parents and siblings, when he graduated from Pittsfield High School, he stayed near home, venturing just twenty miles north to Williamstown. It was a village of stunning natural beauty nestled in the Berkshires of northwest Massachusetts and guarded over by the famed purple hills. It was a community of white steeple churches, fieldstone fences, and long green lawns. The place suited the boy; both were quiet without being deadly somber, handsome without being ostentatious, and industrious without loudly announcing their ambition.

Whittlesey was seventeen when he enrolled at Williams College in September 1901. The school had a tradition of student pranks, but it was foremost a place of education. Max Eastman, who enrolled at the college a year before Whittlesey, recalled the tough entrance exams. He underwent a battery of tests in Latin and Greek, mathematics and science, and of course literature. He wrote his sister that he failed the exam in English literature, noting that one of the essay questions was, "Write on Dryden's religious life." When Charles enrolled the following year, his first-semester courses included Elocution, English, French, Greek, Latin, Geometry, and Algebra. Judging from Whittlesey's transcripts, Williams was not the home of gut courses and "gentlemen's C's."[2]

The month he arrived at Williams his country was beginning a seismic transition. A new century had dawned, and the nineteenth century—the century of Lincoln and Grover Cleveland—was waning. An influx of new peoples, innovations, and ideas had created a new America. Popular writers like Edward Bellamy and Henry George had reimagined the country's social contract, while Thorstein Veblen and Richard Ely attacked classical economic theory. Washington Gladden and Walter Rauschenbusch questioned conventional religious assumptions, while Lincoln Steffens and Upton Sinclair exposed political and economic abuses. Electric ideas illuminated the intellectual landscape in the brave new century and charged Whittlesey's imagination.

All the ideas, energy, and change appeared to coalesce in one man: Theodore Roosevelt. An assassin's bullet placed him in the Oval Office only days before Whittlesey arrived on campus. During the next four years, while Charles studied ancient and modern languages, struggled with biology and advanced mathematics, and excelled in courses on Dante and the Italian Renaissance, "TR," as Roosevelt was popularly called, gave Whittlesey and his friends subjects to debate during late-night discussions. From the beginning, whether the result of breeding or inclination, he was a Roosevelt man, committed to the president's passion for unbridled progress and public service.

"The Strenuous Life," Roosevelt's 1899 speech before the Hamilton Club in Chicago, was a clarion call to Whittlesey's generation. It demanded their best, beckoning them to "enter the arena" and throw their energy into the struggle for goals larger than themselves. "I wish to preach, not the doctrine of ignoble ease," intoned the recent survivor of the Battle of San Juan Hill, "but the doctrine of the strenuous life, the life of toil and effort, of labor and strife; to preach that the highest form of success which comes, not to the man who desires mere easy peace, but to the man who does not shrink from danger, from hardship, or from bitter toil, and who out of these wins the splendid ultimate triumph." Roosevelt's speech praised the rugged men who had pushed the frontier westward and risked their lives for their nation. "We do not admire the man of timid peace," he emphasized. "We admire the man who embodies victorious effort; the man who never wrongs his neighbor, who is prompt to help a friend, but who has those virile qualities necessary to win in the stern strife of life. It is hard to fail, but it is worse never to have tried to succeed. In this life we get nothing save by effort."[3]

For Charles, the strenuous life was not played out on the baseball diamonds and football fields. He was an intellectual in training. The antithesis of an athlete, his classmates never once recalled him with a ball in his hands, and he preferred solitary birding expeditions to team sports. In truth, he looked nothing like the popular image of Roosevelt's strenuous American. He was built for quiet libraries and offices, not the frontier or gridiron. At six feet two inches, thin and gangly, with eyes seeming to bulge through rimless wire glasses, he possessed extraordinarily long, thin legs and large duck-like feet. Many observers later compared him to a stork or crane, an avian look that was further exaggerated by his reserved, occasionally even withdrawn, nature. Max Eastman called him "sharp-edged, impersonal, and unsentimental," but with all that, he was enormously likeable and thoughtful, a man who spoke carefully and truthfully.[4]

Whittlesey embodied contradictions. Even at Williams, classmates recognized the different facets of his personality, referring to him by nicknames, including the familiar "Chick" and the imperious "Count." Universally liked and admired, he was also distant and self-contained. Capable of discussing ideas deep into the night, he gave little away of his inner self. Incisive and analytical, his sangfroid harbored a burning intensity. The world of ideas beckoned him, but as a "Son of Roosevelt" he longed, as Tennyson wrote in "Locksley Hall," to "mix with action, lest I wither by despair."

Toward the end of his time at Williams, Whittlesey had a revealing conversation with Asa H. Morton, a notoriously challenging romance languages professor from whom he took two courses on Dante and another two on the Italian Renaissance. More than an instructor, Morton was a guide into the life of ideas. Middle-aged, with a trimmed iron-gray beard, Morton was thoroughly cosmopolitan in manner and sparkling in conversation. "He brought home from his summers in Europe," remembered Eastman, "an atmosphere of Latin Quarter sophistication not elsewhere to be breathed at Williams."

Seeking advice one evening, Whittlesey visited Morton in his home. He was considering becoming a missionary.

"What qualifications have you?" Morton asked. "Have you mastered any heathen language?"

"No, I haven't," Whittlesey answered.

"Have you made a special study of the Christian religion?"

"No, I hardly know anything about it."

"Have you looked into the life led by missionaries?"

"No, I haven't."

"Well, do you really want to be a missionary?"

"No, but I want to do something that I *don't* want to!"[5]

EASTMAN, ALONG WITH WHITTLESEY'S FATHER and Roosevelt, exerted a pivotal influence on him. Remarkably handsome with brooding eyes and an open smile, he was equal parts committed intellectual, irreverent prankster, and passionate believer, a student questing for something that he could not yet define. Eastman left a record of his regard for Whittlesey. Long after they graduated, Max still thought his fraternity brother "had as brilliant brains and keen a character as anyone I've ever known." Yet he also sensed the contradictions. Whittlesey, he thought, "had seemed more than the rest of us, in the lightning speed and intemperate force of his judgments, designed for fame. And yet he was contemptuous of it. He was contemptuous of all those values that loom so large to the ambitious."[6]

Whittlesey left few traces of his feelings toward Eastman—no journals, no autobiographies, and only a few letters. Yet an investigator can trace the influences of the two on each other—and, more important, Whittlesey's deepest thoughts—in the pages of the *Williams Literary Monthly*. Both were members of the Lit. Board in their junior and senior years, and both wrote regularly for the monthly, contributing poems, short stories, and essays.[7]

They both, for instance, registered their complaints about the social and educational environment of Williams. The vibrant rebellious streak that would mark Eastman's life is evident in his essay "Systematic Suppression of Freshmen." He decried elite colleges' numbing productions of types—Princeton men, Yale men, Harvard men, and Williams men. A senior in a Williams fraternity boasted, "The freshmen in our house are taught silence, then obedience, and finally, if the upper classmen be in sufficient force, total submission to our wills." The system, Eastman thought, was antithetical to the growth of independent thought and individuality. He called for rebellion against the process, demanding *education* not *induction* at Williams. Like Whittlesey, he believed the school's social customs were almost designed on a Confucian model to produce "compulsory reverence" for past traditions rather than thoughtful leaders.[8]

In the essay "Liberal Culture," Whittlesey's contribution to the cause, he excoriated the educational system at his college. Repeatedly he heard alumni assert that "the principal benefit of a college course is the friendships it occasions," an opinion that he could only interpret as an indictment "on the prevailing system." He agreed with Professor Henry van Dyke Jr. of Princeton that the purpose of a higher education was to instill the ability "to judge correctly, to think clearly, [and] to see and to know truth." Whittlesey added another to the list: "To attain the faculty of pure delight in the beautiful." Yet Williams failed to properly inculcate an appreciation in the fine arts of "music, painting, sculpture, architecture, and poetry, or more broadly, literature." Particularly in languages, the school either failed utterly or succeeded "in but a miserably small per-cent of cases." In stilted language that reflected his academic bent, he concluded: "Honesty compels the opinion that the 'intellectual degeneration of the college youth'... is in large part due to the insufficiency for his needs of the intellectual diet offered him."[9] The essay reveals a certain priggishness, an icy distance from his fellow students, and a retreat into books.

His fiction in the *Williams Literary Monthly* uncovers other facets of the future military leader. Stylistically, his short stories are a cross between Bret Harte and O. Henry. Some are tales of miners set on the western frontier; most have plot twist endings. As a whole, however, all reveal Whittlesey's finely honed sense of duty, feelings of isolation, and haunting ennui. In "The Lotos," with its allusions to Tennyson's "The Lotos-Eaters," the protagonist is torn between a quiet life of ease and the strenuous life as a lawyer in Chicago. In "The Ides of November," virtually every decision and action torments the main figure. In "A Lonely Post," a mining engineer longs to escape the tedium of his assignment in Peru. It is only when he gives a friend his chance to return home that he finds tranquility and sees the beauty of the mountain post.[10]

"The Twins Mine," more than the other tales, speaks to Whittlesey's conflicted character. For "ten hard years," prospector Joe Stanley dug for gold, working the same claim fruitlessly day after day. Yet he is not unhappy; quite the opposite. He did, however, form a partnership with two other prospectors who swindle a wealthy, thoroughly crooked miner while Joe is away on business.[11]

Although the swindlers forward Stanley his share of the trans-
action, he is horrified. In his mind rang his father's admonition:
"Joe, be an honest man." Although he had not participated in the
"skinning," he suffered the guilt and vowed to right the wrong, re-
solving that "the trail would never end till death or success fulfilled
his promises." Vengeance became a new quest, and he wandered
the mountain trails, driven by his father's words "to be an honest
man," until ultimately fate rewarded his toil.[12]

Be an honest man. Choose death over dishonor. The reward is
in the task. "The Twins" captures the essence of Charles Whittlesey.
During his long solitary hikes in the hills surrounding Williams
College, he must have wrestled with the story's themes, working
through how he could personally fulfill his father's expectations and
Roosevelt's challenge. Fittingly, Eastman recalled that his friend's
favorite poem was a sonnet by Milton:

Lawrence, of virtuous father virtuous son
Now that the fields are dank, the ways are mire,
Where shall we sometimes meet, and by the fire
Help waste a sullen day, what may be won
From the hard season gaining? Time will run . . .

"Milton's cool-voiced sonnet," as Eastman suspected, exempli-
fied Charles Whittlesey's reserved sociability as well as his broader
commitment. Judged in the context of his life, it is a soldier's poem,
a soldier whose pleasures seem sadly fleeting.[13]

THEODORE ROOSEVELT CAME TO WILLIAMS College on June
22, 1905, for Whittlesey's class graduation. The president was
on friendly turf. An informal survey conducted by *The Williams Record*, the college's newspaper, showed that twenty-five of
thirty-six polled faculty members had favored TR in the previous fall's presidential election. College president Henry Hopkins
told reporters that he preferred Roosevelt but gave no reasons.
Ex-president Franklin Carter also favored the incumbent. "I look

upon Theodore Roosevelt as an honest and able administrator, as the staunch supporter of civil service reform and the true friend of the negro," he said. Furthermore, inspired by the president's call for the strenuous life and advocacy of reform, undergraduates like Whittlesey championed him. At the ceremony, Roosevelt received the school's highest honorary degree, Litterarum Humaniorum Magister, and addressed the gathered graduates.[14]

Fitting the occasion, a large, distinguished group gathered in the stately Congregational Church. Former secretary of war and soon to be secretary of state Elihu Root sat near Roosevelt, not far from the ex-ambassador at the Court of St. James, Joseph Hodges Choate. The president looked fit and energetic as he sang Luther's familiar hymn "A Mighty Fortress Is Our God." Then he spoke. He talked about ideas, emphasizing the foolishness of "fantastic ideals" and the necessity of "practical" ones. He seemed to breathe fire as he discussed the Beef Trust and the Standard Oil Company. Only a strong national government, he suggested, could regulate those powerful entities.[15]

Above all else, he challenged the graduates. "A man should not only work for himself, but for the best expression possible for the reward of his work well done," he said. "We expect leadership from Williams . . . Abroad I wish that it might be said that this nation does not merely talk but acts for righteousness and peace . . . We are now enjoying righteousness and peace because the soldiers of our country dared draw their swords for the maintenance of it." Warming to his message, he stressed, "I demand that in all cases . . . the nation do its duty, accepting the responsibilities that go with greatness and daring to be great. Do not, however, let this nation gain the reputation of doing justice to the weak rather than that of exacting justice from the strong."[16]

Listening to Roosevelt, shaking his hand once he received his diploma, Whittlesey must have certainly recognized a kindred spirit. Roosevelt's themes—selfless leadership, satisfaction in work well done, peace through strength, justice for all—were ones that Whittlesey had expressed in his fiction and advocated among friends. "I want to do something that I *don't* want to!" he said.

He did not yet know what that something was, but Roosevelt appeared to validate the quest.

IN HIS FICTION, WHITTLESEY'S YOUNG protagonists are not wealthy, and occasionally consider career opportunities in the legal profession. It was hardly surprising, then, that he chose that path for himself after graduation. In the fall of 1905 he entered Harvard Law School, the oldest and most distinguished law school in the country.

It was a demanding curriculum with rigorous exams that decided if a student advanced from one year to the next. In his first year, Whittlesey took classes in torts, real property, contracts, civil procedure, and criminal law. Courses in equity and constitutional law came later. It was not an environment that permitted much time for lively fraternity discussions and short story writing.

The Harvard College atmosphere, however, was, like its law school, heavy with fresh ideas and new approaches. The influence of Theodore Roosevelt, class of 1880, seemed as powerful on campus as the reforms of college president Charles William Eliot. It was the Harvard of intellectual giants George Santayana, William James, and Josiah Royce. Progressivism and pragmatism, the role of America in the world, and the influence of the new wealth on the country's body politic—these movements and issues animated Harvard life as its professors and graduates moved in and out of high offices in Washington, DC.

In 1908, when Whittlesey departed Harvard with his degree, he joined the New York law firm of Murray, Prentice & Howland at 37 Wall Street, where he specialized in the increasingly complex field of banking law. Outwardly, he appeared comfortable in the role of a Wall Street lawyer. He mastered the minutiae of the changing regulatory laws and earned a reputation for careful preparation, incisive thinking, and an ability to cut to the core of any case. Yet friends who knew him best believed that he was destined for something more than a Wall Street partnership because money seemed so unimportant to him. They considered him too intellectual, too committed to his ideals, to spend the rest of his life poring over dry contracts.

While his college friends married and began families, Charles preferred life in a boarding house. He was single, a bachelor who was not romantically linked to any woman. His was more of a male-centric world. He willingly scampered hundreds of miles around the Northeast to watch a good football game, and enjoyed the chummy camaraderie of the Williams Club and the Harvard Club. He remained a gifted storyteller with "a keen eye for the ridiculous," and his quiet charm, unassuming nature, and relaxed bonhomie made him an ideal companion for an evening at the club.[17]

His politics, however, did not fit the Harvard Club profile. Even at Williams College, he tended to romanticize outsiders, men and women with unorthodox ideas and strong convictions. In "Brook Farm," an early 1904 essay published in the *Williams Literary Monthly*, he praised the "brilliant Boston minister" George Ripley's communal experiment. Transcendentalists like Ripley who saw "the vast inadequacy of conventional social life," Whittlesey wrote, desired an alternative social contract, one forged on rural solitude, communal pleasures, shared labor, and intellectual pursuits. Describing the Utopian existence, he noted, "As far as work was concerned, there was absolutely no compulsion. In fact, the rustics of the neighborhood maintained that everyone was paid alike—the man plowing in the field and the man at the window drawing a picture of the plowman." Furthermore, he lauded the community's gender equality. Men and women shared voting privileges and engaged in "brilliant and remarkable" conversation. When Brook Farm ultimately collapsed under the weight of its economic mismanagement, he concluded that "there was no one of the old members who did not mourn the end of that merry, carefree time from which had resulted a clearer, a broader mental and moral outlook and a deep, abiding conviction of good fellowship and the happiness of life."[18]

In the years after Whittlesey arrived in New York, the social and political values of Brook Farm had taken root in Greenwich

Village, not far from his Wall Street office but on the other side of a significant cultural divide. In the years before America's entry in the Great War, Greenwich Village looked and felt like an isolated retreat in New York. Its diagonal streets predated Manhattan's grid pattern, and until 1917 it was unreachable by subway. Most of its population was foreign born, but they had already begun to follow the industrial jobs out of the Village. The result was low rents in rundown buildings with spacious lofts and a Bohemian aesthetic, an ideal retreat for aspiring artists, struggling intellectuals, and penniless radicals. On the narrow streets of the Village, playwright Eugene O'Neill rubbed shoulders with the likes of radical journalist John Reed, dancer Isadora Duncan, and artist Marcel Duchamp.

Shortly after Whittlesey began to practice law on Wall Street, Max Eastman settled in Greenwich Village. Whereas Whittlesey never demonstrated a desire for fame and public recognition, Eastman seemed to crave both. By 1913, Max was teaching uptown at Columbia and editing *The Masses*, turning it into the literary centerpiece for socialist politics and the artistic avant-garde. That summer, when Max published *Enjoyment of Poetry*, Charles sent a congratulatory note, one tempered only by Eastman's didacticism. Whittlesey may have departed Williams, but there was still much of the Williams undergraduate in him. Chiding, reluctant to be told what to think, he wrote his friend, "I hadn't suspected poetry of being such a tremendous affair. A pedestrian, charged with the burden of the loss of gravity can't restrain a resentful grunt at having the ether explained to him."[19]

Whittlesey needed no instruction in appreciating poetry, nor did he need guidance in politics. One historian has suggested that "Whittlesey was one of Eastman's converts" to socialism—and it's true that Max may have been an influence. Yet Whittlesey had been leaning left for at least a decade. His views on social equality, his lack of concern for wealth, and his basic idealism all pulled him leftward at a time when the Socialist Party was expanding its base. Perhaps it was one of the reasons he left Murray, Prentice & Howland and went into practice with his Harvard Law School friend John Pruyn in a small office at 2 Rector Street. In any case, in the pivotal election of 1912, *The Masses* threw its support behind the Socialist candidate—editorializing that "every vote cast for Eugene V. Debs is a vote for revolutionary socialism and the class struggle"—and Whittlesey followed suit.[20]

Whittlesey, however, was too independent minded to stay in the socialist fold. He eventually rejected the Socialist Party's dictates about the class struggle and global politics. According to one account, in late 1915 he read a story detailing Socialist Party leaders attempting to press their views on a dissenting majority. Tiring of the affair, he threw down that paper, remarking, "To hell with that crowd!"[21]

It is uncertain what issue led to his decision. But the preparedness debate most sharply divided his worlds of conservative, traditionalist Wall Street and radical, bohemian Greenwich Village. For socialists, the Great War was an imperial land grab that threatened working class solidarity, and they passionately condemned it. For men of Whittlesey's class and schooling, the war, however regrettably, was moving closer to America. They regarded Imperial Germany as a political, economic, and military threat, one the piddling US Army and Navy were unprepared to meet. How, they asked, could an army of only eighty thousand men, poorly equipped and doctrinally impoverished, hope to stand up to a German force more than twenty times as large and markedly better trained and armed? How could a militarily weak nation protect American freedoms and democratic institutions?

For Charles Whittlesey, the sinking of the *Lusitania* changed everything. After a German U-boat sank the ocean liner off the Old Head of Kinsale on May 7, 1915, killing 1,198 passengers, including 128 Americans, interventionists demanded war against Germany. Outraged American politicians and writers charged Germany "with the crime of willful and wholesale murder." Americans denounced the Germans as barbarians, beasts, and "baby killers." Teddy Roosevelt believed that the German assault required a military reprisal from the United States.[22]

The sinking of the *Lusitania* forced Whittlesey to confront something that *he didn't want to do*. The ruthless attack on innocent passengers convinced him that the Germans were inhumane and immoral, and that they had to be stopped. He came from a long line of patriots; men from his family had served in every American conflict since the Pequot War. He had a duty, then, to serve his family and his country with honor. If war came, he concluded, he would fight.

In New York, the Harvard Club on West Forty-forth Street stood at the heart of the preparedness movement. In Harvard Hall and the Grill Room, the library and the billiard room, members railed against the Kaiser's treachery and demanded retaliation. Within days, Grenville Clark, Elihu Root Jr., Theodore Roosevelt Jr., and other club members dispatched a telegram to the White House expressing their conviction that "national interest and honor imperatively require adequate measures both to secure reparations for past violations by Germany of American rights and secure guarantees against future violations."[23]

They knew, however, that words were a poor substitute for action. Men of social and economic standing, educated at Harvard at a time when President Eliot urged graduates to embrace public service, they were raised to believe that concepts like duty and honor were not idle abstractions. Two forceful club members led the charge. General Leonard Wood, who served as army chief of staff under President Taft and still remained on active duty in 1915, took the lead. Hawk-nosed and rugged, a soldier whose chain spurs and dog-headed riding crop struck no one as affectations, Wood did not demand respect because everyone gave it so freely. Grenville Clark, heir to a banking and railroad fortune, was Wood's workhorse. Tirelessly, he organized, writing letters, drafting statements, and proselytizing. Wood and Clark wanted to show that their crowd would lead the movement to prepare America for war. It was to this call that Whittlesey responded.[24]

Five weeks after the *Lusitania* sank, Wood addressed a gathering of more than a thousand members sardined into the main hall at the Harvard Club. He called on them to volunteer for his planned

Business Men's Camp, a one-month initiation into military procedures and life. It was a boot camp designed for men in their thirties
and forties, an extension of a similar program he had begun for
college-age youths. Philip Carroll, a descendant of the Carrolls of
Carrollton and a classmate of Clark's, was among those who answered the summons. So was DeLancey K. Jay, descendant of John
Jay and John Jacob Astor; John Purroy Mitchel, mayor of New York
City; Percy Haughton, Harvard's football coach; Richard Harding
Davis, the nation's famous war correspondent; and Quintin, Archie,
and Ted Roosevelt Jr. Altogether, the names of the roughly 1,300
men who paid their own way to attend the camp on the shore of
Lake Champlain in Plattsburg, New York, read like a list pulled
from the Eastern Seaboard's *Who's Who* and *Social Register*. Wood's
biographer later described the impact the camp had on the 1915
social season, writing, "The butterflies of Newport and Bar Harbor
complained that life was desolate, since the best of their young men
were in Plattsburg."[25]

The first Plattsburg Camp was a raging success. It led to other
camps, and the "Plattsburg Idea" of preparedness won thousands of
converts. At Plattsburg, pressed against the lake and not far from the
Green Mountains, the troops of the Business Men's Regiment—
called the Tired Business Men (or T.B.M.s) by the regular army
officers who trained them—learned to march and salute, mastered
the manual of arms and military verbiage, and practiced firing rifles, mortars, and machine guns. They slept on cots in tents, ate
beans in a mess, and moved through the day on a schedule set by
a bugle. For bankers and lawyers, businessmen and politicians, it
was a demanding month, a taste of TR's "strenuous life," but few
complaints interrupted the course of the days.

At night, beside the lake and lit by flickering lanterns, Wood and
other dignitaries addressed them. The old Rough Rider himself
showed up on August 25. Dressed in a riding jacket, breeches, and
leather leggings, a wide-brimmed hat shading his eyes, he decried
the present administration's timid foreign policy and blasted "the
professional pacifists, the poltroons, and the college sissies who organize peace-at-any-price societies." Although he never mentioned

President Woodrow Wilson by name, there was no mistaking who was in the crosshairs of his address when he asserted that "to treat elocution as a substitute for action, to rely on high-sounding words unbacked by deeds, is proof of a mind that dwells only in the realm of shadow and shame."[26]

The words of Roosevelt, espousing ideals of honor and duty, inspired Whittlesey and thousands of other Harvard men of his generation to enter the arena. More than any college in the nation, Harvard contributed to the war effort. A total of 11,319 Harvard alumni, students, and faculty would serve in the Great War. By the summer of 1917, half of the school's 4,700 students had entered the service. Harvard Law School dropped from 850 students to 250 in a semester; and Harvard Business School's decline was even sharper, from 232 students to 32. With 12 ROTC companies, the war had transformed Harvard into "a Government military school."[27]

If Harvard men inspired the Plattsburg movement, thousands of Americans followed them as the war seemed to encroach ever closer to US interests. Sixteen thousand men attended the camps in 1916, including Charles Whittlesey, who made his first trip to Plattsburg that July. He completed the thirty-day course and emerged as a private in the US Army Reserve. In his discharge papers, his commanding officer noted that his service was "honest and faithful," and his character "excellent."[28]

Several months after America's entry into the war, he returned to Plattsburg for the three-month program, again receiving high praise from his commander. By the summer of 1917, the program had produced "ninety-day wonders" like sausage links. Always a perfectionist, Whittlesey trained with a grim determination to succeed. By the end of the course, the army had placed him high on the list of those promoted to captain, US Army Officer Reserve Corps. Again, he received a discharge, but with the pressing demand for troops and officers, he knew that it was only a matter of weeks until the government called him into service.[29]

2

Muck Raking

INSIDE THE DOWNTOWN OFFICE OF THE *PROVIDENCE JOURNAL*—
"the Rhode Island bible"—John R. Rathom, editor and "patriot
of the highest order," stored thousands of telegrams, letters, checks,
photographs, and deciphered codes in a secured vault. During
the Great War, he kept more than seven thousand index cards of
names, including hundreds of American citizens he suspected were
working for the Kaiser, traitors living among neighbors and friends.
Known throughout the country for their investigations, Rathom
and the *Journal's* muckraking reporters documented a vast network
of German spies working in the United States. He planted agents
in German embassies and consular offices in Washington, New
York, Boston, Chicago, and other cities. He'd become so successful
exposing German conspiracies against America that a German dip-
lomat orchestrated an assassination plot against him. At least, that
was the story he told the world.[1]

Rathom lived by a simple motto: "Raise hell and sell newspapers." By the time the United States had entered the Great War,
he had become one of the most influential propagandists in the
nation, spinning tales on the speakers' circuit and in his syndicated columns about German intrigue. A self-promoting "super
spy hunter," Rathom published sensational exposés about German

In 1917, Karl Muck, the world-famous German conductor of the Boston Symphony Orchestra, became entangled in a scandal when citizens in Providence, Rhode Island, accused him of refusing to conduct "The Star-Spangled Banner" during a concert at Infantry Hall. *(Courtesy of the Boston Symphony Orchestra Archives.)*

operatives in the United States, warning the country about "cunning plots to kill our people, sink our ships, dynamite our factories, and disrupt our national life." His stories, described by one magazine writer as "more thrilling than fiction," were stitched from the same cloth as the "yellow journalism" that dominated during the 1890s circulation war between Joseph Pulitzer and William Randolph Hearst.[2]

The American public was, in the words of Hearst, "more fond of entertainment than ... information." Rathom, a large man with a round, fleshy face, weak chin, and a retreating hairline, also recognized that war propaganda could satisfy Americans' insatiable appetite for drama. During the Great War, selling newspapers meant exploiting American fears of German spies and saboteurs. Undoubtedly, in 1916 and 1917, German agents were responsible for dynamiting several bridges and munitions plants. So whenever an American factory or supply ship mysteriously exploded or caught fire, the press immediately blamed the Kaiser's agents, stoking the flames of anti-German hysteria.[3]

Spy mania pervaded the country. Newspapers saturated the public with stories about German schemes on American soil. The

Providence Journal carried the same editorial day after day, warning readers about the insidious peril lurking in cities throughout the nation: "Every German or Austrian in the United States, unless known by years of association to be absolutely loyal, should be treated as a spy." Reminding citizens to remain on high alert, the *Journal* declared, "We are at war with the most merciless and inhuman nation in the world. Hundreds of thousands of its people in this country want to see America humiliated and beaten to her knees, and they are doing, and will do, everything in their power to bring this about."[4]

Rathom was particularly concerned that the Boston Symphony Orchestra (BSO) would be performing in Providence on October 30, 1917. The BSO, a prestigious ensemble of international renown, was not only a German institution, he thought, but a threat to democracy itself. Its famous conductor, Karl Muck, was a loyal German and a friend of the Kaiser's, while the orchestra itself comprised a dozen nationalities, with more than half of its musicians from Germany or Austria. In 1917, when most conductors of American symphonies were either German born or German trained, nativists associated orchestras with Prussian militarism, barbarism, and apocalypse. "German music," opined a writer from the *Los Angeles Times*, "is the music of conquest, the music of the storm, of disorder and devastation."[5]

In Rathom's suspicious eyes, Muck's standard concert program, featuring the great German composers—Beethoven and Wagner—demonstrated his plan to spread the Hun's "Kultur." Preoccupied with uncovering alien enemies, he began a campaign against Muck that would change the conductor's life.

On the morning of the concert, before the Boston Symphony Orchestra's afternoon train arrived in Providence, Rathom published an editorial that drew the attention of the city's most enthusiastic patriots. "Professor Muck is a man of notoriously pro-German affiliations," he began, "and the programme as announced is almost entirely German in character," a sure sign that the conductor endangered the city. The provocateur told readers that Muck had not played any patriotic American songs during his concerts—and then he issued a challenge: "The Boston Symphony Orchestra should play 'The Star Spangled Banner' in Providence Tonight."[6]

Responding to his column, the Rhode Island Liberty Loan Committee wired the BSO, as did a group of nine local women's clubs, requesting that the Symphony Orchestra play "The Star-Spangled Banner." Before the concert, "scores of prominent men and women" appeared at Infantry Hall expecting to buy tickets. Fearing protests, Charles Ellis, the BSO's resolute business manager, turned them away, claiming that the concert was sold out, despite rows of empty seats. "We have sold all the seats we care to sell," he announced. When a reporter from the *Journal* asked him if the BSO would play the anthem, Ellis answered, "I think not."[7]

Although the concert continued without incident, the next morning the *Providence Journal* ran a front-page story accusing Muck of ignoring requests to play the anthem. None of the reporters had spoken to him, but the newspaper insisted that he had refused to play the national air. But was that really true?

Nothing Muck had said or done publicly suggested that he had even been informed of the request to play the anthem, let alone that he posed any threat to the United States. American audiences had no reason to distrust him before the Providence concert. But as the war intensified and vigilantes bullied anyone suspected of aiding the Kaiser, he feared the inflamed passions against his country would engulf him. Paranoid that Americans who claimed to be his friends would turn on him, Muck could hardly trust anyone. Increasingly, he felt "surrounded by enemies who hate me from the depth of their heart because I am a German."[8]

The war made Muck question his place in America, and seriously doubt whether his career could survive it. While legions of journalists villainized the Germans, he increasingly felt unsafe in the United States and resentful of Americans who smeared the Kaiser. Preparing for a rabble, he stashed incriminating letters beneath his home's floorboards and stockpiled his house with guns and ammunition. He fantasized about an armed confrontation. "I could easily hold my house against a cowardly mob for a few hours until the police could come," he wrote. "That would be great sport."

A HUB OF LEARNING, SOCIAL reform, and high culture, Boston revered its artists, intellectuals, and musicians. "In Boston," a music critic observed in 1906, "the leader of the orchestra is a good deal bigger man than the mayor." It was against this backdrop, at a time when American connoisseurs of classical music worshiped a Germanic canon, that Karl Muck became the leader of the Boston Symphony Orchestra. Decades before his arrival, during the nineteenth century, classical music came to the United States when European transplants, mostly German musicians, and American proselytizers like Boston critic John Sullivan Dwight promoted the music of symphony orchestras and operas. The city's enlightened aristocracy developed a deep reverence for German romanticism, especially the great composers—Beethoven, Brahms, Schumann, and Wagner. This "sacred" music could be heard throughout the city: in churches, schools, theaters, and concert halls.[9]

The domain Muck inhabited, the one constructed by Boston's cultural elites, could be found along Huntington Avenue—a nearly two-mile corridor of institutions devoted to the arts, a sanctuary of high culture stitching together the Old World and the New World. At the turn of the century, the Boston Brahmins, an exclusive group of WASP authorities, built six large buildings—shrines to the cultural centers of Europe—including Symphony Hall, the Museum of Fine Arts, and the New England Conservatory. Cultivating a prestigious and refined culture meant dividing Americans into categories of highbrow and lowbrow—and policing that division. The leaders of Boston's cultural institutions complained vociferously of the unwashed masses attempting to turn drama, literature, and music into "popular" entertainments. For the elites, the majority of Americans were ignorant and incapable of appreciating the beauty of art and classical music, and were better suited to the simplistic entertainments of vaudeville theaters, amusement parks, and sport stadiums.[10]

In Boston, the most influential figure in the city's high culture was Henry Lee Higginson, a quixotic philanthropist and founder of the Symphony Orchestra. Since 1881, when he established the BSO, Higginson, an elder statesman sporting a bristly gray Vandyke, had built it into a world-class institution. An influential banker whose family heritage traced back to the Brahmin clans— the Lees, Cabots, Lowells, and Putnams—Higginson was well connected, a friend of the city's power brokers, US congressmen, and cabinet members, though he held no partisan fealty. Intolerant of unions and outside interference, Higginson, the sole proprietor of the BSO, viewed the orchestra as *his* property. The benevolent patriarch demanded the absolute best from his musicians, requiring them to sign contracts that allowed him to summarily dismiss anyone who failed to meet his exacting standards.[11]

Higginson needed a conductor who could inspire brilliance and discipline from the orchestra's musicians. In 1906, he hired Muck, then serving as the world-renowned Kapellmeister of the German Royal Opera. Born in Darmstadt in 1859, Muck learned the violin as a child, studied classical philology at Heidelberg, and later developed into a superb pianist at the Leipzig Conservatory. Although he never formally studied conducting, he became a master of the craft, serving opera houses in Zurich, Salzburg, Graz, Prague, and elsewhere. Appointed by the Kaiser to be the first conductor of the Berlin Royal Opera in 1892, he emerged as one of the most esteemed maestros in Europe. Although Muck initially declined Higginson's offer, he ultimately agreed after his employer, Kaiser Wilhelm II, an admirer of Harvard, released him.[12]

Muck proved immensely popular in Boston, and he enjoyed performing in the United States. "I like the American audiences," he told a *New York Times* reporter. He impressed Higginson, too, particularly with his unified programs. Higginson came to believe that Muck surpassed every conductor he had ever hired. How exactly, the *Times* reporter asked, did the self-taught conductor command an orchestra? Muck answered that he had a gift. "How can I say? It all lies in the gift of interpretation. If one has that he will know the truth when he has found it. That's all there is to it."[13]

After two years conducting the BSO, however, Kaiser Wilhelm called Muck home. Yet the maestro soon became unhappy in Berlin, where he clashed with the Royal Superintendent. Seeking autonomy over his career, he took every opportunity to conduct orchestras outside the German capital, often failing to return from his vacations on time. Although he maintained close ties with the Kaiser, he no longer wished to serve as director of the Royal Opera. In 1912, when Higginson offered Muck an opportunity to rejoin the BSO on a permanent basis, providing him a substantial salary of $28,000, the maestro eagerly accepted, knowing he would enjoy greater artistic and personal freedom in America.[14]

Muck seemed to devote his entire life to the Symphony Orchestra. He showed little interest in socializing with strangers. Sometimes he pretended that he could not speak English so that he could avoid conversations with people who interrupted his work. Studious and austere, he carefully reviewed compositions, obsessing over every note as he marked up scores with color-coded annotations in red, blue, and green pencil. He possessed a remarkable feel for tempo, rhythm, and balance. Radiating authority, he imposed Prussian discipline and structure on the orchestra. A temperamental chain-smoker, he spoke directly, and sometimes harshly, to musicians who tested his patience. Once, an exhausted violinist complained about arm pain during a rehearsal, asking the maestro what to do. Muck snapped, "Cut it off!"[15]

In a time when conductors directed with great flair, he appeared stoic and unsentimental on stage, usually wearing a perfectly tailored suit with a high, stiff collar and a long black coat. A short, slim man with black hair combed straight back, hawk nose, and a prominent chin, he conducted with a minimalist style. Cool and distant, he carried himself with military authority, demanding perfection from his musicians, rarely uttering a word of praise. The dueling scar across his cheek suggested the fearlessness of a German officer, a man ready for battle.

When the Great War broke out in July 1914, Muck and two dozen other musicians from the BSO were traveling throughout Europe. That summer he had returned to Germany to conduct

at the Bayreuth Festival, where he performed every year. A patriotic German, he was determined to serve the Kaiser. Knowing
Muck's devotion to his country, Higginson feared losing him and
dispatched Charles Ellis to persuade the conductor to return to
Boston. Muck's wife, Anita, loved their life in the Hub and desperately wanted to return. When her husband tried to enlist in
the Kaiser's army, the wizened fifty-five-year-old was denied on
account of his age and physical fitness. Later, he received a telegram
from the Imperial Headquarters, ordering him to resume conducting in the United States, where he could serve as an instrument
of propaganda, using his platform to shape American perceptions
about Germany during the war. Reluctantly, after Ellis assured him
a safe voyage across the Atlantic, in September Muck and his wife
sailed for Boston.[16]

Higginson's immediate concern was that the war would
fracture his beloved orchestra. Despite his sympathies with the
Allies—his firm, Lee, Higginson, & Co., financed loans for England and France—he echoed President Wilson's idealism, stress-
ing the importance of neutrality. In October 1914, he addressed
the orchestra, reminding them that they must remain unified,
regardless of their political differences. "We are of many nationalities," he said, "including Americans, and we are all on American soil, which is neutral. Therefore, we must use every effort
to avoid all unpleasant words or looks, for our task is to make
harmony above all things—harmony even in the most modern
music. I expect only harmony in your relations to one another."[17]

He knew that quarrels between the musicians could easily ig-
nite. The war was on everyone's mind, and the musicians spent
an extensive amount of time together, rehearsing, performing,
and traveling on long train rides. He also understood that he had
to censor himself if he was going to maintain peace from within
and avoid criticisms from patrons. Publicly, he avoided taking any
stands, but privately he denounced the Kaiser "as an enemy of the
world."[18]

The Germans' assault on the *Lusitania* infuriated him. He insisted that the United States should respond firmly. "I would do

everything except to make war," he wrote a friend in May 1915, arguing that the government should cease trading with Germany and force German ambassador Johann von Bernstorff to leave the country. Had Higginson asked Muck about the *Lusitania*, he would have been horrified by the conductor's views, which he expressed candidly in a letter to a friend: "The ship had to be destroyed," he wrote. Germany could not be blamed for the passenger deaths, he maintained, since the imperial government had warned Americans to avoid ships traveling the Atlantic. "It was not Germany's fault but the fault of England and America."[19]

In October 1915, Higginson, a former Union major during the Civil War, joined the "preparedness" campaign, arguing that the United States needed to build an army and navy that could protect the American shores. Serving as the chairman of a Boston preparedness parade, in the spring of 1916 the former Harvard student implored youths to join the Plattsburg movement. "*Go to Plattsburgh!*" he urged.[20]

Throughout the 1915–1916 season, music critics and newspaper writers praised the BSO as a model symphony orchestra, proof that music could unify men whose countries waged war. Increasingly, however, the American musicians resented the way Muck favored the Germans in the orchestra, promoting them over others who were more deserving. But as Muck saw it, he was the orchestra's dictator. Not even Higginson could rein him in.[21]

After the sinking of the *Lusitania*, no one publicly questioned Muck's politics or his relationships with German officials. It did not seem relevant for reporters to ask the maestro about the war, especially since he had never expressed any anti-American sentiments. Privately, though, he confessed that he felt incredibly stressed, worrying about his family and friends back in Germany. Filled with guilt for not doing more to aid his countrymen, he resented living in America. "This whole country," he complained in 1916, "is ruled by a crowd of bums who are tainted with English money." Deep down, he thought that the Allies' propaganda against Germany would pull the United States into the Great War. "My only hope," he lamented, "is that the American people will wake up again and hang the few dozen bums to the highest tree which grows in this country."[22]

ON FEBRUARY 1, 1917, GERMANY resumed its policy of unrestricted submarine warfare. That meant that without warning its submarines would attack any ships found in designated waters around Great Britain, France, and Italy. It also meant that the United States, an officially neutral country, would have to surrender its right to trade with the Allies, and any American ships bound for Europe could be torpedoed. In response, two days later, President Wilson severed diplomatic relations with Germany, and the German ambassador, Count Johann von Bernstorff, was given his passport and ordered home.[23]

Bernstorff's primary objective was to keep the United States from joining the Allies, a difficult task because German submarines prowled the Atlantic. The ambassador knew America well, and he was certain that US military forces would give the Allies an advantage in the war. Combatting prejudices against his country, he conducted a propaganda campaign, paying American journalists to plant pro-German articles in the nation's newspapers. A tall, charming aristocrat, he spoke perfect English with no accent. His warm blue eyes and inviting personality disarmed Americans, including his beautiful American wife. The dashing emissary became a popular socialite, befriending influential Americans in Washington and New York City. He also maintained close ties with prominent Germans living in America, including Karl Muck.[24]

On February 12, two days before Bernstorff departed for Copenhagen on the *Frederick VIII* of the Scandinavian-American Line, Muck traveled by train to Washington to see his dear friend one last time. "I have a very painful hour to go through tomorrow—this goodbye of Bernstorff and two other old acquaintances in the Embassy," he wrote a confidant, "but it means shutting my teeth together." For the sake of his career in America, Muck knew that he could not publicly express his anger over the German ambassador's expulsion. He had already taken great risks meeting with Bernstorff, as the Bureau of Investigation (the precursor to the FBI) kept close tabs on German activities in the United States. In fact, the Bureau had compiled a list of nearly one hundred Germans who it believed should be interned the moment the United States entered the war, and another list of 1,300 Germans it planned to investigate.[25]

A few weeks after Bernstorff vacated the German embassy, an international scandal hit American newsstands. On March 1, the *New York Times'* front-page headline blared:

GERMANY SEEKS ALLIANCE AGAINST U.S.

ASKS JAPAN AND MEXICO TO JOIN HER

The *New York World* ran a series of subheads that screamed halfway down the front page:

MEXICO AND JAPAN ASKED BY GERMANY

TO ATTACK U.S. IF IT ENTERED THE WAR;

BERNSTORFF A LEADING FIGURE IN PLOT

The sensational story divulged German foreign secretary Arthur Zimmermann's cable to Bernstorff, informing him of Germany's proposed alliance with Mexico and Japan in a joint war against the United States, promising to help Mexico regain "her lost territory in Texas, Arizona, and New Mexico" with "generous financial support." Bernstorff had received the message and transmitted it in code to Heinrich von Eckardt, the imperial minister in Mexico. British intelligence had intercepted and decoded the infamous Zimmermann telegram, and delivered it to President Wilson, whose cabinet now favored a declaration of war against Germany.[26]

In the aftermath of the telegram's publication, the US government disclosed intelligence exposing Bernstorff as the head of a spy agency operating in America. While the ambassador maintained official diplomatic relations and courted influential Americans at dinner parties, he also recruited agents for a vast German spy network. Operating out of New York, a city that had one of the highest concentrations of Germans in the United States, Bernstorff approved clandestine missions to bomb bridges, factories, piers, canals, and supply depots.[27]

When President Wilson asked Congress for a declaration of war on April 2, he was convinced that it was necessary not only to secure peace in Europe, but to protect the country from German saboteurs and disloyal German-Americans. Fighting the war on the home front required vigilance against the enemy. The day Wilson signed the war resolution, April 6, he delivered the Presidential Proclamation on Alien Enemies, which gave the government wide latitude to classify Germans who were suspected of aiding the Kaiser or endangering public safety as enemy aliens. Those designated as enemy aliens were barred from writing, publishing, or uttering a single word critical of the US government, the armed forces, or the American flag. Enemy aliens also had to surrender all firearms, weapons, and wireless radios. And they could not travel within a half mile of any "military installation," which included munitions factories and seaports. Furthermore, the law gave the government the right to arrest, jail, imprison, and intern anyone suspected of violating the provisions—without a trial.[28]

Hardly two months after the United States entered the war, on June 14, 1917, President Wilson addressed the nation during the annual celebration of Flag Day, revealing his deep fear over Bernstorff's spy network. The Germans, he charged, "filled our unsuspecting communities with vicious spies and conspirators." Worse, "their agents diligently spread sedition amongst us and sought to draw our own citizens from their allegiance—and some of these were men connected with the official embassy of the German government." As far as Wilson was concerned, the German Empire left him no choice: "What great nation in such circumstances would not have taken up arms?"[29]

The following day, the president signed the Espionage Act, an omnibus bill that had very little to do with espionage. The law suppressed opposition to the war, prohibiting people from making statements that interfered with the armed forces or incited disloyalty, an especially important measure given the unpopular reinstatement of the draft. The penalties were stiff: anyone who obstructed the activities of the military or aided the enemy could face fines up to $10,000 and a prison sentence of up to twenty years. The law also empowered Postmaster General Albert Burleson, an intolerant but loyal Democrat, to crack down on individuals, political groups, and publishers that disseminated antiwar literature through the mail. One victim of these provisions, Charles Whittlesey's friend Max Eastman, was forced to shut down his left-wing magazine *The Masses* after he was accused of printing "treasonable material."[30]

The US declaration of war against Germany unleashed a campaign of "100 percent Americanism," a crusade rooted in hypernationalism, xenophobia, and nativism. Prior to the Great War, native-born Americans viewed Germans as the most productive immigrants and the most capable of assimilation. Germans held esteemed positions in every professional field, including engineering, science, medicine, music, and higher education. In Boston, in 1903, a sociologist identified Germans as the most respected immigrants in the city. But the proponents of 100 percent Americanism wanted to "purify" the nation, to cleanse it of all German influence. Denouncing the "hyphenated American," those dangerous German-Americans and others with divided national loyalties, Teddy Roosevelt maintained, "There can be no fifty-fifty Americanism in this country. There is room here for only 100% Americanism, only for those who are Americans and nothing else."[31]

Building Roosevelt's "America for Americans" required purging every vestige of German culture from the country. Americans burned German books and newspapers; they began calling hamburgers "liberty sandwiches" and sauerkraut became "liberty cabbage"; school districts prohibited teaching the German language—"a language that disseminates the ideals of autocracy, brutality and hatred." Many states and cities banned German operas, bands, and symphonies. The war transformed classical music—and especially the work of composers like Bach, Beethoven, and Wagner—into dangerous Germanic propaganda. Fearing hostility from patrons, a number of symphonies refused to play any work by German composers. Some made German musicians sign loyalty oaths, declaring their complete support for the United States. In Boston, anti-German hysteria had become so intense that the Boston Pops stopped selling pretzels because they were the favorite snack of enemy aliens.[32]

In a climate of rising hostility toward Germans, Muck considered resigning and returning to Germany. Without him, though, Higginson believed that he would have to disband the BSO. Higginson received numerous letters warning him about Muck's wickedness, but he defended his conductor, certain that he had committed no crime. "If he is dangerous," he wrote Harvard president Charles Eliot, "so are many others of the Orchestra, and, if he goes, the Orchestra goes, too, for I cannot replace him." Looking ahead to the BSO's 1917–1918 season, Higginson remained uncertain about the future of his orchestra. The war on the home front convinced him that he could control its fate as much as "a leaf in the storm."[33]

THAT STORM, HIGGINSON'S BIOGRAPHER BLISS Perry wrote, "first broke in Providence." Muck did not learn that the town's citizens had requested that he conduct "The Star-Spangled Banner" until he returned to Boston on October 31, 1917. After the United States joined the Allies, Americans increasingly came to believe that the patriotic song should be played at every public gathering—in schools, at sporting events, and especially at concerts. Although Congress did not declare "The Star-Spangled Banner" as the national anthem until 1931, Americans already revered it, as Woodrow Wilson had designated it the national air for official military events in 1916. Because many orchestras included a significant number of German musicians, they deflected charges of disloyalty by playing the anthem at the beginning of every program. But when the BSO business manager showed Higginson the telegram from Providence requesting that his orchestra play "The Star-Spangled Banner," he deemed it a superfluous request from people who were not subscribers. "Why should they play it?" he asked. "It has no place in an art concert."[34]

The group of Providence women's clubs that had made the demand in the first place denounced Higginson's response, many of them claiming that they were regular subscribers of the Symphony Orchestra. Leading the charge against Muck, the clubwomen demanded that local police bar the Symphony Orchestra from the city. Made up of white, middle-class and upper-class women, these social clubs recast themselves during the war as influential political groups. The Great War coincided with a Progressive Era reform movement in which women claimed expanded rights of citizenship—working in wartime industries, fighting for suffrage, supporting the preparedness movement, volunteering for the Red Cross, and raising money for Liberty Bonds.[35]

During the war, music clubs like those in Providence focused their energies on "Americanizing" immigrants through song and encouraging public displays of patriotism at all manner of concerts. The Providence clubwomen, then, felt they were merely fulfilling their patriotic duty in demanding to hear the national anthem at Infantry Hall. Voices of intolerance, these clubwomen led the choir of 100 percent Americanism, fighting to maintain the purity of American music. On the home front, American wives and mothers of sons fighting in Europe became the conscience of the nation, sounding the alarm against the dissemination of German culture.

After the Providence concert, John Rathom's newspaper portrayed Muck as a treacherous enemy intent on spreading the Kaiser's propaganda. On November 1, the *Journal* published a scathing political cartoon on the front page under a bold heading: TIME TO DO A LITTLE MUCK RAKING. The drawing portrayed Uncle Sam, the fierce defender of America, picking Muck off the stage with a giant pair of tongs.

"There is no room for a man like Muck on the concert stage of America," the newspaper declared. "Dr. Muck should be withdrawn at once and forever from the American stage and placed where he belongs—behind bars in an internment camp."

The *Providence Journal's* scathing editorial implied that the government should treat Muck as an enemy spy. Tom Harwick, a special agent with the Justice Department, told the *Providence Journal* that he planned to request that his superiors in Washington investigate Muck. A few days later, the Justice Department announced that it would scrutinize him to determine "the real reasons" behind his refusal to play it. When reporters pressed him about the anthem, he maintained that "The Star-Spangled Banner" was "a political composition," and it had no place in an artistic concert. "Does the public think that the Symphony Orchestra is a military band . . . ?" he asked rhetorically. "No!"[36]

Bombarded with letters from friends, politicians, veterans, soldiers' wives, and concert subscribers, Higginson feared that the Symphony Orchestra would not survive the outrage against the conductor. *The Chronicle*, a New York journal for high society, reported that BSO subscribers were "in revolt against Muck." In a letter to Higginson, one Boston attorney said paying the conductor's salary was the equivalent of sending a check to the Kaiser. Speaking to roughly a thousand patriots at the Boston City Club, the largest gathering ever held there, John Rathom attacked Higginson, accusing him of being a German sympathizer. Captivating the audience with stories about how he had uncovered German spies working for Ambassador Bernstorff, the editor admitted that he orchestrated the anthem requests from Providence citizens. The fact that Higginson protected Muck suggested something more sinister in the city, he alleged. "In my judgment, there is no city in the United States, with the single exception of New York, where German and Austrian propagandists are more dangerous or persistent than here in Boston."[37]

The growing criticisms against the BSO left Higginson with no other option than to confront Muck. On November 2, he met with him at Symphony Hall, where an American flag flapped outside in the breeze. He asked Muck if he would be willing to play "The Star-Spangled Banner." The conductor replied, "What will they say to me at home?" Higginson did not know, but he said, "When I am in a Catholic country and the Host is carried by, or a procession of churchmen comes along, I take off my hat out of consideration—not to the Host, but respect for the customs of the nation." Muck thought for a moment. "Very well," he said, "I will play the Star-Spangled Banner."[38]

Muck may have agreed to play the anthem, but he couldn't imagine standing on the American stage much longer. He submitted his resignation, though Higginson would try to delay the conductor's departure until the end of the season. Muck was certain that he wasn't safe in America. "Suppose I should be interned?" he asked. "That is most unlikely," Higginson scoffed.[39]

The mounting stress made Muck increasingly agitated. He felt trapped. He didn't really want to play "The Star-Spangled Banner." Doing so seemed like a betrayal of his artistic integrity and his loyalty to his country. Why would Americans even want a German conductor to perform it? He simply didn't understand. The pressure to play the anthem rattled him, and it also drove a wedge between him and his wife, Anita. "You are to blame for this!" he shouted at her. "It is you who made me come to America."[40]

Higginson hoped that if he spoke directly to the people of Boston that he could regain their trust. On November 2, the same day as his confrontation with Muck, before the evening's concert began, he addressed the audience and announced that Muck would play "The Star-Spangled Banner." In fact, he explained, the conductor had never refused to play it in the first place. When Higginson told the crowd that Muck planned to resign, the audience gasped. Then, when the conductor took the stage, the house welcomed him warmly, showering him with applause. The two men shook hands and Muck later closed the program conducting "The Star-Spangled Banner."[41]

Yet zealots vilified the German maestro and "his Symphony of hostile aliens" for daring to play *America*'s anthem; it was a "contamination of our national hymn," one writer charged. Another critic assailed Muck for conducting it with "manifest ill will." At that point, it did not matter whether he performed the anthem or not, or how he conducted it. All that mattered was that he was a German—and that John Rathom had convinced the nation's patriots that Muck hated America.[42]

While Muck performed the anthem in Boston, Teddy Roosevelt visited Public School 45 in New York, where he listened to
school children sing "America." If Muck was once known as a distinguished conductor of a prominent symphony orchestra, he was
now a potent symbol of the Kaiser's reach across the ocean. After
listening to the children, Roosevelt gave a speech in which he
argued that enemy aliens like Muck had to be contained. "Muck
ought not to be allowed at large in this country," he bellowed. "He
ought to be interned at once, as should anyone who refuses to play
'The Star-Spangled Banner.'" If the Boston Symphony Orchestra
wouldn't play the national anthem, he added, then it ought to be
shut down.[43]

The former governor of Maryland agreed. When Edwin Warfield, a longtime Democrat and president of the Fidelity Trust
Company, learned that the BSO was scheduled to perform in Baltimore on November 7, he condemned Muck, vowing that a mob
would prevent the conductor from stepping one foot in Francis
Scott Key's home state. Warfield organized a rally at the Lyric Theater, where a rabble of three thousand denounced Muck. When the
governor suggested that the German be placed in an internment
camp, a man yelled, "A wooden box would be a better place!"[44]

By the end of November, after the government implemented
President Wilson's regulations against enemy aliens, Muck and
twenty-two other members from the BSO were barred from the
nation's capital, and multiple concerts were cancelled. Whenever
the orchestra did travel, the foreign musicians had to obtain permission from the Justice Department to leave the state. Conducting an investigation into Muck, agents in the Justice Department
had already begun tracking his movements. In September, naval
officers visited Muck in Seal Harbor, Maine, where he rented a
summer cottage. The Seal Harbor postmaster, F. H. Macomber,
had reported that in the middle of the night, Muck's neighbors
heard strange hammering sounds and saw flashes of light coming
from his window. Perhaps, they thought, he was signaling German submarines skulking off the Atlantic Coast. When the naval
officers visited the house, they found the entire third floor wired,

raising further suspicions that he used a secret radio transmitter to communicate with German officials. But it turned out that a previous resident had installed the wires, not Muck. Nonetheless, the officers reminded him that foreigners were not allowed to go near the shore and reported their interview with Muck to the Bureau of Investigation.[45]

In Boston, George Kelleher, a special agent with the Bureau and a special assistant to the attorney general, judged Muck's activities devious. Serving all of New England, the Boston Bureau field office was filled with proponents of 100 percent Americanism, agents who were determined to thwart radicals, pacifists, and Germans. Kelleher, an Irish Catholic who had worked with the Bureau since 1910, instructed a field agent named John B. Hanrahan to interview the naval officers and Postmaster Macomber in Seal Harbor. Writing in his report afterward, Hanrahan warned, "It seems gross carelessness to allow *a trained enemy alien* who despises the United States, to install himself on the sea coast of the country, in a house from which he could easily signal to enemy submarines."[46]

A trained enemy alien? What exactly did that mean? Did the Bureau have evidence that Muck was in fact a secret agent? Was he working for Bernstorff? In the aftermath of the Providence controversy, as the allegations against Muck put pressure on the Bureau to do something, its agents began digging into his private life and compiled a dossier on him. In early November, a New York field agent interviewed an informant—an attorney named Greenberg—who provided valuable intelligence: Muck held "secret meetings" with Ambassador Bernstorff at the Biltmore and the Ritz-Carlton hotels.[47]

But there was something more. Muck had a twenty-two-year-old mistress, Rosamond Young, an aspiring soprano who traveled with the Boston Symphony Orchestra. According to the informant, Young kept a safety deposit box in a bank that contained letters from Muck "that might be of some value" to the Bureau. The New York field agent added nothing else in his report, but there was now an intriguing and obvious question: What was in the letters?

3

Out of the Cage

EVEN DRUNK IN THE EARLY MORNING, DRIVING AN UNFAMILIAR automobile with another man's wife on the seat beside him, Babe thought he could make it. Close to the Kenmore Street subway station, two trolley cars of the Newton and Brighton lines were approaching each other and going entirely too slowly for the Red Sox ace. Judging the distance between the two trolleys, Babe entertained the notion that there was just enough time for him to speed between them. He was wrong. He struck one streetcar, knocking it off its tracks, and ricocheted into the other. Both trolleys sustained considerable damage, and the car was "smashed to a shapeless mass." Babe escaped from the vehicle with booze on his breath but unscratched.[1]

The same could not be said for two women in the accident. The crash hurled Cora Walker off her trolley seat into the side of the car, injuring her chest and hip, and sending her to the City Hospital. Mrs. Harriet Crane, Ruth's late-night companion and the owner of the automobile, suffered facial lacerations and bruises. She took a taxi to the hospital, apparently without Babe. From the brief reports in the next day's papers, the reader could only glean that he drove as he pitched—fast and with great dash. One reporter even applauded the ballplayer's nerve, commenting that throughout

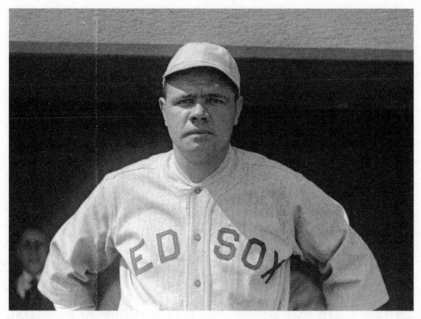

George Herman Ruth, the "Babe," the Boston Red Sox's irrepressible left-handed pitching ace. After spending years in a Catholic orphanage, on his release he seemed determined to make up for stolen time. In Boston, he pitched and hit as he lived—fast and all out. *(Courtesy of the National Photo Company Collection, Library of Congress.)*

the wreck, he "heroically stuck to the wheel," attempting through sheer willpower to salvage a winning result.

Readers could almost forgive Ruth for his lapse in judgment. It was November 1917, and the twenty-two-year-old pitcher had just finished a phenomenal season, winning twenty-four games and compiling an earned run average (ERA) of 2.01. In the American League, he finished first in complete games, second in victories, and third in innings pitched, more than validating his billing as the finest southpaw in the game. Equally remarkable, never once in all those innings did his manager Jack Barry pinch-hit for Ruth, who proved more than capable with a bat in his hands. Hitting .325, including eleven extra-base hits, no pitcher could match his prowess at the plate.[2]

By then the name Babe Ruth was on baseball fans' lips wherever the game was discussed, but the player was far better known than the person. Sportswriters had transformed him into a character from the pages of Dickens or Horatio Alger, a cross between Oliver Twist and Ragged Dick. "Charles Dickens might have written a story of the early life of George Ruth, a story of simple but dramatic power," wrote John J. Ward in 1916. "A boy born in humble circumstances, with the most meager advantages, he was sent when but seven years old to an industrial school, where he was committed until he was twenty-one."[3]

Well, yes, that was partly true, but the passive voice construction implies that everything happened *to* him, not that he was the author of his own story. And as much as any man of his times, George Herman Ruth Jr. was self-created, inventing and inhabiting a larger-than-life persona.

GEORGE RUTH WAS BORN IN the dead of the freezing winter of 1895 and raised in Baltimore, near the brackish waters of the Chesapeake Bay, close to the smell of the dead fish and ship tars of the harbor. The sixth-largest city in the nation, Baltimore advertised itself as "the Liverpool of America," a place where ships, goods, and people came and went, a hub for natives and immigrants, businessmen on the make, and day laborers struggling just to get by. Thick black smoke from steamers filled the air, and horse-drawn wagons clogged the narrow cobblestone lanes near the six long city piers. The bustle and cacophony of that world, the traffic-flowing, deal-making, oath-shouting, pleasure-taking confusion of harbor life, soaked every fiber of Ruth's being. Although he would leave Baltimore in his early twenties, Baltimore never left him.

Ruth was a child of the inner harbor district, a section of Baltimore known as Pig Town, a name that came from the herds of swine that roamed the filthy, garbage-strewn lanes. In his first ghostwritten autobiography, *Babe Ruth's Own Book of Baseball*, published in 1928, Ruth recalled his early days there as a glorious adventure. Casting himself as a Huck Finn–like figure, he described the "dirty, traffic-crowded streets," the wagon drivers who "cursed and swore and aimed blows with their driving whips at the legs of kids who made the streets their playground." Wild street urchins responded with profanity of their own, hurling rotten apples at the drivers before disappearing into narrow alleys. Altogether, he judged, his Baltimore was "a rough, tough neighborhood, but I liked it."[4]

Baltimore, and particularly Ruth's Baltimore, had a decidedly German feel. It had "a pleasantly beery, wurst-full, kraut-smelling" ambiance, noted Ruth biographer Marshall Smelser. Ruth's Café on 38 South Eutaw Street, a gathering place for working-class union members and German immigrants, was close to the harbor and served German dishes. Germans made up the city's largest ethnic group, and street toughs like Ruth were as likely to swear at a shopkeeper or wagon driver in their native language as in English. Even as an adult, when he was several decades past his Baltimore roots, Babe occasionally spoke the language. Baseball writer Fred Lieb, for instance, was surprised to hear him converse in German with Lou Gehrig's German-born mother. Babe "spoke almost as well as Lou Gehrig, who was raised to talk German with his parents, and he even got some indelicate German words and phrases into his conversation." Lieb recalled that Ruth also spoke German with his own father. Babe later told the writer that it was in his father's saloon that he first learned German and English cuss words, chewed tobacco, and tasted beer and alcohol.[5]

Only in retrospect could Ruth have discovered a carefree romance in his early years. In reality, it was a grim life. The occasional stinging pain from a dray driver's whip was the least of George's worries. Angry, often violent drunken men stumbled nightly from a hundred saloons. Periodic epidemics of cholera killed children by the thousands. Germ-plagued birthing beds, open sewers, unlit streets, rabid dogs, uncovered wells, spoiled food—there were endless opportunities to be injured or infected or killed. We know very few specifics about Ruth's early years, but according to George's sister Mary they were the only children in the family (of eight total) to survive childhood. The young Ruth's German Baltimore was a far cry from some innocent Black Forest adventure. It was closer to a dark Grimm tale that ends badly.[6]

In *The Babe Ruth Story*, another ghostwritten autobiography, published the year that he died, Ruth was more forthcoming about his early life, though still vague in details. He claimed he had "a rotten start" and was "a bad kid." "Looking back on my boyhood, I honestly don't remember being aware of the difference between right and wrong." He avoided schools, roamed the streets, pilfered food, cursed, fought, smoked, and drank. He ran wild. His mother, Katherine, was usually pregnant, often ill, and emotionally distant from her son. "My mother hated me," he later told a sportswriter. His father was an overworked waterfront saloonkeeper, swift to anger and quick to dish out punishment. Young George quickly learned to avoid him as much as possible. As far as he could tell, home life and street life were equally dangerous.[7]

Little is known about Ruth's early years, except that love was in short supply and violence ever present. A neighbor recalled seeing the father beat his son with a billiard cue. Ruth's sister Mary, called "Mamie," remembered her dad's violence: "Daddy used to whip him something terrible," she said decades later. "He just wouldn't mind Daddy, that was the problem." Or perhaps the problem was the family's poverty, or the hundred-hour weeks that Ruth Sr. spent drawing beers and serving meals, or the troubled relationship he had with his wife. All that remains of Ruth's youth are a few stories: he learned at an early age to take the last sip of a beer or whiskey left on a table; he stole money from his father's cash register; and he was as uncontrollable as his father's temper.[8]

When Ruth was seven years old, he got an unlikely break. In June 1902, Friday the 13th, his father discarded him. He loaded his boy onto the Wilkens Avenue trolley, traveled about three miles west, and dropped him off at an imposing, five-story stone structure that looked like a prison. The iron gates at St. Mary's Industrial School for Orphans, Delinquent, Incorrigible, and Wayward Boys must have seemed a world away from his old neighborhood where he had been free to roam the city streets. Inside the main building, George Herman Ruth Sr. had a conversation with the head of the facility, and then dumped his son on the Xaverian Brothers who ran the school.

In the first few years after his internment at St. Mary's, there were several attempts to reincorporate George into the family. They never lasted long. "Why?" sportswriter Bob Considine later asked him. "You know, I'd do things." What things? "Drinkin'." Undoubtedly, he was not a lush at nine or ten, but even then he was apt to "do things," and each time he returned home his father soon shipped him back to St. Mary's. Eventually the sojourns home ended altogether. He spent most of the next thirteen years inside the walls of the reformatory. His family members visited infrequently, and undoubtedly his later fame and wealth was the only reason that he remained attached to his father and sister Mamie at all. Classmate Louis "Fats" Leisman recalled that no one visited Ruth. "Well, I guess I am too big and ugly for anyone to come and see me," he said to Leisman on one lonely visiting day.[9]

He never said why his father left him at St. Mary's. All he said was that one day he was "a loose jointed, gangling dirty-faced kid in knee pants playing in the street" and the next he was shut inside of something akin to a penitentiary, told when to get up, when to eat, when to go to class, and when to go to bed. All the instructions were a new experience, and not particularly welcomed. "I liked the freedom of the street; liked the gang of youngsters I played with and prowled with," he recalled. He missed the crowded lanes of the docks, the color and noise of the streets. He even missed the police and "the beatings that came from the shopkeepers when [he was] unfortunate enough to fall into their clutches."[10]

The rigid world of St. Mary's proved harsh and uncomfortable. The brothers labored to educate and wring the wildness out of their wards. Some of them went about their task with a heavy hand, others with kind words. All expected obedience. One can only imagine what it must have been like for Ruth—abandoned by his parents, among the youngest of eight hundred boys, subject to a long list of rules, a life dictated by an inflexible schedule. His flat moon face and thick nose and lips gave rise to his nickname.

Malicious kids called him "Nigger Lips." He hated the moniker, so of course it stuck. What impact did the taunts have on him? He never said, but even during his years in the Big Leagues, he was sensitive to insults, ready to fight players who called him names.[11]

Eventually, Ruth adjusted to the taunts of the other boys and the regimen of St. Mary's. At least outwardly, he accepted that his parents had abandoned him, and he fit into the daily routine well enough. He attended the usual classes. Little of the content rubbed off, though he did develop a fine Catholic school script. He performed better in vocational classes. He tried his hand at carpentry and even cigar rolling. Oddly, for a boy with large, meaty hands, he apprenticed as a shirt maker. He enjoyed the work, and an appreciation for a finely tailored shirt stayed with him for the rest of his life. But the lasting impression that one gleans from Ruth's academic and vocational training is that he was uniformly unexceptional, the kind of big, loud kid that probably would get lost in the machinery of an institution the size of St. Mary's.

And he unquestionably would have if he had not seen Brother Matthias Boutlier hit a baseball. Matthias was a big man, maybe six feet six inches and well over 250 pounds. He was in charge of school discipline, but had none of the martinet qualities normally attributed to the position. Rather, the boys he supervised respected and admired him, especially on the days when he led them to the upper yard and hit baseballs. He was a thick, wide-hipped man, but he had an amazingly graceful swing. With a bat cocked in his right hand, he would hit soaring moon-shots to the schoolboys waiting deep in the field. One after another, the balls would climb high in the sky and arch—deep, deep, deeper—eventually falling toward the outstretched hands of the laughing fielders. Finally, in a pyrotechnic finale, he would hit a series of balls with dazzling speed. Another brother recalled, "The balls kept falling down like snowflakes over the entire yard."[12]

In an age when baseball reigned supreme as the national game, what boy could resist such a performance? Ruth must have watched with sheer wonder, dreaming of being able to hit like Matthias. "I think I was born as a hitter the first day I ever saw him hit a baseball," he said. "He was the greatest man I've ever known." Almost immediately, Ruth began to imitate Brother Matthias. He ran with the same petite, pigeon-toed steps; he swung the bat with the same long, uppercut motion; he even considered a life in the church. It didn't take long for Ruth to conclude that the Xaverian Brotherhood was not for him—but baseball was another story.[13]

"Idle hands are the devil's workshop," reads Proverbs 16:27. The brothers at St. Mary's took the maxim to heart by putting bats and baseballs into their boys' hands. As much as an educational and vocational facility, the school was a baseball factory. Separate teams represented floors in the dormitories, shops, classes, and age levels. There were advanced teams that played in city leagues and all-star teams that competed against high school and college squads. In 1909, for example, there were twenty-eight St. Mary's teams in uniform, and the playing season ran as long as ten months. Skilled, dedicated players could compete in more than two hundred games in a year, honing their skills under the tutelage of knowledgeable brothers and older students. Few places in the country offered a better education in the game of baseball.[14]

Furthermore, few students of the game were more naturally suited for it than George Herman Ruth. He matured into a raw-boned, well-muscled teenager over six feet, with long arms and legs, exceptional hand-eye coordination, and competitive fire. He began playing at the school as a left-handed catcher wearing a right-hander's mitt, but it soon became apparent that he could play any position, including pitcher. He was an outstanding hitter, but then, as today, a superior left-handed pitcher was a prize to be cherished and nurtured. By the time he was eighteen, he ruled St. Mary's baseball diamond, and word of his phenomenal talents had spread beyond the walls of the institution. By 1913, Baltimore newspapers had begun to report Ruth's pitching, hitting, and catching feats. As a pitcher, he didn't lose a contest; as a hitter, he belted a home run in almost every game.[15]

Soon Jack Dunn, the manager and owner of the International League's Baltimore Orioles, heard about Ruth. Stories vary about where and when he first saw the prodigy. Perhaps he saw Ruth pitch against Mount St. Joseph's College of Baltimore, witnessing the kid strike out twenty-two batters in a 6–0 victory. Or maybe he heard some stories, met Ruth at St. Mary's, and liked the size and look of him. In any case, what we know is that on a cold, snowy Valentine's Day in 1914, Dunn visited St. Mary's and signed Ruth to a professional contract. Dunn agreed to pay Ruth $600 for a six-month season and serve as his legal guardian until he turned twenty-one. A few weeks later, Brother Matthias quietly assured the boy who had spent most of the previous thirteen years as an inmate at St. Mary's. "You'll make it, George," he said.[16]

Then Ruth went out of the same gate he had entered in 1902. "He was free," wrote biographer Robert W. Creamer. "After all those years he was finally out of the cage, and nobody was ever going to get him into one again."[17]

WHEN RUTH CHECKED OUT OF St. Mary's, he spent a frigid weekend at his father's saloon on Conway Street, and then boarded a train for spring training in Fayetteville, North Carolina. It was a good day to leave Baltimore. A blizzard had dumped a foot of snow on the city, toppled the steeple off a Methodist church, shattered windows, and leveled fences. The town looked war-torn, and anyone leaving from Union Station headed south must have felt fortunate. Ruth was on the train, the first of thousands he would board in the following decades, and early the next morning he got off in Fayetteville, where the weather was only slightly better than Baltimore's.

Thousands of games inside the walls of St. Mary's had admirably prepared Ruth to play professional baseball. In the Orioles first intersquad game played with the team's young prospects, he came to bat in the second inning. Swinging like Brother Matthias, he clouted a ball deep over the head of the right fielder into a cornfield outside of the fairgrounds. As the fielder scrambled to retrieve the ball, Ruth walked around the bases. A memorable hit, it astounded the spectators. A few years earlier, Jim Thorpe, playing for the Fayetteville team, had blasted the longest home run anyone in town had witnessed. But Ruth's, the townsfolk agreed, was longer by at least sixty feet. A Baltimore reporter wrote that the home run "will live in the memory of all who saw it. That clouter was George Ruth, the southpaw from St. Mary's school."[18]

The next week, when Jack Dunn and the rest of the team arrived in Fayetteville, Ruth's hit left tongues still wagging. "Wait till you see this kid," the manager told his regular players. Ruth impressed everyone. At the plate he swung with the free, natural grace of "Shoeless" Joe Jackson, and on the mound he displayed an electric fastball and a sensational curve. "He has all the earmarks of a great player," Dunn told reporters. "He's the most promising young ballplayer I've ever seen."[19]

Dunn was struck by the youthful player, who wasn't so much a diamond in the rough as just a diamond, perfectly formed and in no need of further cutting. He talked about Ruth incessantly. "Dunnie's Babe," the other players began calling the new player. Shortened simply to "Babe," the nickname stuck, capturing the youth and naiveté of the man-child. "George" seemed too adult for the kid. "Babe" fit him better. It connected Ruth to the folkloric power of Babe the Blue Ox and seemed to suit his round-faced, wide-eyed innocence. While the Orioles were still in Fayetteville, Baltimore writers began to talk about the new kid, "Babe Ruth." "George Ruth" was now just an overworked bartender in a down-at-the-heels saloon near the Baltimore waterfront.

"Dunnie's Babe" didn't last long with the Orioles. The team was hemorrhaging money, and that made Ruth a valuable asset that could solve the owner's financial problems. In 1913, the Federal League, which styled itself as the "third major league," opened for business, and a new Baltimore team, the Terrapins, began competing with the Orioles head-to-head for the city's baseball fans. Dunn's franchise struggled. Even though Ruth was a young sensation, few fans noticed. Only eleven paying customers, for instance, witnessed him pitch a shutout against Rochester. Dunn reportedly was losing $1,000 a day. His only hope of survival was to sell his most valuable players, Babe among them. In early July, Dunn struck a deal with Boston Red Sox owner Joseph Lannin. Although the exact cash amounts vary with the telling, for somewhere between $10,000 and $25,000 Dunn sold the rights to veteran catcher Ben Egan and young pitchers Ernie Shore and Babe Ruth to the Sox. On the morning of July 13, Ruth arrived in Boston with a small suitcase of personal items, ready to play.

When Ruth entered the clubhouse at Fenway Park, he seemed apprehensive around the men on his new team. He was nineteen, lacking confidence and worldly experience, surrounded by strangers. On a team of mature men, he was an overgrown kid, making friends with the young boys who showed up at the ballfield to watch team practices, borrowing their bicycles to peddle around town, and gobbling as much ice cream as he could. His teammates were mostly hardened baseball men, who treated all rookies with disdain, and young talented ones with a cold, distant aloofness that often spilled over into outright hostility. Ruth and the other Baltimore players, after all, had traveled to Boston to take the jobs of established regulars. If Babe succeeded, some veteran, who had friends on the squad, would either be traded or released. Here one day, gone the next—that was the cruel law of the business.

Veterans routinely hazed Babe. They muscled him out of his turn in the batting cage, and one day when he showed up in the locker room he found his bat sawed in half. Worse yet, they vulgarly attacked his looks and behavior. Teammates called him a "caveman," nicknaming him "the Big Pig," "the Big Baboon," and "Tarzan, King of the Apes." At first, he liked the Tarzan moniker— at least until he learned that it implied that apes had nurtured and raised him. Soon, the "Nigger Lips" taunts began, as older teammates suggested that he had black ancestry. The mere suggestion that Ruth had black ancestors implied that he was inferior, that he was less than a man. Ruth bristled at the charge, threatening to fight anyone who openly insulted him.[20]

Ruth's Catholicism didn't help matters. The Red Sox, like much of Boston, divided along religious lines. Friends and roommates Smokey Joe Wood and Tris Speaker headed a faction known as the "Masons," championing America's Protestant heritage and displaying open contempt for the team's Catholic players, whom they called the "Knights of Columbus." By 1914, the contentious Speaker was one of the finest fielders and hitters in the game, but Wood had injured his throwing hand the year before and his position in the pitching rotation was uncertain. Ruth threatened his place on the team, adding to the religious hostility he and Speaker felt.[21]

Ruth presented an easy target for mean humor. If baseball came naturally to him, nothing off the diamond did. Judging from his behavior, St. Mary's had a limited civilizing influence. He was a creature of extremes. Robert W. Creamer wrote, "He disliked rules, objected to authority, and most of his adult life did what he damned well wanted to." All of which was true, but he openly defied the most basic levels of hygiene, decorum, and social norms as well. Babe thought nothing of grabbing a roommate's shaving brush—or toothbrush in some stories—if he didn't have one of his own, showering after a game and putting on the same sweaty underwear he had pitched in, or crudely explaining to the wife of a teammate that he had an unexpected groin itch. In 1914—and, indeed, for the remainder of his career—he lacked anything that could be called sophistication, but he just didn't care.[22]

Teammates and opposing players often employed animal metaphors to describe Ruth. They compared him to apes, bears, and other large beasts. When the Xaverian Brothers released him from St. Mary's, one teammate commented, "it was like turning a wild animal out of a cage." Rube Bressler, who played in the majors from 1914 to 1932, recalled that Ruth played the game innately. "He played by instinct, sheer instinct. He wasn't smart, he didn't have any education, but he never made a wrong move on a baseball diamond." In fact, Bressler thought, "he was like a damn animal. He had that instinct. He knew when it's going to rain, things like that. Nature, that was Ruth!"[23]

Players said Babe consumed everything in life with instinctual gusto. "Lord, he ate too much," recalled Boston teammate Harry Hooper. "He'd stop along the road when we were traveling and order half a dozen hot dogs and as many bottles of soda pop, stuff them in, one after the other, give a few big belches, and then roar,

'OK, boys, let's go.'" Consuming hot dogs and sodas and belching in a low, loud rumble was not the only thing he did in excess. He ate raw meat, seldom flushed toilets, treated farts as gifts to be admired, and enjoyed telling stories of his sexual exploits. A disgruntled roommate labeled him "the noisiest fucker in North America," and once Babe proudly announced from the shower, "The ladies from Boston, they'd recognize this cock anywhere."[24]

In calling the women of Boston in his circle "ladies," Babe stretched the definition of the word. Hooper suspected that when he arrived in town he had never had sex. "Once he found out about it, though, he became a bear." He married about the first young woman he met in Boston—a sixteen-year-old waitress at Lander's coffee shop named Helen Woodford—but behaved in 1914 and for the remainder of his career like a randy bachelor. Frequenting the brothels on Governor's Square, he had no sense of discrimination. One willing woman seemed as good as the next. Marshall Hunt, a *New York Daily News* sportswriter, later observed that many of Ruth's escorts "would really only appeal to a man who was just stepping out of a prison after serving a 15-year sentence." He sought forsaken women—companions who came from the same hardscrabble world that he did. Working girls serviced him regularly, and didn't complain if there was a teammate in the next bed or if Ruth munched peanuts or smoked a cigar during the act. For Ruth, women were sources of momentary pleasure, easily discarded and left behind with the keys to a hotel room.[25]

Respectable women and wives of teammates wanted nothing to do with him. Nearly everything that came out of his mouth was offensive. "He was foul-mouthed, a show off, very distasteful," recalled the wife of one Boston teammate. "The kind of person you would never dream of having to dinner." Another player's wife agreed. "He used so many swear words it embarrassed you, and believe me, I don't embarrass easy."[26]

Even when he tried not to offend, he often did. Later in his career, he attempted to navigate one formal dinner, watching what he said and trying his best to observe social niceties. Ford Frick,

Babe's ghostwriter who attended the affair with him, said that the meal began with a fine asparagus salad. Ruth hesitated, carefully selecting the right fork to use, and poked at the salad without eating any. When the host inquired from across the table if he did not like the salad, Ruth answered, "Oh, it's not that. It's just that asparagus makes my urine smell."[27]

Although Ruth seemed surrounded by women wherever he went, he knew very little about them or how to express real intimacy. "There's something about women that scares me to death," he once said. "I'm not afraid of any man on earth but almost any little scrap of woman can knock the nerve out of me." Raised mostly by men, he "hardly knew" his mother, a woman who offered little affection. According to George Sr., Katie Ruth drank heavily—"she was always drunk"—and carried on extramarital affairs. In 1906, the court found her guilty of "having unlawful sexual intercourse with another man not her husband." The infidelity and drunkenness was too much for her husband to bear. He filed for divorce and the court awarded him custody of the children. By that time, though, young George was a ward of St. Mary's, a boy abandoned by his family.[28]

Ruth's teammate Harry Hooper, a quiet, intelligent man, could not relate to the unsophisticated, loud-mouthed rookie. Unlike most ballplayers, he had a college degree in engineering and had worked as a surveyor on the West Coast. And unlike Ruth, who had a singular talent, he did not need to play baseball for a living. But when he realized that he could make more money playing professional ball than working for the railroads, in 1909 he signed with the Red Sox. Although he played on four World Series championship teams and earned induction into the National Baseball Hall of Fame, for all his success and the honors he received, he is best remembered as having been a witness to Ruth's formative years. More than that, Harry Hooper played a role in the creation of the Ruth legend.

"You know, I saw it all happen from beginning to end," he told a baseball writer who interviewed him late in his life. A half century later, Hooper was still mystified by what he watched unfold:

Sometimes I can't believe what I saw: this 19-year-old kid, crude, poorly educated, only lightly brushed by the social veneer we call civilization, gradually transformed into the idol of American youth and the symbol of baseball the world over—a man loved by more people and with an intensity of feeling that has perhaps never been equaled before or since. I saw a man transformed from a human being into something pretty close to a god. If anybody had predicted that back on the Boston Red Sox in 1914, he would have been thrown into a lunatic asylum.[29]

RUTH'S TALENT WAS OBVIOUS, HIS potential unlimited. Standing on the mound, a ball in his left hand and a sneer on his lips, he looked to St. Louis Browns second baseman Del Pratt "like a prizefighter ...That was the way he was built." His pitching rhythm—fast and aggressive—reflected his personality; there was little nuance or subtlety about it. He pounded the catcher's mitt with fastballs that popped like firecrackers. In 1914, Joseph Lannin sent him to his Providence Grays for seasoning in the minors, but Babe was back in Boston by the end of the season. By 1915, he became part of Boston's regular rotation. Most of his starts came against weaker American League clubs, another sign of his youth and inexperience, but there was no arguing with his performance. He compiled an 18–8 win/loss record with a 2.44 ERA, struck out 112 batters, and surrendered the second fewest hits in the league.[30]

In 1916, Ruth became the ace of Boston's celebrated pitching staff. He won 23 games, boasting 170 strikeouts, a league-leading 1.75 ERA, and a record-breaking 9 shutouts. After winning World Series titles in 1915 and 1916, Boston failed to win a third straight in 1917. Nevertheless, that season Ruth dominated on the mound. He tallied a 24–13 record, finishing the season first in complete games, second in victories, and third in innings pitched and in fewest hits per nine innings. He had firmly established himself as the team's most valuable player.

Ruth's behavior and desires had not changed much since walking out of the gates of St. Mary's, but he now swaggered with confidence. He was the best left-handed pitcher in the game, the favorite of Red Sox fans, and a draw in every American League stadium. His early career pitching statistics outshined those of Walter Johnson and Christy Mathewson. Between 1915 and 1917, he had won sixty-five regular season games, and lost only thirty-three. His winning percentage was an impressive .663. Yet Babe did something more. His batting average was .299, and he had hit nine home runs, remarkable achievements for a pitcher. Writing about Babe in 1916, John J. Ward remarked, "Ruth [is] dreaded for his tremendous wallops almost as much as for his pitching skill. He seems to have a natural batting eye, and [is] as likely to make a home run as an ordinary pitcher [is] to scratch out a freak single."[31]

As great as he was as a pitcher, his hitting made him unique. Walter Johnson threw harder, and Eddie Cicotte had a greater command of the strike zone. But no pitcher, and perhaps no batter, could hit the ball farther than Babe. The time was approaching when Red Sox management would have to confront a basic question that would decide the future of baseball: Was Babe Ruth a pitcher or a hitter? No player could live in both worlds.

ON THE AFTERNOON OF JANUARY 11, 1918, Ruth arrived at the Red Sox's Dexter Street offices dressed in the latest fashion and looking for more money. Although he had lost one of his rubber galoshes somewhere in the snowy streets of Boston, a coonskin coat and the thought of a new contract had kept him warm. When he had thrown his other galosh out of the window and taken off his coat, reporters noticed that he looked trim and healthy. He told them that he had spent the early winter at his farm in North Sudbury hunting, hiking, and chopping down trees. Not scrawny cherry trees "like Washington flattened," he said, comparing himself with America's first president. He had chopped "cords and cords . . . a small-sized forest" of sturdy New England wood.[32]

The Davy Crockett raccoon coat and George Washington comparisons bespoke a man whose time had come. "The mighty hunter and woodsman from North Sudbury" had become the slayer of American League batters. "He is the most colorful player, the best individual drawing card on the Boston team," wrote Burt Whitman. Like Walter Johnson and Ty Cobb, he had become a star attraction in every American League city. "Ruth's power as a turnstile clicker is well known," commented the *Boston Herald* reporter. "When he takes a swing at the ball, it is Homeric indeed, and one can hear the swish and the grunt in the back of the grandstand."

His prowess with the bat, as well as on the mound, was not lost on Babe. It was what set him apart from every other player. Whitman praised Ruth's strength—the way he bent metal and his crushing handshake—and his elemental spirit of a boy. Furthermore, in Babe he saw something more, a quality that no athlete—certainly none since the "Boston Strong Boy" John L. Sullivan—possessed. A generation before Ruth, "The Great John L.," the most famous pugilist in America, would burst through the doors of a saloon and announce, "I'm John L. Sullivan and I can lick any son of a bitch in the house!" He was a perfect emblem of the boisterous, aggressive nation that America had become—uninhibited, impulsive, and gregarious. He drank as hard as he fought and lived like there was no tomorrow. His power in the ring was legendary. And now, in Sullivan's city, Babe Ruth was exhibiting the same characteristics and tendencies. Although he had not yet achieved the same iconic status as John L. Sullivan, he stood on the precipice.[33]

Babe arrived at the team office convinced that club owner Harry Frazee should reward him with a generous new contract. Behind closed doors, the two negotiated. Although he was portrayed in the press as an innocent, he was no babe in the woods. He fully understood his value and was determined to get his $3,500 salary doubled. Frazee played the "war card," musing that there might not even be a 1918 season and, if there were, attendance would probably be sparse. Besides, demanding more money during the war seemed more than greedy; it was unpatriotic. The owner countered with $5,000 and the suggestion if Ruth had another good year that they could discuss a significant raise. "Babe was not unreasonable exactly," noted a reporter, "but it took a long time before owner and player came to terms." Eventually Ruth accepted the offer. Although the more than 40 percent increase was less than what Babe wanted, he had little leverage and finally agreed, making him the first Red Sox player to sign a 1918 contract.[34]

He was motivated to sign the contract in large part because of the war. Even a cursory glance through Boston newspapers underscored the repressive, anti-German mood sweeping the city and the country at large. The controversy surrounding Karl Muck, federal charges against "alien enemies," vigilante attacks against German-Americans—all attested to a building sense of paranoia and frustration. About a week after Ruth signed his contract, a *Boston Globe* writer warned that "German spies might be lurking at almost every corner or railroad trestle or munitions or food factory yard," and every loyal American should be on the lookout for enemy activity. It was not a propitious time to be a German-American in the United States, especially one in the public gaze.[35]

Before America's entry into the war, Ruth showed little concern about his German heritage. In 1916, when a reporter asked him about his family name, he casually responded, "I guess it's a German name; sounds like it, any way. But it serves all right. I never found it hurt my batting average or was a burden to me with men on base. Ruth is my name, and Ruth it will stay, so far as I'm concerned."[36]

George Herman Ruth—a child of German heritage, paid handsomely to entertain the American public, a fixture in newspapers across the country—had good reason not to hold out for a few thousand dollars more. The increasing use of "Babe" served him well; it made him seem more American and removed the taint of guilt by association. But Babe was not blind to the delicacy of his situation. A misstep in public, a planted story by an angry baseball official, any hint that he was not doing his part in the war could shatter his popular image.

4

The War Game

HARRY FRAZEE MADE A FORTUNE TAKING RISKS. AFTER THE United States declared war on Germany, the owner of the Red Sox bet $2,000 that the conflict would be over before the 1918 season began. But during the winter months of 1917, his hubris turned into nervousness. As the war escalated and the demands for American manpower intensified, he feared that the draft would deplete his roster and derail his business. A full 90 percent of Major League players were eligible for conscription. By January 1918, the Red Sox had already lost eleven men to the military effort—the most in Major League Baseball. What could he do?[1]

Publicly, he delivered a patriotic message: Baseball players were not above making the same sacrifices as other Americans—and they certainly should not receive an exemption from the draft. Country came before baseball. "We want to win the war, don't we?" he asked a reporter.[2]

On the eve of the 1918 baseball season, with the war weighing on every business decision he made, Frazee held grave doubts about whether he could even field a team. In the world of musical theater, Frazee, a successful producer, had learned that life was a gamble. No matter how much experience he had, staging a winner at the box office was never a sure thing. The same was true in baseball.

So what could he do? He could roll the dice one more time.

THE BEST PART ABOUT BOSTON, Frazee thought, was leaving it. He may have been the owner of the Red Sox, but he belonged in Gotham. He made a name for himself on Broadway. From the time he had his first job as a theater usher in his hometown of Peoria, Illinois, he longed to be in show business. When he was just sixteen years old, he became the assistant manager of the Peoria Theater, booking shows, selling tickets, and seeking publicity. The following year, he worked as an agent for a touring production, hustling his way across the Midwest. And during his late teens he managed the Peoria Distillers, a semi-professional baseball team. Barnstorming with the club, Frazee discovered that baseball, like the theater, was really about selling entertainment, and he could turn a profit doing both.[3]

Restless and ambitious, he returned to musical theater, building his career around a string of successful light comedies. He understood what drew people to the theater. "The rank and file," he said, "go to the theater for diversion, and I try to give them what they want." Comedies and farces provided joy and relief, an escape from the ordinary. He was not interested in tragedies. "There are enough undertakers' announcements in the papers," he said. By 1907, the twenty-seven-year-old vaudeville impresario, known as the "king of one-night stands," had become so prosperous that he built his own playhouse in Chicago—the Cort Theatre.

Yet he remained intrigued by the possibilities of peddling sports. In 1909, he approached Red Sox owner John I. Taylor about buying the team. When Taylor declined, Frazee turned to boxing, profiting from the national interest in "the Fight of the Century"— a contest between Jack Johnson, the first black heavyweight champion, and Jim Jeffries, the "Great White Hope." Exploiting the country's deep racial divisions, Frazee and boxing promoter

Jack Curley organized a troupe of pugilists and wrestlers featuring Jeffries. In 1910, Frazee made a small fortune hyping Jeffries as the savior of white America, the man who would redeem the race in the boxing ring. Although Johnson pummeled Jeffries on Independence Day, Frazee had already made $58,000 off white Americans' hopes.[4]

"Handsome Harry" Frazee had a very good year at the box office, too. By midsummer, he had moved to New York and soon thereafter produced *Madame Sherry*, a sensational hit that made him $250,000 in profits. Flush with cash, he opened the Longacre Theater on Broadway, and in the coming years, he produced popular shows, including *A Pair of Sixes*, *A Full House*, and *Nothing but the Truth*. An innovative producer, Frazee developed the concept of "flying matinees," where his companies played in towns close to New York City during the afternoon and returned later that evening for a show on Broadway. Expanding his business holdings, he built more theaters, dabbled in the stock market, and purchased investment properties. By 1916, the former usher from Peoria had become a millionaire overseeing a theater enterprise that extended from New York to Chicago.

Success, money, and power made him among the most influential figures in American theater. Living on Park Avenue, he rubbed elbows with Manhattan socialites and the most prominent actors, playwrights, and composers. A gregarious, hard-drinking womanizer, Frazee pursued the company of aspiring actresses when his wife was away. Short, shaped like a bowling ball, with dark features and a large head, he possessed boundless energy and irrepressible confidence. A fast-talking P. T. Barnum of a salesman, he knew how to command a room. Wearing the finest suits, he often conducted business with a stiff drink in hand. "Frazee never drew a sober breath in his life," said songwriter Irving Caesar. "He made more sense drunk than most people do sober."

Since he had first tried to buy the Red Sox, Frazee made subsequent offers to purchase other Major League teams, including the Chicago Cubs, the New York Giants, and the Boston Braves, but none of the deals materialized. Then, less than a month after the

Red Sox won the 1916 World Series, the team's second championship in two years, owner Joseph Lannin decided that it was time to sell. In his three years as owner, Lannin, a real estate developer and hotel proprietor, reportedly had earned $400,000. But with the war escalating in Europe, he foresaw trouble for Organized Baseball, despite President Wilson's campaign promise to keep the nation on the sidelines. The stress of owning the Red Sox had exacerbated his heart trouble, too. "I'm too much of a fan to own a ball club," he told manager Bill Carrigan after the Series. "It's had me on edge all summer, which has accounted for my outbursts from time to time."[5]

Shortly after the Series ended, Frazee learned that Lannin was interested in selling the club. In a complex business arrangement, Frazee and his business partner, Hugh Ward, paid Lannin $400,000 in cash and pledged a three-year note for $262,000. Frazee also assumed a $188,000 mortgage on Fenway Park. Under the agreement, Fenway Realty Trust, a company established by former owner Charles Taylor, held the mortgage on the stadium. Convinced that buying a winner was a sound investment, Frazee said that purchasing the Red Sox made as much sense as financing "a show that had already opened to good reviews."[6]

For the producer, owning a baseball team did not seem that different from managing a theater. The bottom line was giving the public what it wanted. The baseball diamond served as a stage where the players, like actors, entertained spectators in an unscripted drama. "Baseball," he said, "is essentially a show business. If you have any kind of a production, be it a music show, or a wrestling bout, or a baseball game that people want to see enough to pay money for the privilege, then you are in show business and don't let anyone tell you any different."

Not everyone in the sport shared Frazee's views. Byron Bancroft Johnson, the "czar of baseball," regarded him as an interloper. He saw the theater producer as a threat to his authority, an outsider who was neither a friend nor a malleable supplicant. Since founding the American League in 1903, Johnson had recruited every owner and endorsed every team sale, but Lannin, frustrated by Johnson's meddling in the club's business affairs, did not seek his approval. Still, Johnson, nicknamed the "Benevolent Autocrat" by *The Sporting News*, firmly believed that the league's existence—and its prosperity—depended on his ability to supervise the business operations of each team.[7]

Johnson's critics likened him to Theodore Roosevelt, an egotistical leader full of self-praise and self-righteousness. Built like the Bull Moose, "Ban" Johnson, a rather large man with a round, fleshy face, spoke in a forceful, stentorian manner. An avid reader of poetry and military history, he appreciated a lively debate and "never missed an opportunity to make a speech." According to one writer, "No matter how often Ban made a speech it was always the same speech; all about how he, singlehanded and alone, had made baseball a gentlemen's sport, and it must be kept forever clean because sportsmanship spoke from the heart of America and he would lay down his life to save our beloved nation, at which point he would begin to cry."[8]

Temperamental and petty, described by Cleveland owner Charles Somers as a man who "never forgets an enemy," Johnson vowed that he would get the best of Frazee. Once Johnson failed to persuade Lannin to renege on the sale, there was nothing that he could do except make life difficult for the new Sox owner. Soon, however, Johnson and Frazee would find themselves embattled in a war—not against each other, but for the game's very survival.

"AN OFFICIAL DECLARATION OF WAR will sound the death knell of practically all branches of sports in this country," the *New York Times* predicted in March 1917. By that time, the Germans had resumed unrestricted submarine warfare against all US ships in the Atlantic, and Americans had learned about the Zimmermann telegram, Germany's proposed alliance with Mexico. In the weeks before opening day, the press speculated that the global crisis would force the owners to concede the season.[9]

The Great War seemed to threaten baseball, a sport that embodied the nation's democratic values. Echoing President Wilson, journalist Benjamin DeCasseres maintained, "The world ought to be made safe for baseball." Without it, America would cease being recognizable. But as long as the game endured, DeCasseres wrote, "the Kaisers and Trotskys would strike out" and "the country that would win the war was the country that produced" the sport's greatest players—"Christy Mathewson, Ty Cobb, and Babe Ruth."[10]

According to baseball's proponents, the national pastime promoted the country's ideals of competition, equality, self-reliance, and solidarity. Citizens from every part of the country enjoyed the game. Baseball united spectators sitting in the grandstands, melting the hometown crowd—immigrants from the old country and native citizens alike—into a community devoted to a single cause. "The spectator at the ball game is no longer a statesmen, lawyer, broker, doctor, merchant, or artisan," journalist H. Addington Bruce wrote, "but just a plain everyday man"—an American.[11]

By the Great War, baseball had become something more than a popular spectacle. It was, philosopher Morris Cohen wrote, "a national religion." The game touched every corner of the country. Boys and young men played it on city lots and open fields. Newspapers detailed the successes of local teams while national magazines published stories about players, owners, and pennant races. Writers glorified the game in books, poems, and songs. In a time of war, Cohen suggested, baseball served a higher purpose. The game cultivated "hope and courage when we are behind, resignation when we are beaten, fairness for the other team when we are ahead, charity for the umpire, and above all the zest for combat and conquest."[12]

The country's most famous evangelical preacher at the time, Reverend Billy Sunday, believed that baseball was more important during the war than in peacetime. "The idea that baseball is a luxury that ought to be postponed until after the war is over is ridiculous," he wrote in 1917. Described by his biographer Robert Martin as "a prophetic pugilist battling for righteousness," Sunday delivered sermons with his sleeves rolled up, shaking his fists as beads of sweat dripped from his brow. The former professional ballplayer hypnotized audiences as he stormed and shouted, hurling imaginary baseballs and sliding across the stage like it was home plate. He had no tolerance for cowards and called for pacifists to be executed.[13]

Convinced that sports prepared men for war, Sunday contended that the best soldiers were ballplayers. "What are soldiers worth if they're not good athletes?" he asked. "What is a battle but a showdown of athletic skill of a terrible intensity?" Competing on the field helped men develop a fighter's instinct. Even General Pershing attributed American soldiers' proficiency for throwing grenades to playing baseball. Sunday insisted that Americans needed the sport now more than ever. "Baseball," he declared, "*is a war game.*"[14]

Ban Johnson agreed. Not only would the American League conduct normal operations during the 1917 season, but every team would also perform military drills before each game. The idea of turning baseball players into citizen soldiers came from Yankees co-owner T. L. Huston. He believed that the drills would help prepare the players for the service and argued that baseball players should serve as role models for America's youth, exemplars of patriotism worthy of emulation.[15]

The owners' decision to have players conduct military maneuvers was not based purely on patriotic sentiments, but rather a desire to protect their business interests, too. Baseball executives hoped that if the players received formal military training of some sort, then the War Department might allow them to remain on their respective clubs until they were absolutely needed in the service.

Thus, baseball officials went about turning stadiums into theaters of war. On April 19, 1917, "Wake Up America! Day," a national campaign for military recruitment, Ban Johnson announced that teams would encourage fans to enlist in the armed forces at every ballpark. Throughout the war, elaborate military parades and recruiters appeared on the fields before games. Marching bands played patriotic songs, including Harry Von Tilzer's "great base ball war song," titled "Batter Up: Uncle Sam Is at the Plate." Fans cheered and sang along: "The Allies and the Huns / Have made a lot of runs / Put Sammy in to hit / And watch him do his bit . . . " In Chicago, White Sox players sang the national anthem before

During the Great War, proponents of the preparedness campaign believed that athletes made the best soldiers. Using rifles instead of bats, here the Cleveland Indians parade across the field under the direction of a drill sergeant. *(Courtesy of the National Baseball Hall of Fame and Museum.)*

the games began. And every team owner organized Liberty Bond drives, Red Cross donations, and charity exhibition games.[16]

In May, Ban Johnson announced that the owners were willing to do whatever was necessary to support the war effort, and that every player who felt compelled to volunteer for the armed forces should do so. Later that month, Congress passed the Selective Service Act, requiring all men between the ages of twenty-one and thirty to register with the government. Among the 9.6 million men who appeared at more than four thousand registration sites on June 5 was twenty-three-year-old George Herman Ruth, who registered in Boston, though he would later receive an exemption as a married man. In July, Johnson suggested that the draft might force the owners to cut the season short, but few players were called up before season's end. Although the Red Sox finished with an impressive ninety wins, the White Sox took the pennant and beat the New York Giants in the World Series.[17]

Baseball survived America's first season at war, but by the late fall of 1917, Johnson sensed an escalating crisis on the horizon. By November the Selective Service had drafted ten players from the Cleveland Indians and cut into many other teams' rosters. Given the indiscriminate nature of the draft, Johnson noted, some teams were hurt more than others. "Baseball," he said, "cannot be maintained at its present high standard unless we can retain a fair proportion of the star players who have been developed by years of training." Therefore, he suggested that each club should preserve its roster with an exemption of eighteen players—the very best ones—totaling 288 men from all teams. Baseball executives, owners, and fans denounced Johnson's plan, calling him "selfish" and "unpatriotic." "I would not go one inch toward Washington to ask President Wilson or the Secretary of War for special favors for baseball," said National League president John Tener.[18]

Provost Marshal Enoch Crowder, the head of the Selective Service, dismissed Johnson's proposal, too. "That must be a pipe dream," he said. "There certainly is no warrant in the law for exempting baseball players from the draft, and there is nothing in the regulations to warrant making exceptional rulings for men liable to service who make baseball their livelihood." Crowder made clear that he had not received an official request from Johnson or any other baseball executive. Facing intense criticism, Johnson backpedaled and explained that he had not actually petitioned the government for player exemptions. Rather, he was simply offering a potential solution that would allow Major League Baseball to continue as President Wilson had hoped that it would.[19]

The truth of the matter was that all of the owners were busy scheming about how to keep baseball stadiums open for business. On December 14, 1917, the owners from the American League and National League met in Chicago at the Congress Hotel "to consider various matters of joint interest to the two leagues." They had become increasingly alarmed about how the war and the government's entertainment admission tax might diminish attendance for the upcoming season. In 1917, attendance declined throughout Major League Baseball by nearly 20 percent. Less than half of the sixteen teams turned a profit that season, and the owners feared that 1918 would be worse. Initially, the owners agreed to play a full season, though they later reduced it from 154 games to 140. They also agreed to cut player salaries, trim rosters from twenty-five players to eighteen—not because Johnson suggested it, but because it would save the owners money—and raise ticket prices across the board to offset the 10 percent "war tax."[20]

Still, no one knew what to expect for the coming season. "Facing the year which waits just over the crest," Grantland Rice wrote in December, "the two major leagues are up against the greatest uncertainty they have ever known."[21]

"NO ONE," HARRY FRAZEE SAID, "ever made any money in this world unless he took a chance." Despite the grim outlook for baseball in the winter of 1917–1918, Frazee made it known that he was optimistic. Scrambling to assemble a full roster, he had to replace the eleven men who had already enlisted in the service. Knowing that he was willing to take a risk and that the Philadelphia Athletics had lost $60,000 in 1917, Ban Johnson facilitated an arrangement that would benefit both clubs. Carrying enormous debt and one of the highest payrolls in baseball, Connie Mack, the penurious manager and part owner of the Athletics, was desperate for relief. Fortunately for Mack, his friend Johnson had found a profligate investor in Boston who could solve his financial problems.[22]

While most team owners feared bankruptcy during the war, Frazee wagered that Americans would be more inclined to seek a diversion in a time of war. "People must be amused," he said. "They must have their recreation despite the grim horrors of war." Determined to build a winning team, Frazee gave Mack $60,000 in cash and three journeymen in exchange for pitcher "Bullet" Joe Bush, catcher Wally Schang, and outfielder Amos Strunk—all valuable players who could help the Red Sox win. The *Boston Globe* called it "one of the biggest baseball deals that has been pulled off in years." But Frazee wasn't done dealing. He made another arrangement with Mack, paying "a substantial sum" that brought first baseman John "Stuffy" McInnis, a talented hitter, to the Red Sox. "Boston," Frazee said, "has been educated to expect winners in the American League, and when I discovered that the war had deprived the Red Sox of their best players, I was compelled to act or play to empty benches."[23]

Critics complained that Frazee had tried to buy the American League pennant, exploiting the hardships confronting the owners. But that was not the harshest charge against him. Although Frazee publicly stated he would not request special favors for his club from the government, in December he contacted Captain William R. Rush, commandant of the Boston Navy Yard, seeking a deal. Offering to donate the entire receipts from a series of exhibitions that would benefit the Navy Relief Fund, Frazee hoped that the games would help him buy exemptions for Red Sox players already serving in the navy.

Awaiting a reply from Rush, Frazee also lobbied Franklin D. Roosevelt, the assistant secretary of the navy. He wanted Roosevelt to authorize a deferment for player-manager Jack Barry and left fielder George "Duffy" Lewis, both of whom were already enlisted in the naval reserve. Writing FDR on January 23, he reminded him of President Wilson's stated desire that Organized Baseball continue uninterrupted, providing Americans a source of diversion and entertainment. But without the services of eight players already serving in the navy, he wrote, "I might as well shut my gates." Roosevelt sympathized with him and wrote Captain Rush, suggesting that they consider helping Frazee but only if the commandant agreed that it was appropriate.[24]

When rumors spread throughout Boston that members of the Red Sox had received preferential treatment from the navy, sportswriters excoriated Frazee. Publicly, he denied seeking exemptions for Barry and other members of his team. He told the Brockton chapter of the Knights of Columbus, "I have not asked for furloughs for any of my players and I don't intend to." But when reports surfaced that Congressmen James A. Gallivan, a devout member of the Royal Rooters—the Red Sox fan club—and a friend of Frazee, had also pressured Navy Secretary Josephus Daniels on Frazee's behalf, the Red Sox owner feigned ignorance. "I don't understand it," he said. "There must be some kind of mistake."[25]

Frazee had run out of political capital. Neither Roosevelt nor Gallivan could help him. Besides, none of the players serving at the Boston Navy Yard wished to return to the club. And even if they had agreed to Frazee's plan, the public would have vilified them as slackers and draft dodgers who had betrayed their country. Frazee had no choice but to field a team without them.[26]

5

Bang That Old Apple

FOREVER RESTLESS, BABE RUTH HAD A SERIOUS CASE OF CABIN fever. After a dreary winter spent with his wife Helen at "Home Plate"—their farm in Sudbury—he was ready for a change. Spring training in Hot Springs, Arkansas, promised to be the perfect remedy. It was Babe's kind of town—small enough to be cozy, big enough to find some action, and thoroughly wide open. It boasted a racetrack and several casinos, and though it didn't advertise its brothels, they were easy enough to find and their doors were open all night. After the dull winter, he anticipated stretching his legs and loosening up his arm on the baseball diamond, while also finding some fun. What he didn't expect—what no one imagined— was that simply by having more fun, he would transform the game of baseball.

On March 9, around noon, when Ruth arrived at the South Station, snow dusted the Hub. A blizzard sweeping across the Great Lakes threatened the first leg of the trip as the team headed west toward Albany. Loaded down with two large bags and a set of left-handed golf clubs, Babe greeted his traveling companions. Most of the players had made other travel arrangements, but a bevy of sportswriters, cartoonists, and photographers boarded the train

When the Boston Red Sox arrived in Hot Springs, Arkansas, for spring training in 1918, new manager Ed Barrow (standing second from the left) expected that Babe Ruth (standing fourth from the left) would serve almost exclusively as a pitcher. Yet with a roster decimated by the draft, Barrow desperately needed hitters, and Ruth was ready to fill the void. *(Photo by Carl Horner, Courtesy of Heritage Auction Gallery.)*

with Babe in Boston. When it reached Albany, Harry Frazee and his new manager Ed Barrow, along with infielder Johnny Evers and several other players, joined the Boston group. In the club cars, journalists and players planned on passing the time drinking, smoking, and gambling. Edward Martin of the *Globe* wrote, "No arrangements had been made for any golf matches on the train, but it is understood that there may be other games played."[1]

While Babe and his group settled into their seats, the weather worsened. West of Albany, heavy snow and winds created drifts along the route, delaying the train's arrival in Buffalo by five full hours. Missing the connection for the Hot Springs Special, one writer blamed the holdup on an engineer who drove as though he were commanding a tank through the trenches on the Western Front. Instead of rolling west toward Akron and St. Louis, the Red Sox contingent pounded the cold off their feet inside the station, waiting for a 2:00 a.m. connection. Making matters worse, especially for nighthawks like Ruth, Ed Barrow gave a first indication of what kind of manager he would be when he announced that he would run a strict, no-nonsense training camp. There would be "no late sleepers," he said. Every player had to be out of the dining room by nine. "Babe Ruth was very dejected when he heard the sad news," Paul Shannon reported.[2]

Once past Buffalo, the mood lightened again. The players bantered and laughed. Some read, others gambled, but most drank. Heavy drinking and alcoholism has always been part of the "drink hard, play hard" culture of baseball, but it was probably worse before 1918 than after. The stories of such heavy drinkers as Rube Waddell fill pages in the history of the sport, and reporters of the era generally treated them as a source of humor rather than pathos. In Boston and on the road, Ruth was a heavy, usually gregarious drinker. As the train plowed west toward St. Louis and then south toward Little Rock and Hot Springs, he was the center of the action—consuming feasts in the dining car, dropping money at the card table, and greeting virtually everyone who boarded, especially the soldiers who got on at every stop. He "was the life of the party and fraternized with a lot of soldier boys from Camp Devens," commented Martin. Ruth "passed around his cigars and did not overlook any of the lads in khaki."[3]

Babe enjoyed his role as the bell cow, even when he was the object of the humor. According to one newspaper account, when a member of the Red Sox group commented on the beauty of the landscape, Babe cut in, hoping to get the final word on any subject. "This is nothing," he said. "The best scenery goes by when we are sleeping."[4]

If sportswriters occasionally reported Ruth's gaffes, it was all in good fun. The pleasure they took in his uninhibited behavior gave

life to their columns, and they regarded themselves as hero build-
ers, not myth busters. The *Globe's* thirty-four-year-old "Eddie"
Martin, born and raised in South Boston, led the group of Ruth's
acolytes in the press. He was an authority concerning Babe and
baseball, a master of the most arcane trivia. "If Eddie says so, it is
so," was the saying around the *Globe's* office. At the same time,
he was apt to exaggerate and engage in some harmless "godding
up" of Boston's star—and his reports from spring training and the
coming season were instrumental in shaping the popular image of
Babe Ruth.[5]

Not everyone shared in the mirth of the ride to Hot Springs.
Even in the best of times, Ed Barrow rarely cracked a smile or
appreciated a joke, and March 1918 was not the best of times.
Frazee departed for the Ozarks feeling uncertain about how his
reconstructed team would perform under a new manager. When
his former manager Jack Barry had enlisted in the naval reserve in
1917, Frazee knew he needed a baseball man who could help him
rebuild the team. This was when he turned to Barrow—informally
at first—who was serving at the time as the president of the International League. Then, early in 1918, after several disagreements,
the International League team owners effectively forced Barrow
out of his position when they cut his salary by two-thirds, and
Frazee formally hired him as the Red Sox's manager. As the skipper sat on the train to Hot Springs, mulling over how to forge a
winning squad out of desperate parts, he found little comfort in the
childish antics of his best pitcher.[6]

Though he shared few characteristics with his star player, they
did have two things in common: both were products of a grim
childhood and a love for baseball. Edward Grant Barrow—named
after his father and the victorious Union general—was born in
Springfield, Illinois, while his family was in the process of moving
to Nebraska. After six bleak, unproductive years farming on the
Great Plains, his family moved to Iowa, near Des Moines. Barrow spoke little about his early years—the struggles of his family,
the hardships of farm life, his efforts to contribute to the family
income, and an early, brief marriage. But he did open up on the

subject of baseball. He claimed he had been a good high school and sandlot pitcher; that is, until he injured his arm throwing on a cold, wet day. After that, he stayed in the game the best he could by organizing barnstorming tours, managing or buying a stake in minor league squads, and working in various front office positions. For a short time, he even managed the Detroit Tigers.[7]

Barrow often moved from town to town and job to job because of his abrasive, nearly dictatorial personality. *New York Times* columnist Arthur Daley wrote, "He was a big, broad-shouldered man who feared no one and could argue as forcefully with his fists as his tongue." With an eye for typecasting, Frazee referred to him as "Simon," after Simon Legree, the cruel slave driver who enjoyed beating and breaking the spirit of his chattel in Harriet Beecher Stowe's novel *Uncle Tom's Cabin*. Barrow certainly looked the part. He had a pugnacious face—weary eyes, boxer's nose, and smirking lips framed between a square chin and bushy, black eyebrows. He frequently spoke of his love for the sport of boxing—second only to baseball—and claimed that no man had ever bested him in a fight. His look, fiery temper, and heavyweight physique encouraged few to test his record. No doubt, he knew baseball, but his brutal managing style ensured conflicts with such lawless players as Babe Ruth.[8]

Under his regime, Barrow announced, rules would be strictly enforced. All card games, he proclaimed, would be nickel-and-dime affairs that ended no later than 11:00—no high-stakes contests that lingered into the early mornings. Shortly after noon on March 11, when the train arrived in the Valley of the Vapors, the boss issued several other edicts. He refused, for instance, to let the players take a car to the ballpark. He insisted that they walk the two miles from the hotel to the practice field. After three hours of work on the diamond, they trekked back to the hotel over the mountain trail. They followed the march through the afternoon heat with hot spring baths and an hour and a half break before dinner. Lights were to be out by 11:30.[9]

His puritanical rules struck Ruth as a mite extreme. For Red Sox players, spring training was a highly anticipated opportunity to escape the frigid New England winter for the more hospitable climes of southern resort towns like Hot Springs and Tampa. As much as a time to shed winter weight and regain the previous season's form, for many players—and Ruth was certainly among them—spring training meant gambling on cards and horses, spending nights with prostitutes, and enjoying a bachelor's life, whether they were single or married. Barrow's rules, then, were a disappointing setback, to say the least, and Ruth bristled under them. If he could resist the casinos and the brothels and the racetrack on the edge of town, he did not try. His only problem, he told the *Globe*'s Martin, was that the racetrack and the golf course were on opposite ends of Hot Springs, making it impossible to enjoy both activities in one afternoon.[10]

Realizing that with an ersatz team with so many recent arrivals, he had to give—at least for the moment—some maneuvering room to his best player, Barrow ignored infractions by Babe and a few others. Soon after his boot camp regimen began, he eliminated the mountain trail hikes, giving his boys more free time in the afternoons. And he stopped enforcing bed checks. Harry Hooper recalled that despite Barrow's rules, Ruth continued losing money at the track and courted venereal disease in the brothels. Yet his nighttime activities didn't seem to interfere with his work on the diamond. His pitching was sharp, and he attacked training sessions, and even the few mountain hikes, like a hungry rookie.[11]

Swinging a bat, Ruth discovered more joy from hitting the ball than from anything else he did on the field, and he entertained his teammates and spectators alike, hitting deep shots to the outfielders. He hit long, high balls, difficult for the fielders to judge, and he "had the boys racing around for a lot of leg exercise."[12]

At the start of the exhibition season on March 17, the full Red Sox squad was not in camp, and Barrow humored Babe by starting him at first base against the Brooklyn Dodgers. "His play at first was sensational," reported Martin, who compared him with Hal Chase, the great Chicago White Sox first baseman. "The big fellow plucked [baseballs] from the ozone, dug them from the dirt and reached everywhere for them in real Chase fashion."[13]

Babe made his most spectacular impression at home plate, not first base. In the fourth inning, he launched a ball high toward deep left center where it landed in a pile of lumber for a home run. He came to the plate again in the sixth inning. This time, he hit the ball even farther. It traveled over the right-field fence and finally landed in the middle of an alligator farm. "The intrusion kicked up no end of commotion among the 'Gators,'" noted Martin.[14]

It also stirred the imaginations of the spectators. Admittedly, Brooklyn did not use its first-string pitchers in the contest, and it was a meaningless exhibition, but the distance of Ruth's blasts defied the standards of the day. There was palpable excitement among spectators who watched Ruth pound the ball. Martin could hardly contain the rush he felt when he wrote his lede: "What a wallop when the lid was pried off the 1918 baseball season here this afternoon!" Although Barrow saw the performance as a lark, Ruth and several other teammates had a glimmer of something more significant. Babe could do more than just throw a ball across the plate. He was an athlete who could field, and he could hit the ball farther than any other player. Harry Hooper must have sensed the shift. He had just arrived in town and only watched the contest, but would soon become Barrow's leading advisor for on-field strategy and the greatest champion of making Babe Ruth a full-time hitter.[15]

Hooper—along with teammates, reporters, and spectators—kept watching Ruth. At the plate, he generated interest with every twist of his body, turning dull, routine swings into a carnival performance. A few days after his barrage of home runs, the Red Sox worked out on a chilly, damp afternoon. Low clouds threatened rain, and playing baseball smacked of misery. Then Babe stepped to the plate for batting practice. After taking a few swings, he "calmly announced" that he was going to hit one out of the park. No sooner had he said it than he did it, driving the pitch over the fence.[16]

The audacity of the called shot staggered the imagination. No one before that time *tried* to hit a home run. The game in the Dead Ball Era was one of limited expectations. Players choked up on their thick-handled war clubs, took short, chopping, flat swings, and concentrated on making contact. They bunted singles, moved a runner from one base to the next with sacrifices, and occasionally slashed line drives into the gaps for doubles or triples. It was a game of hitting behind the runner and guarding the strike zone like a lion does her cubs. Players and fans alike treated home runs as gifts from the baseball gods, when in fact they were often the result of an outfielder who played too close to the infield or tripped pursuing a deep fly ball.

In truth, the swings of such great batsmen as Ty Cobb and Honus Wagner were not conducive to hitting home runs because the baseball used in the games was difficult to hit with a long, powerful, uppercut stroke. It was the job of pitchers to punish the baseball before putting it into play. They took the clean, white, round ball and simply abused it—nicking it with their nails or belt buckle, smearing it with dirt, tobacco-laced saliva, or some other agent, transforming it into a dark, misshaped, almost spheroid object that they could throw with a variety of spins to make it move, drop, and curve with great accuracy. It was that forlorn "ball" that they would throw one hundred or more times a game. Actually trying to connect with such a maltreated object for a home run was lunacy.

Yet that was precisely what Ruth did, transforming the conventional batter's swing in the process. Instead of choking up on the bat and chopping at the ball, Babe gripped it low, his right hand down to the knob, unleashing a whipping undercut swing that could launch a baseball farther than any man ever had. When he swung the bat with all his might, he fully intended to crush it. His majestic home runs—and the very threat of his power—would soon redefine the way that batters played the game, journalists reported it, and fans understood it. His hitting philosophy was simple: "Just bust 'em," he said. "Take a good cut and bang that old apple on the nose."[17]

On March 23, Babe showed off his revolutionary approach toward hitting before several hundred doughboys when he and the team played an exhibition against the Dodgers. Both teams left their quarters in Hot Springs early in the morning, took a train through the hills of Arkansas to Little Rock, and then traveled by automobile to the army cantonment at Camp Pike for the game.[18]

No sooner had the Red Sox arrived at Camp Pike and taken the field to warm up than dark clouds swept in and the skies opened, followed by lightning flashes and low rumbles of thunder. Although the managers cancelled the contest, they still held a batting practice, and Babe's performance was thoroughly entertaining for "the khaki boys." He swung like Brother Matthias had at St. Mary's. To the immense enjoyment of the soldiers, in a Homeric session he drove five balls over the right-field fence. The feat was so unusual that a *Boston American* headline blared: BABE RUTH PUTS FIVE OVER FENCE, HERETOFORE UNKNOWN TO BASEBALL FANS.[19]

The next day he added to his growing reputation as a hitter in another game against the Dodgers. In the third inning, facing Brooklyn's pitcher Al Mameau, with the bases loaded—a full house—Ruth hammered the ball over the right-field wall. Writers had not yet invented the phrase "grand slam," but Ruth would inspire a whole new language to describe his exploits on the field. All the players who witnessed the hit agreed it was the longest they had ever seen. "The ball not only cleared the right field wall," reported Martin, "but stayed up, soaring over the street and a wide duck pond, finally finding a resting place for itself in the nook of the Ozark hills." Paul Shannon of the *Post* disagreed only on a few of Martin's finer points. He claimed the ball cleared the fence by about two hundred feet and dropped in a pond beside the alligator farm. In either case, "the spectators yelled with amazement," much to Babe's pleasure. As he rounded first, he laughed and said, "I would liked to have got a better hold of that one."[20]

Scattering ducks, astonishing soldiers, angering alligators— Babe Ruth at the plate was becoming a figure of folklore. He was Paul Bunyan with an ax, Davy Crockett with a rifle, Mike Fink on a keelboat—an American capable of accomplishments beyond mortal man. A *Boston Herald* reporter claimed that if an alert trolley driver had not seen one of Ruth's home runs sailing over the fence and taken evasive actions, the ball "would have knocked the trolley car off the tracks." Clearly, several journalists concluded, the army needed heroic "Colossuses" like Ruth.[21]

YET THE STORIES OF HIS exploits contrasted sharply with the news of American troops reaching France. Only a few days after Babe had begun to scatter the gators outside Majestic Park, the team of Hindenburg and Ludendorff launched the *Kaiserschlacht* (Kaiser's Battle) against the British and French lines on the Western Front. Freed from war in the East after the Bolshevik Revolution pulled Russia out of the conflict, Germany had shifted fifty divisions to the west, determined to overwhelm the Allied Powers before the United States could get its army in place. More troops combined with tactical and weaponry innovations led to predictably grim results. Boston newspapers echoed the dire concern of America's allies. The war, many allied leaders feared, might be lost.

For all the newspaper space devoted to Ruth's hitting, Ed Barrow viewed the performances as mixed blessings. During spring training, Ruth hit four home runs in twenty-one at bats, a remarkable achievement for the era. Furthermore, his moon shots attracted attention and lured fans into the ballpark. They also encouraged Ruth to think of himself as a hitter, a development that worried Barrow. Babe was a great pitcher and not much more than a sideshow performer as a batter, the manager thought. In addition, Babe's thinking was juvenile, and if he latched onto a harebrained notion, he was apt to hold it tight.

In any case, that problem was still down the road. By the end of spring training, Barrow, a cold man who tended toward a glass-half-empty worldview, was sanguine about his team. Except for one curious development: toward the end of March, George Whiteman and Sam Agnew fell ill with the grippe, and several other players soon became sick. "The reign of grippe and sore throat continues," Martin noted from Hot Springs. The same day, Henry Daily of the *Boston American* reported, "A perfect epidemic has run through the entire city, and almost everyone complains."[22]

A reign of grippe? A perfect epidemic? Or just the flu—sick for a few days then back to work? No one on the team seemed too concerned. Yet out in Haskell County, Kansas, a physician named Loring Miner had recently contacted the US Public Health Service to report some strange influenza patterns. There seemed to be a new kind of flu. And it killed.

6

The Keys

IT WAS THE SEASON OF THE GREAT WITCH-HUNT, A TIME OF widespread persecution, all across the country, targeting pacifists, radicals, and "German sympathizers." Thousands of Americans joined in, from federal and state law enforcement officials to local citizens concerned about the incursion of Germans, socialists, and communists. At the center of the effort was the Bureau of Investigation, which was fighting its own secret war against German operatives on American soil. Short on manpower due to the draft, the Bureau recruited more than 250,000 zealous volunteers who joined the American Protective League, an extralegal vigilante network intent on suppressing dissent.[1]

At the top of the witch-hunting pyramid was the director of the Bureau of Investigation, A. Bruce Bielaski. A short, trim bundle of energy, Bielaski had overseen the prosecution and conviction of black heavyweight boxing champion Jack Johnson. His campaign against the boxer led to a prison sentence and encouraged him to flee the country. Now he targeted Karl Muck.[2]

In Washington, DC, Bielaski, a lawyer and former Pinkerton detective, had followed the sensational accusations against the German conductor, whom the Department of Justice had identified as an enemy alien, barring him and twenty-two other BSO musicians from the capital. Muck, he decided, warranted closer examination. So he assigned Thomas Flint, one of his most trusted agents, to investigate Muck and determine whether the German conductor had violated the Espionage Act or any other laws. On January 15, 1918, Flint filed his report and concluded that Muck posed no danger to the United States. Writing Bielaski, he called the allegations against the conductor "a frame-up of the Providence Journal."[3]

Nevertheless, Bielaski directed Bureau agents in Boston to continue their persecution of Muck. A day after Flint wrote Bielaski, George Kelleher, assistant district attorney and the special agent in charge, learned that in New York a "volunteer operative" with a pro-war political group called the American Defense Society, which advocated 100 percent Americanism, had offered information about the maestro. Investigators in the American Defense Society had arranged for Kelleher to interview the volunteer, Herwegh von Ende, who was also the eminent director of New York's Von Ende School of Music. Endorsed by Muck, von Ende advertised his music school as a "Most Attractively Equipped Home for Young Ladies Under Proper Chaperonage." One of those young ladies was the conductor's mistress, Rosamond Young, a talented singer with a rich, full voice.[4]

Von Ende supplied the Bureau with details about the relationship between his former student and Muck. As he explained it to Kelleher, the German regularly corresponded with Young and she kept their letters in a safety deposit box at Harriman National Bank. How von Ende discovered this sensitive information remains unknown. But Rosamond Young, a statuesque woman with a round face, short brown hair, blue-gray eyes, and porcelain skin, was "extremely infatuated" with the famous conductor and would do anything for him. Muck could be quite shrewd, von Ende suggested, but he was careless about protecting his secrets. An American citizen related to German nobles, von Ende admitted that he knew Johann von Bernstorff. But Muck, he warned, was even more dangerous than the German ambassador.[5]

Although he did not doubt that Rosamond's parents were loyal Americans, von Ende indicated that she was "somewhat pro-

German," since she was completely manipulated by Muck. Her parents were wealthy Republicans who favored prohibition. A prominent oil manufacturer and distributor, Frank L. Young and his wife, Minnie, were actively involved in Boston politics and civic affairs. An advocate of women's suffrage, Minnie served on the boards of various associations, including the Dorchester Women's Club and the Woman's Christian Temperance Union. Prudish Victorians, they knew nothing about their daughter's relationship with the conductor. They would have been horrified if they had read one of his passionate love letters. "My family was in total ignorance of the seriousness of my affair with Dr. Muck and of the compromising nature of the letters," she later confessed.[6]

In New York, an alarmed mother, Mrs. Susan Dakin, contacted District Attorney Francis G. Caffey to report her concerns that Muck had tried to seduce her daughter. She provided Caffey with Muck's suggestive letters. A flirtatious roué, Muck had eagerly pursued the daughter, Miss Susan Herter, persisting with letter after letter, urging her to meet him. When she did not immediately reply, he became impatient. Caffey forwarded the letters to the attorney general's office in Washington, but the Justice Department concluded that the correspondence did not reveal any violations of federal law and returned the letters. Undeterred, Caffey forwarded the letters again, this time to officials in Boston, and encouraged them to investigate the German conductor's alleged corruption of young American women.[7]

Muck suspected that government agents—"Rathom men," he called them—kept close tabs on him. "In these days," he wrote Rosamond, "when the beast-like agents of the Department of Justice are following my every footstep we must make our plans with care lest these hunters will have a chance to draw our friendship before the public gaze." Shadowed by government agents, he could not risk being seen with her in public, so he rented a secluded apartment where they could meet. "I will see to it that you have a duplicate key to the apartment, and after we have talked over every detail we can meet at our new nest as often as it is mutually convenient and safe for you."[8]

The private apartment may have reassured Rosamond that their tryst would remain a secret. But Karl Muck couldn't hide from the Rathom men much longer.

IN EARLY MARCH, MUCK INFORMED BSO founder Henry Higginson that he planned to leave the country, though he would conduct the orchestra for the remainder of the season and would perform later that month in New York. Higginson recognized that Muck's association with the orchestra had hurt attendance at Symphony Hall and agreed that it was time to help him secure safe passage to Europe. On March 13, 1918, he wrote John Lord O'Brian, special assistant to the attorney general, and requested passports for Muck and his wife, Anita, to travel to Germany in early May. Charged with running the War Emergency Division of the Justice Department, O'Brian supervised the enemy alien regulations. During the war, he prosecuted the most important cases under the Espionage Act, including one against former Socialist Party presidential candidate Eugene Debs for an antiwar speech. Although Muck was a naturalized Swiss citizen, O'Brian ruled that he was a denizen of Germany and therefore an enemy alien. Surprisingly, O'Brian informed Higginson that he had no objections to Muck's application. But it was not up to him. To obtain a passport, O'Brian explained, the conductor would have to go through the Boston office of US district attorney Thomas J. Boynton.[9]

Boynton, a loyal Democrat and former Massachusetts attorney general, was overwhelmingly focused on apprehending treacherous Germans. When Muck's passport application reached Boynton's office, the staffer responsible for reviewing it, Assistant DA Judd Dewey, was already inclined to believe that the German conductor was concealing a nefarious past. Working with Bureau of Investigation agents, Dewey surmised that if the conductor had mailed incriminating letters, then he might be able to prosecute him for violating postal laws or the Espionage Act. Although Boynton reminded him that O'Brian found no reason to withhold the passport, Dewey decided to dig into the conductor's private life.[10]

While the Massachusetts district attorney and a group of special agents from the Bureau expanded their investigation into Muck, Lucie Jay, a widow, prominent New York socialite, and founder of the Anti–German Music League, organized a campaign to prevent him and the BSO from performing at an upcoming Carnegie Hall concert. The daughter of a German immigrant turned shipping magnate and the only female director of the New York Philharmonic, Jay was motivated in part by a desire to make sure that no one questioned her loyalty to the United States. Her crusade against German music had begun in November 1917, shortly after Muck's appearance in Providence provoked a backlash from clubwomen. But Muck was not her only target. She attacked many of the most visible Germans in American popular culture: musicians, opera singers, and actors. "No American woman," *The Chronicle* declared, "has done more, individually, than Mrs. William Jay in exposing German propaganda in this country."[11]

Writing Higginson, Lucie Jay demanded to know why Muck remained the conductor of the BSO when he had submitted his resignation. Furthermore, she could not fathom why he should be allowed in New York City if he was barred from Washington, DC. Higginson defended his conductor, claiming that Muck was a Swiss citizen who had no connection with the German government. Jay, however, demanded that Muck prove his Swiss citizenship. Supported by the Daughters of the American Revolution and the American Defense Society, she accused the BSO of harboring enemy aliens. Muck's concerts were "always filled with German sympathizers," she maintained. Two days before the BSO's concert, Jay again vowed that Muck would not perform in New York.[12]

When the day of the concert, March 14, arrived, the city's newspapers anticipated a culture clash at Carnegie Hall: "Mrs. William Jay Moves to Stop Muck's Concerts—Patronage of Boston Symphony Orchestra Is Largely Pro-German, She Says, Moving to Silence Orchestra"; "Muck and His Enemy Aliens Here

Tonight—Patriotic Societies and Loyal Citizens by Thousands Protest in Vain—Kaiser's Director and Band Reach the City."[13]

Outside of Carnegie Hall, dozens of patrolmen and plainclothes officers monitored the crowd, fearing that an attack on the "Kaiser's director" could spiral out of control. The police prepared for the unruly protestors, but the moment the conductor appeared on stage the anxious audience inside the auditorium welcomed him with a rousing ovation. Then, when the crowd fell silent, Muck stood at the podium and raised his baton, all eyes fixed upon him, and led the orchestra in playing "The Star-Spangled Banner." The patrons cheered enthusiastically. Throughout the evening they offered generous applause, the *Boston Globe* reported, though "some of it [was] a little forced and prolonged by what seemed to be the German portion of the audience—a good sized portion."[14]

In the end, the orchestra was able to finish the concert without disruption, but Lucie Jay's protests made living in America unbearable for Muck. "The last New York scandal has made the whole pack still more rabid," he complained to Rosamond. He could not imagine conducting in the United States much longer, not with the hounds on his trail. "I am like a shabby dog here in this country, where every cut-throat may assail me with impunity," he fumed.[15]

His world seemed to be spinning out of control, an uneasy feeling for a man of great confidence and authority. For as long as he could remember, he had lived according to his own desires. Obedient musicians, admiring patrons, and adoring fans worshipped him. He commanded hundreds of musicians, dictating when and how they played. They answered to *him*. And the women in his life—his wife, his mistresses, and his idolizers—also deferred to him.

Yet ever since the fall of 1917, after the Providence concert, it seemed that women controlled his fate. Leading the campaign against Muck, the clubwomen of Providence had organized the first public protests opposing the BSO; then Lucie Jay and the society women of New York escalated the attacks. In the coming weeks, as federal agents investigated every aspect of his life, he would have to depend on two women to protect him, the two women who knew all of his secrets—his wife and his lover.

The public scrutiny Muck faced made it nearly impossible for him to see Rosamond. She began doubting his love, wondering how much longer they could carry on the dalliance before the nativists dragged him off to an internment camp. He reminded her that a married man could not publicly confess his love for another woman. If the world knew about their affair, it would harm her family's reputation and cause them both great suffering. "It is possible," he wrote, "that one visit might pass by without the pack getting wise to it. But is this the time, this the situation, where one may risk *so much* for the sake of a possibility?"[16]

It was a time of indecision. Rosamond fretted about their future and the danger she risked being with him. Muck shared her trepidation, knowing that "his enemies would rejoice" if they discovered his secrets. Rosamond couldn't be too careful, he cautioned. "Our relationship must be guarded until I am free to make you my own, darling." Should his enemies expose them, he promised that he "would be only too proud to shoulder it all."[17]

Deep down, though, he must have known that it was a promise he couldn't keep.

ON MARCH 20, 1918, ABOUT a week after the Boston Symphony Orchestra performed at Carnegie Hall, Assistant US Attorney Kelleher sent Boston Bureau agent Norman Gifford to New York to retrieve the letters that Rosamond Young kept in a safety deposit box at the Harriman National Bank. Armed with a search warrant, Gifford introduced himself to James Keenan, a bank employee who he hoped could open Young's safety deposit box. Uncomfortable with the agent's request, Keenan explained that he couldn't open the box unless Gifford produced the keys. When Gifford stressed the importance of unlocking it, Keenan said that he wanted to cooperate, but he needed authorization from his absent supervisor. The agent knew he could not return to Boston empty-handed. He was so desperate to obtain the letters that he even considered sawing the box. Ultimately, after a few telephone calls to the Bureau's division superintendent, Gifford announced that he would return with Rosamond's keys.[18]

That same day, Kelleher had dispatched two federal agents to Young's family home in Dorchester, an affluent streetcar suburb on the Neponset River. Special Agent Feri Weiss, a mustachioed "America First" advocate, eagerly accepted the assignment. An Austrian immigrant who married "a proper" New England woman and adopted her nativism, Weiss was an outspoken proponent of immigration restriction. He often complained that most Bureau agents did not take their jobs as seriously as he did. Worst of all, he lamented, too many incompetent agents allowed the law or the chain of command to prevent them from apprehending subversives and radicals, the "vermin" who contaminated the country.[19]

While Rosamond was out horseback riding, Weiss and another agent presented her mother with a warrant to inspect the premises. After some discussion, Minnie Young escorted the agents up the stairs to her daughter's bedroom where they searched her desk and dresser drawers. As Weiss combed through the drawers, Minnie sat on a window seat, watching him, wondering what exactly the agent was hoping to find. Weiss wondered, too, if Muck had already instructed Rosamond to destroy their correspondence. Sure enough, he uncovered a note dated five days earlier—March 15, 1918—indicating that Rosamond had burned letters. Muck thanked her for igniting a "bonfire," warning her that government agents would search the property of anyone who knew him.[20]

As Weiss inspected the room, he hoped Minnie would rise from the window bench. Then the doorbell rang. The mother excused herself to greet her son Harold at the door. While she was gone, Weiss and his partner lifted the seat cover and discovered a black tin box, locked shut. When Minnie returned to the bedroom with Harold, the agents inquired about the keys to the tin box, but Rosamond's mother said that she did not know anything about them.[21]

Wearing her riding costume, Rosamond finally returned home to the front steps and found her mother distraught. "Officers from the Department of Justice are here!" Minnie shouted. Rosamond had dreaded this moment, but Muck warned her that it would come. Minnie insisted that her daughter had committed no crime, but the agents now knew that Rosamond had burned Muck's letters, which they suspected incriminated him. They were all but certain that she was involved in some kind of cover-up.[22]

Rosamond panicked. She did not know what to say. She followed her mother and brother into the library, where she saw the two agents in dark suits. Her eyes searched the room until she spotted the black tin box sitting on a table. Defiant, Rosamond protested the intrusion. "What a contemptible insult!" she shouted. Weiss placed his forefinger over his lips, admonishing her to speak quietly so that the servants could not hear their conversation. Harold encouraged her to listen to Weiss and do as the agent asked. Then Weiss requested that she unlock the box. "Must I?" she asked. "Oh, God, must I?"[23]

Realizing she had no choice, Rosamond left the room for a moment and returned with a key. Fighting tears, she opened the box, lifted the cover, and threw herself into a chair. Inside the box Weiss found a trove of letters between Young and Muck, a photograph of the conductor, and more keys.

"What are these for?" Weiss asked.

"They are safe-deposit vault keys," she answered.

"What's in the vault?"

"Letters."

"From Dr. Muck?"

"Yes."

More letters? Inwardly, Weiss must have smiled. He told Rosamond that she would have to accompany him to the banks where the boxes were kept—in both Boston and New York. She hesitated, maintaining that the intimate letters were written before the war, and that there was nothing political about them. Weiss guaranteed that the Bureau had no intention of publicizing her relationship with the German—*if* she cooperated.[24]

The next day Weiss and his partner escorted Rosamond to the Old Colony Trust Bank Company in Boston. One of them pulled a piece of a paper out of his pocket and told her that the Bureau had a warrant to open the vault, though he never showed Rosamond the document. She wondered later if the agent had duped her into opening the safe-deposit box. Rosamond explained that the bank records would show that she began renting the box two years before the United States entered the war and that she had not opened it since 1915. Again, she pleaded with them—the letters were "merely of a personal nature and had not the slightest connection with politics."[25]

But the agents ignored her appeal and once the box was opened, they began stuffing the letters into a briefcase. Inexperienced and naïve, she hoped that the missives would reveal Muck's innocence; there was nothing in them that indicated he had broken the law or worked for the German government. "Perhaps," she thought, "even though this brings me everlasting shame it may free Dr. M from suspicion—If so, I can bear it!"[26]

The next day, she accompanied agents to New York where they compelled her to unlock another safe-deposit box at Harriman National Bank. She admitted later, "I had not the slightest suspicion that I was putting the final evidence into their hands for just what they were after—serious and compromising personal scandal."[27]

Rosamond lived in fear. The agents warned her about helping Muck. "I was carefully watched and judiciously threatened," she wrote. The Bureau's agents "impressed the fact that if I or my family made a single move—they would make the whole affair public." She cringed knowing that the agents were reading dozens and dozens of intimate letters exchanged between her and a married man. "Oh, those letters! Well, did they smack their lips over such food!"[28]

Back at 45 Milk Street, the Bureau's Boston office, Feri Weiss translated letters written in German. What the agents found were statements Muck wrote to Rosamond between 1915 and 1917 that revealed his disgust for Americans—"dogs and swine," he cursed them—and his devotion to the Kaiser. He penned numerous anti-American statements and made references to meetings with

Ambassador Bernstorff and other German officials. Weiss was certain that Muck worked for the Kaiser's propaganda network. The German conductor fantasized about attacking American munitions plants, a sure sign that he belonged to Bernstorff's cabal of saboteurs: "How easy a German spy could throw a little bomb into [an American] factory."[29]

Convinced that Muck threatened public safety, District Attorney Thomas Boynton moved to detain him under the President's Proclamation on Alien Enemies, which allowed the government to apprehend any German the Justice Department deemed a threat to national security. It did not matter if the government lacked evidence of an actual crime; if the Justice Department had "reasonable cause to believe" that a German was aiding the enemy or *might* aid the enemy, then the suspect could be arrested, jailed, imprisoned, or interned.[30]

On the evening of March 25, 1918, Dewey called the police lieutenant at the Back Bay station, requesting assistance as federal agents planned to arrest Muck. After meeting with officers at Station 16, Weiss dispatched a messenger boy to Muck's stately redbrick home at 50 Fenway to determine if he was there. The conductor, it turned out, was still at Symphony Hall. Shortly thereafter, the agents briefly visited his house, confirmed his whereabouts, and proceeded to Massachusetts Avenue. When they arrived at Symphony Hall, Charles Ellis, the BSO's business manager, informed them that the orchestra had not finished rehearsing. Promising his cooperation, Ellis pleaded with the federal agents, asking them to delay the arrest until the end of rehearsal so as not to disturb the musicians. The agents agreed. Then the officials fanned in all directions, occupying the corridor.[31]

Weiss drifted into the auditorium and found a seat. The voices of the chorus singing Bach's "St. Matthew Passion" filled the hall. He studied Muck, watching the conductor's deliberate movements on stage as he directed the orchestra with total control. The maestro had spent the last six months preparing the "St. Matthew Passion" for a concert that was scheduled to take place the following evening. And the hard work had paid off: the orchestra and chorus rehearsed magnificently. But it was the last time Muck would stand in front of the Boston Symphony Orchestra.

THEY HAD HIM SURROUNDED, AND he didn't even know it. Federal agents and police officers had blocked every exit to prevent Muck from escaping Symphony Hall. When the rehearsal ended around 10:30 p.m., Ellis told him that they needed to have an important meeting in his office. Weiss followed closely behind Muck, and when they reached the office he placed him under arrest. The conductor said little more than goodbye to his wife. Then the agents placed him in a car and took him to the Back Bay station.[32]

Word spread throughout the Theater District: the Justice Department thumbed Karl Muck for a German operative. Hurrying to their offices on Washington Street—"Newspaper Row"—Boston reporters rushed to file the biggest story in the city. The following morning, the *Boston Traveler* announced: MUCK ARREST MOST IMPORTANT OF THE WAR.[33]

7

Family Traditions

FROM HIS POSITION NEAR THE FRONT IN FRANCE, CHARLES
Whittlesey's brother Elisha watched the skirmishes play out overhead. German and French planes circled each other like hawks
as artillery fire went back and forth. "It is interesting to see those
fellows scoot along when little white puffs (French air-shells) or
black puffs (German shells) appear out of nothing in the air about
them," he wrote his mother, Anna. Distinct sounds accompanied
the white and black puffs—the French guns emitted a "sharp, dry
crack," while the German weapons gave a "rather heavy sound."
The speed of the dogfights, the stillness of the observation bal-
loons, and the dangerous thud-thud-crack-crack of the guns stirred
something in the young poet's soul. Somehow, in the center of the
war, surrounded by crippled buildings and scarred earth, doomed
men and pointless offensives, Elisha found beauty.[1]

He was one of the doomed men. He knew it—his penetrating
eyes had a haunting quality—and so did his family and friends.
His Harvard classmates had called him Tim, a name that suited
him more than that of the biblical prophet Elisha. He possessed,
a member of his class said, "the magic touch of real friendship."
Maybe it was because of his grave health. His heart was weak, and
in an age long before transplants, bypasses, and angioplasties, there

was nothing much a physician could do for him, save counsel a life of inactivity. He was not generally inclined to heed that advice, determined to live a full if short life without sadness or regret. "He was essentially a poet and a joyous one," a friend judged. "He spent his life capital completely, but it was not a prodigal show; it was a deep investment for friends and for society."[2]

His record at Harvard attested to his streak of fatalism. After attending Phillips Andover Academy, illness prevented him from enrolling at Harvard for several years. Yet once there he evinced a passionate interest in everything to do with the institution. "He was the most loyal and enthusiastic member of the class," a fellow student recalled. In addition to serving on boards of the *Harvard Monthly* and the *Harvard Advocate*, he was an active member of D.K.E., the Signet Society, the Stylus Society, and the Poetry Society. Classmates thought he "showed unusual literary talent," and that his poetry and stories in the *Harvard Monthly* were exceptional, a claim made all the more singular given that John Dos Passos and E. E. Cummings were also writing for the literary publication. Significantly, however, he was a lackluster student, occasionally on probation and appearing to regard his class work as secondary to his other interests. Once again, his serious physical condition dictated choices: he picked friendships and service over the pursuit of exceptional grades.[3]

Seldom had grades seemed less important than during Elisha's years in Cambridge. He enrolled there in the fall of 1914, six years after his brother Charles had received his law degree. The Great War had turned the world topsy-turvy, and students at Harvard debated with passionate intensity the course their country should take. The death of poet Alan Seeger (Harvard 1910) on July 4, 1916, fighting for France on the Somme, stirred the patriotism of faculty and undergraduates alike. A consensus emerged that Harvard students would, as they had in past conflicts, defend their country and its institutions. "To what a magnificent tradition of war service do Harvard men fall heir," wrote an editorialist in the *Harvard Advocate* at the beginning of the fall 1917 term. "The tablets in Memorial Hall and the Union which commemorate those who gave their lives in former wars, are constantly before our eyes . . . Already some five or six hundred undergraduates have left the University for active service." The editorialist maintained that it was imperative that the other students prepare to follow their classmates to France so that each "can feel sure that to himself, to his college, and to his country he has not been remiss."[4]

By the time that editorial appeared, Elisha had already left for Europe. Although he had attended a Plattsburg Camp, he remained too weak to enlist in the US or French armies. Instead, as soon as Congress declared war, he prepared to leave Harvard and join the American Ambulance Corps, one of the school's officially approved national service options that allowed students to abandon college activities and still receive credit for the year's work. On May 11, 1917, he wrote Dean H. A. Yeomans of his plans to go abroad the following week. He asked the dean to excuse him from the week's classes to return to Pittsfield, see his family, learn to drive a car, and get a license.[5]

By the end of the month, the newly licensed Elisha was in France driving a Camion truck for the American Field Service on the deadly Soissons front. In letters home, he attempted to soothe his family's concerns, describing his five-ton vehicle as "a huge lumbering beetle," and telling stories about Whiskey and Soda, the lion cub mascots of the Lafayette Escadrille. Whiskey, he wrote his mother, "lumbered up and chewed my sleeve and pawed me. I scratched his ear. The beast is a bit more than a year old; and he is like a big Newfoundland puppy."[6]

Whiskey and Soda presented fewer hazards than the Germans. Dangers stalked Elisha's duties, waiting around every turn as he trucked shells, bombs, ammunition, and other supplies to the front, lurking in the soil and crater pools soaked by oily, long lasting mustard gas. The Germans, he rapidly concluded, were in the war for the long haul. One day he inspected deserted frontline Boche trenches. "They were wonderfully done," he wrote his family. "Those fellows evidently expected to stay there. At one place, and there are many like it, some of us went down four flights of stairs, 100 steps in all along a passage and came up in another trench.

They are all buttressed very well with beams, willow wattling, concrete and corrugated iron, and seem to ramble on forever." They were more like homes than trenches, and as he was poking about, Elisha found helmets and ammunition as well as clothes, dishes, magazines, cards, dice, and other evidence of soldiers who had settled in for a long stay.[7]

He also discovered the humanity of the enemy. "I found a German book of selected poems, minus the cover." Relying on his two Harvard courses in German that Elisha had barely passed, he translated the officer's favorite poems. "I can read most of them and they are wonderful lyrics. From his choice it is evident that he was quite a sentimental cuss."[8]

Mostly, however, Elisha came across destruction. "Shell craters are scattered about everywhere," he wrote, visible reminders of the power of modern weapons. Where once there was a town, now there was "merely an outline" of one. In a village, German artillery had blown the roofs off all the homes, and turned walls into rubble. One church especially touched him. "There's something about a steeple with the top bitten off, a half-moon of masonry ripped from it, that impresses one, especially when the main structure looks like an over-worked Swiss cheese."[9]

Still there were signs of life. Families living in holes, people going about their business in shelled towns while soldiers prepared for battle—everywhere the detritus of war was scattered around them. "I guess that the Germans thought that their rights had been infringed," Elisha wrote, but he didn't venture a guess on what rights. Instead, he drove through the night delivering shells to the French soldiers who were defending their rights, trying to avoid the fifteen-feet-deep potholes along the road and hoping that the next turn would not be his last.[10]

Elisha's letters arrived intermittently at the Whittleseys' Pittsfield home at 38 Pomeroy. Bureaucratic red tape delayed the delivery of mail, and too often the censors were "not overly generous." His family "cherished" the missives, but the weeks between news from Elisha were slow. Making matters worse, two other Whittlesey boys, Charles and Melzar, had reported to training camps.

Anna Whittlesey put up a good front, but her husband, Frank, wilted under the heartache of having a feeble son on the Western Front. In October, the *Pittsfield Eagle* reported that Frank had suffered a nervous breakdown. He was recovering in Nantucket. And worse news was still to come.[11]

THE FAMILY WAS FAMILIAR WITH tragedy. Frank and Anna's first son, Frank Russell Jr., had died when he was four, and their only daughter, Annie Elizabeth, had died of black diphtheria a few months before her ninth birthday. Their fourth child, Russell, also fell ill with the disease, recovered, but died in 1911 at the age of twenty-three. Furthermore, it was clear early on that Elisha suffered from a life-imperiling condition. The deaths of their children, especially Annie, cast a shadow over the entire family. Anna never fully recovered from the loss. Nor did Charles.[12]

As the eldest surviving son—every inch of Milton's "virtuous father virtuous son"—Charles assumed his burdens and responsibilities diligently. Elisha especially showed Charles's influence. Although he lacked his brother's seriousness in the classroom, Elisha wrote for various campus publications, and passionately debated the crucial issues of the day. He also embraced—as his Whittlesey ancestors had done for almost three hundred years—the opportunity to serve and defend his country. Although eight years younger than Charles, Elisha was the first to step onto French soil.

Elisha was still hauling shells and ammunition along bombed roads near Soissons as his brother completed the ninety-day officers training course in Plattsburg and reported to Camp Upton for active duty. By the end of the first week of September, Captain Whittlesey was placed in a staff position as commanding officer of the Headquarters Company of the 308th Infantry, part of the National Army's newly formed 77th Division. Virtually everything about Camp Upton, the National Army, the 77th Division, and its junior officers and draftees was new—and that was the rub. New did not mean sleeker, improved, and better; far more often it meant untried, unprepared, and disorganized.

The army had built Camp Upton, one of sixteen new cantonments established across the country, on a desolate ten-thousand-acre tract in Long Island's Suffolk County, a stretch of blowing sand, ugly scrub oaks, and forlorn pines that was inundated with flies and mosquitos. The closest village was Yaphank, which, as far as the army was concerned, was noteworthy only for being a featureless stop on the Long Island Rail Road. Visitors said that to see Yaphank was immediately to forget it. But it had what the army wanted: deserted land where it could build a camp and train soldiers away from the trappings of civilization.[13]

The soldiers were part of the National Army. Unlike the regular army and the National Guard, which combined volunteer enlistees with conscripts, the National Army was composed entirely of draftees. They were men who did not voluntarily answer President Wilson's call to serve their nation; in many cases, these were men who had no stake in Wilson's war aims, the cause of the Allies, or the eventual outcome. Many were immigrants or sons of immigrants from Germany or Austria-Hungary who had ties to their homelands; others were Jews from Russia who felt utter disdain for the land of their birth. For many Americans inside and outside of the government, the very notion of *e pluribus unum*—out of many, one—was a rhetorical reach. As historian Richard Slotkin framed the question: "Was it possible to create from such diverse and even dissident elements a new democratic army, large enough to contest a world war and loyal enough to see it through?"[14]

In no unit was this question stickier than the 77th Division. Its conscripts came largely from New York City, the most ethnically and politically diverse place in the United States. The company officers had the look of men whose families came to America on the *Mayflower*. In almost all ways, they resembled Charles Whittlesey—English heritage, establishment families, Ivy League educations, Plattsburg graduates, and as members of the strenuous generation, true "Sons of Roosevelt." Crawford Blagden of the 307th Infantry had been a football standout at Harvard, and W. Kerr Rainsford of the same unit was the son of an Episcopal rector, as well as an athlete and Harvard graduate. George McMurtry, another Harvard man who would serve with Whittlesey in the 308th Infantry, fought with TR in Cuba. L. Wardlaw Miles, who wrote the history of the 308th Infantry, had earned both a medical degree and a Ph.D. in literature from Johns Hopkins, and had resigned his professorship at Princeton to attend Plattsburg and enlist in the army. These men belonged to the same clubs, wore similar school ties, had worked in the same tightly knit professional communities, and were often related by marriage. In short, they spoke the same language.[15]

In many cases, they literally could not understand the languages of the conscripts they commanded. One survey reported that soldiers from forty-three different nationalities served in the 77th. Although census reports indicated that more than 95 percent of native white American citizens were literate, the officers in Camp Upton sadly discovered that a fourth of their conscripts were "unable to read the Constitution of the United States or an American newspaper, or to write a letter in English to the folks at home." Nor was their spoken English much better. The first roll calls were disasters. One officer called out, "Morra, T."

"Here!" came the answer.

Then he called, "Morra, R."

"Here," responded the same man.

"Does your first name begin with a T or an R?" the officer pressed.

"Yes, sir," the soldier answered.

"Is your first name Rocco?"

"Yes, sir."

"What is your first name?"

"Tony."[16]

At least that officer got a verbal response. Others received just blank stares. One officer was shocked to discover that a draftee knew only three words in English: "Merry Christmas" and "fuck." Others knew two fewer words. Nor was the fault only with the conscripts. Sometimes even a Harvard education had not equipped officers to pronounce the names of men born in "Transylvania and Morocco, Venezuela and Bulgaria, Sweden and Mexico, and dozens of other countries."[17]

The 77th Division was in every sense an American melting pot, as diverse and chaotic as New York City. Julius Ochs Adler, an officer in the unit and future general manager of the *New York Times*, wrote in his *History of the Seventy Seventh Division*, "Every type was represented—the gunman and the gangster, the student and the clerk, the laborer and the loafer, the daily plodder, the lawyer. They could be divided into two large classes—the man of muscle and the man of brain. From the variety of languages spoken one might have imagined himself at the Tower of Babel. These diverse types, accustomed to every condition of life, knowing for the most part no master, were to bow down before the military God, *Authority*, and emerge from the melting pot of training, an amalgamated mass of clear-thinking, clean-living men of whom America might well be proud."[18]

Communication was not the only problem. With the exception of several minor conflicts, Congress had largely ignored the army for more than a half century, content to maintain a small force to guard the western frontiers and handle occasional flare-ups with Indian tribes or unruly radical malcontents. Therefore, when Congress declared war against Germany, the US Army faced an appalling shortage of everything. Although conscription dramatically increased the size of the army, there were too few experienced junior-grade and noncommissioned officers to train them. Compounding the personnel problems, commanders confronted a dearth of rifles (especially M1903 and M1917 Springfields), artillery, and other ordnance. Finally, the senior officers were doctrinally impoverished on both operational and tactical levels. The best the leaders could hope for was that American industry would fill the material needs and that the soldiers and officers would learn on the job.

Whittlesey and the other Plattsburg-trained officers tried their best. At Plattsburg, Charles had earned a reputation for precision. He wanted to know not only the what of military procedure but also the why—the theory and reason for different strategies and decisions. To others, he seemed a bit persnickety, a conclusion reinforced by his thick glasses, precise speech, and lawyerly exactitude.

Initially, the men under his command chafed under his meticulous enforcement of the rules and formal manner. They regarded him as "one of those half-frozen New Englanders," constipated by rules and regulations. Behind his back, they made fun of their gangling officer, calling him without affection "The Stork" and "Galloping Charlie."[19]

Gradually, however, the men's views of Whittlesey changed. "He wasn't the cold fish that he seemed to be at first," wrote Samuel T. Williamson in the *New York Times.* "He looked after his men." He demonstrated his concern, for example, during a Liberty Bond drive. Government officials and ranking officers routinely pressured junior officers to buy bonds themselves and to forcefully encourage their men to do the same. Whittlesey knew the regulations, and there was nothing in the book about purchasing Liberty Bonds. He also realized that most of his men came from poor families, sent part of their meager pay home, and had little left in their pockets at the end of the month. They had been drafted and would soon be sent to France to fight in a war. Many would not return; others would come home seriously injured in body or mind. He refused to encourage his soldiers to buy bonds that they could not afford and that they did not want.

As the months of training passed, respect for Whittlesey turned to admiration. Walter Baldwin, one of his noncoms, remarked, "We knew that if he was bossing a job, it would be done right." Then something akin to the love a soldier has for a superior officer replaced admiration. "By his officers he was respected and beloved more than any man in the regiment," noted Wardlaw Miles. Recalling the last days at Camp Upton, Miles remembered Whittlesey: "Tall, lank, serious, and bespectacled. He listens judiciously or talks quietly in the same level tones which he will never lose in the face of danger and despair."[20]

By the end of 1917, during an exceptionally cold winter, soldiers and officers became cohesive platoons and companies, battalions and brigades. The 77th Division, newly minted just months before, took on a personality and character all its own. Some journalists called it the Melting Pot Division, others dubbed it the

Metropolitan Division, the Statue of Liberty Division, or just the Liberty Division. It was all the same. The 77th was "New York's Own," the division that encompassed the Harvard and Yale Club aristocrats as well as the Bowery bums. They had graduated from Ivy League institutions or the School of Hard Knocks, their parents summered in Newport or had never left Italy, they were destined for the Senate or prison. But for the moment, they were one, and would risk their lives for each other.

By February 22, 1918, the men of the 77th Division had been training for over five months, and the bodies and minds of diverse rag-tag draftees had hardened. They had become soldiers, untested in combat to be sure, but pounded into fighting shape and ready to ship across the Atlantic for their baptism by fire. Before they departed, however, their officers packed ten thousand of them, including the 308th Infantry, onto trains and delivered them to New York City for the Washington's Day Parade down Fifth Avenue. It was a final opportunity for "New York's Own" to

Off for the adventure of a lifetime. New recruits from New York bound for Long Island's Camp Upton. For many, the thought of combat must have seemed a distant, romantic notion. Letters home talked more about drinking and playing cards on the train ride than plans for combat. *(Courtesy of the National Archives.)*

march in full battle gear in front of their mothers and sweethearts, fathers and friends.[21]

Snow fell hard when the 77th began the main parade march down Fifth Avenue from Fifty-ninth Street to the bottom of Madison Square on Twenty-third Street. Enormous crowds, packed six or more people deep, lined the avenue, and above those shivering spectators, others stood behind gaping, open windows. The *New York Times* called the gathering "one of the greatest throngs ever assembled in the history of the city," estimating that more than one hundred thousand people stood along the main route and upward of five hundred thousand turned out for the other events. Fifth Avenue was a canyon of sound and color, a cacophony of cheers, shouts, clapping, and music mixed with falling snowflakes, raining confetti, and waving flags.

As soon as they hit Fifth Avenue, the Divisional Band struck up George M. Cohan's "Over There," the popular 1917 song that had come to symbolize American expectations for the Yanks' role in the war. Some spectators joined in on the chorus:

Over there, over there,
Send the word, send the word over there
That the Yanks are coming, the Yanks are coming
The drums rum-tumming everywhere.
So prepare, say a prayer,
Send the word, send the word to beware—
We'll be over, we're coming over,
And we won't come back till it's over, over there.

Others just watched the largest display of patriotism in memory. Officials had made sure that mothers, sisters, and wives received prime viewing spots, but emotions seemed to register on every spectator's face. One person recalled, "From sidewalk to skyline the Avenue was banked with faces as the repeated ranks passed in review. There were radiant faces, curious faces, admiring faces, tear-stained faces, and smiling faces that hid weeping hearts."

Along the route, bullhorn-voiced New Yorkers shouted encouragement. "Good luck boys," yelled many. "Go get the Kaiser" or "Pop old Hindenburg one for me," bellowed a few others. At St. Patrick's Cathedral, "a loud-voiced man of ample proportions" boomed, "You are all right, boys, and we know you will fight to a finish when you get over there." Struck by the throng of well-wishers and the shouts of support, a regimental officer remarked, "No matter what else happens, we will never forget the good-will New York has shown us today."

The reviewing station stood on a flag-draped platform in front of the main entrance of the Public Library. There Secretary of the Navy Josephus Daniels stood between Brigadier General Evan M. Johnson, acting commander at Camp Upton, and Alfred Smith, acting mayor of New York. "This has been one of the finest sights I have ever witnessed," Daniels said after the event, "and I am sure that every American who saw the parade glories in these boys. He would not be an American if he did not feel a surge of pride as he saw those splendid fellows come swinging by." Al Smith agreed: "These are New York boys and they made a marvelous showing."

Row after row they marched, more soldiers than virtually all of the spectators had ever seen. As snow flecked their khaki uniforms and full packs before melting, they gripped their Enfield and Springfield rifles, and marched past the dignitaries. A chorus of cheers greeted Whittlesey and the other members of the 308th Infantry. But New York's 367th Infantry—a National Guard unit composed of black troops commanded by white field officers—received the loudest reception. As their band played "Dixie," cheers echoed up and down Fifth Avenue. "It seemed that every man in the regiment was over six feet in height, and there was not a 'stomach' in the whole command," noted the *New York Times*.

The Washington's Day parade whipped up the sort of enthusiasm for the war effort demanded by the Wilson administration. It was for that reason that Secretary of War Newton Baker had ordered all divisions to hold themselves "available for parades or reviews in towns or cities near their training centers." The sight of men in uniforms; the pleas to support the war effort portrayed in the Howard Chandler Christy and James Montgomery Flagg posters slapped on public walls; the chance to play soldier and climb into antiseptic and safe trenches dug in American soil; the high-spirited beat of "Over There" and "Tipperary"; the opportunity to experience war vicariously in such silent films as *Pershing's Crusaders* and *The Kaiser, the Beast of Berlin*—all roused patriotism, promoted unity, and conjured an image of a righteous war that bore no resemblance to the slaughter on the Western Front. Yet it was that war, that conflict too hideous to discuss openly, into which Captain Charles Whittlesey and the 308th Infantry Regiment would soon be thrust.

PART TWO

THE STORM

8

The Mad Brute

"THE CAGE" HELD ALL OF BOSTON'S HARD CASES—DOPE PUSHERS and rapists, bootleggers and slackers, robbers and confidence men. After federal agents arrested Karl Muck late in the evening on March 25, 1918, he spent the night in the Back Bay police station, and the next morning he was taken to the deputy marshal's office at the Federal Building. Occupying the dingy pen, "rubbing elbows with the motley gathering," was humiliating for the conductor, a man more accustomed to consorting with Boston Brahmins. Pacing the cell floor, Muck subsisted on "high grade cigarettes" and water from a tin cup, wondering what the government wanted from him.[1]

What they wanted were answers. Judd Dewey, the ambitious assistant DA who had now been pursuing Muck for months, had recently been given an expanded role in investigating Boston's alien enemies. While he oversaw Muck's interrogation, Justice Department agents scoured the maestro's home near the Back Bay Fens as well as his office at Symphony Hall. Other agents reviewed his correspondence. Reporters, meanwhile, speculated that he would be prosecuted as a spy. When asked by a reporter how serious the case against Muck was, Dewey simply answered, "We don't arrest all enemy aliens."[2]

The press plastered Muck's face on the front page of every Boston newspaper. Scathing headlines overshadowed news from the Western Front. DR. KARL MUCK IS ARRESTED SPENDS NIGHT IN CELL, the *Boston Post* blared. Reporters and photographers snooped around the Federal Building, prodding officials for details about the evidence against Muck, who was in no mood for taking pictures. "I am not inclined to pose for anything," he groused.[3]

According to the *New York Times*, "hundreds" of visitors packed the corridor of the Federal Building, hoping to catch a glimpse of him. Dozens of curious women appeared in support of the famous conductor. In the offices of the Justice Department, the presence of infatuated women furthered Muck's image as a wolf preying upon sheep. "His position and reputation has made it easy for him to carry out his designs because these young women are carried away by any slight attention they may receive from a matinee idol," wrote an agent with the Bureau of Investigation.[4]

Yet Muck's devoted wife, Anita, stood by him. "My husband's arrest is preposterous," she exclaimed with a German accent. "I have no knowledge of what the charge could be, and I am sure it will prove to be a farce." She was confident that he would be exonerated and soon released. Standing in the marshal's office, Anita greeted him with affection and a kiss. Outwardly, she presented an image of cheerfulness and faithfulness, smiling during her brief chat with Karl. But she knew that their lives were in tatters.[5]

Federal agents treated the couple with skepticism. They interviewed musicians and friends who testified about a troubled marriage. Compiling a dossier on him, informants told investigators that Muck slept with the wives of BSO musicians, including the concertmaster's wife. One informant suggested that Muck's affair with the wife of violinist Adolf Bak, "a rather loose woman," divided the Germans in the orchestra. Albert Spalding, a Harvard music professor, knew Muck well and told an agent that he was "grossly immoral," carrying on multiple affairs for years.[6]

After spending most of the day smoking cigarettes in the US Marshal's detention room, late in the afternoon authorities whisked Muck away in a police car, and then locked him behind bars in the

East Cambridge jail. His cramped cell contained a wooden frame bed and a mattress made of straw. The putrid smell coming from his waste bucket polluted the air. Every morning, he recalled, "I had to line up in the hall to wash shoulder to shoulder with robbers, burglars, murderers, white slavers, [and] negroes." He could hardly bear the humiliation of standing naked next to criminals, stripped of his humanity. Symphony Hall seemed so far away from his cold, drab cell; the uplifting melodies of the "St. Matthew Passion" seemed now only a distant memory. Sitting silently, the jarring sounds of prisoners wailing and shouting interrupted his thoughts. Nothing seemed more devastating than the daily ritual of his iron cell door slamming shut—a cold reminder that he had become a prisoner of war.[7]

KARL MUCK, A NOTORIOUS CHAIN-SMOKER, now suffered confinement without his cigarettes. When the sheriff banned his favorite cigarettes, he learned to smoke a pipe in jail. He spent his days packing it with French tobacco, puffing away, and reading newspapers, disgraced by the daily articles speculating about his crimes. In the Theater District, musicians, artists, and patrons gossiped about the case. Rumors spread throughout the Back Bay that Muck coordinated a mysterious wireless operation with German spies. Anita and BSO business manager Charles Ellis visited him regularly, though Henry Higginson had fallen ill and was unable to travel to the prison. Higginson's doctor had apparently been summoned and arrived at his grand home on Commonwealth Avenue to find him "slightly indisposed." The stress of Muck's arrest wracked his body. The octogenarian aged rapidly, rarely leaving his house. He felt betrayed by people who accused him of harboring an enemy, a scourge on the nation. "I regret to say," he wrote a friend, "that these attacks and rows have stirred up trouble inside of my own body."[8]

On April 1, Muck returned to the Federal Building where District Attorney Boynton and his assistants interrogated him for two hours. He arrived sullen and weary, anxious about his future. Boynton began the interview explaining that he had questions for him, though the conductor had the right not to answer them. However, if Muck did respond to the questions, Boynton explained, then the government could use his statements against him. He understood the risks. Then Boynton began questioning him about his citizenship, his life in Germany, and his position in the Royal Opera.[9]

"Is the conductor of the Royal Opera an official of the German Government?"

"No," Muck replied. "The Royal Opera House is an absolutely private institution. It is subsidized by the Kaiser privately."

"Do you claim German citizenship?" Boynton asked.

"No, Swiss."

"Have you ever claimed German citizenship?"

"No."

"When did you become a Swiss citizen?"

"When I was seven years old," Muck answered. He explained that his father did not have to live in Switzerland for their family to become citizens; he just needed to own property there.

Then Boynton began presenting Muck with letter after letter—thirty in all. Every time the DA introduced one, he asked him if he wrote it and if he deposited it in the mail. Muck answered affirmatively each time, but admitted nothing else. Reading the private letters he wrote Rosamond, he squirmed in front of Boynton and the other men, fearing her involvement might bring her legal trouble. "I would prefer not to discuss any personal matter concerning a lady," Muck said.

The letters revealed that when Rosamond tried breaking off their relationship, Muck persisted with passion, making a statement that the federal agents could hardly believe: "It will perhaps surprise you to learn that to a certain extent Mrs. Muck knows our relationship," he wrote. "She has a noble heart and her mind is broad beyond the comprehension of the swine-like people among whom we must live a little while longer."[10]

Did Anita really know about her husband's tryst? Did she understand his desire for other women? Or was he simply manipulating his lover's emotions?

Soon, he wrote Rosamond, "our gracious Kaiser will smile upon my request and recall me to Berlin." Then he would obtain a divorce, and they would return hand-in-hand to "the Fatherland," where he would make her "my own." He refused to let anyone deny him what he wanted most. "Must we, for the sake of foolish sentiments that are imposed on us by others, forsake the love that is divine and inexpressible by common language?" he asked her. "No, a thousand times no! You are mine and I am your slave and so I must remain."[11]

Boynton did not press him for more details about his relationship with Rosamond. The letters told him everything he needed to know. The former chief postal inspector for New England simply wanted to establish that Muck had violated federal postal regulations. "All I am asking you is whether you wrote this letter and whether you deposited it in the mail."

"Yes," Muck said.

As the interview continued, Boynton questioned him about missing letters. Rosamond had already admitted to federal agents that she destroyed some because he wrote scathing critiques of the United States. She told an agent that he expressed outrage over the internment of German sailors and that he had tried to help them. Yet Muck denied asking her to incinerate the letters. "I think she wrote that she had burned some letters that I wrote to her," he said. "I know I expressed some approval."[12]

Frustrated by Boynton's line of questioning, he fumed about the federal agents assigned to his case—"the Rathom men." Initially, when the Bureau of Investigation director Bruce Bielaski designated Washington agents to investigate Muck, they found no evidence that the German conductor had violated the Espionage Act. One of the agents described the accusations against him as a "frame up" by Rathom. However, Bureau agents in Boston working with Boynton and his assistant attorneys continued investigating him after the Providence concert. "Of course," Muck groused, "the whole trouble against me started from Rathom . . . with that rotten lie that I had refused to conduct the anthem."

"What gave you the impression that Rathom men were employed by the Department of Justice?" Boynton asked.

"I heard that many times," Muck said. "I mean that Rathom himself says he has, in every branch of the National Service, his men."

Yet Rathom was not the spy-catcher that he claimed to be. His exaggerations fanned the flames of German hysteria, but they also earned him the scorn of Attorney General Thomas Gregory, who called Rathom's spy stories "pure and unadulterated fabrications." Incensed over Rathom's claims that the *Providence Journal* had a wireless operation that was more effective at intercepting German secrets than the US government, the attorney general threatened prosecution against the editor. Gregory compelled him to sign a confession, admitting that he had lied about placing informants inside the German embassy and consular offices throughout the country.[13]

In any case, Boynton certainly did not need Rathom's assistance to intern Muck. He had a case for imprisoning him under federal regulations of alien enemies. Muck's failure to register as an enemy alien violated the law, and he had expressed outright hostility toward the United States in his letters to Rosamond. The Justice Department countered Muck's claim of Swiss citizenship, citing numerous letters where the conductor referenced "My Germany," and his "German Citizenship." After interviewing him, Boynton wrote the attorney general, explaining that he did not yet find evidence to prosecute Muck under the Espionage Act, though he considered the German "a menace and a danger to the public peace and safety."[14]

What the public did not know in 1918 was that Muck's correspondence with Rosamond gave Boynton other grounds to prosecute him. The documents provided evidence of violations of the Comstock Act, which, among other things, prohibited people from mailing "obscene, lewd, or lascivious" letters. The district attorney also had enough evidence to charge him with violating the "White-Slave Traffic Act," a law that barred the transportation of women in interstate or foreign commerce "for the purpose of prostitution or debauchery or for any other immoral purpose." Armed with the incriminating correspondence, Boynton believed that the "indecent" letters proved that Muck had violated postal laws, and had lured Rosamond into a life of debauchery.[15]

The White-Slave Traffic Act, better known as the Mann Act for its puritanical author, Illinois congressman James Robert Mann, evolved out of the hysteria of the early twentieth century, an age of rapid industrialization, immigration, urbanization, and the changing role of women. When the Mann Act became law in 1910, middle-class and upper-class reformers feared that large numbers of foreign men were preying upon young white women in the nation's cities, coercing them into a life of near enslavement. The panic over sex trafficking escalated ever higher as more young single women left the protection of the home and moved into crowded cities where evil men and temptation lurked.[16]

In Boston during the war, reporters published stories about the "insidious minions of the White Slave traffic," coaxing young women into servitude under the guise of the Red Cross. Throughout New England, concerned parents and friends reported missing young women, many of whom said that they were going into the Red Cross as nurses. With rising concerns about soldiers contracting venereal disease, authorities launched an anti-vice crusade, cracking down on brothels and organized gangs of traffickers.[17]

Nativism inspired muckraking journalists who published stories about innocent white women who were lured, kidnapped, and smuggled across state lines by foreign men. During the war, propagandists and politicians exploited the obsession over white slavery and fears that German men would degrade American women. Federal investigators suspected that Karl Muck operated his own trafficking scheme, sending lewd women carrying syphilis to Camp Devens, a wild charge that had no basis in fact.[18]

It did not matter that he had never coerced Rosamond Young into prostitution. The ambiguous language of the Mann Act's "immoral purposes" clause allowed federal agents to charge men who engaged in consensual sexual activity outside of marriage. In theory, any man who traveled across state lines with a woman

other than his wife and then had sex with the woman risked prosecution. A man violated the law the moment he crossed state lines
with the woman. Even if he did not have sex with her, simply
intending to cross state lines for any "immoral purpose" made him
subject to a crime. Although US attorneys often ignored the moral
transgressions of offenders, they used the Mann Act to blackmail
men who posed a larger threat.[19]

The case served as a reminder for the purpose of the Mann Act.
"Congress," a federal judge explained, "passed the Mann Act to
protect 'weak women from bad men.'" No "Boche," the agents believed, could get away with defiling the virtue and purity of American womanhood. Like illustrator Harry Hopps's giant, drooling
gorilla stomping on the shore of America, wielding a club and
carrying the limp, half-naked body of a blond woman, Muck was
the "mad brute" incarnate. He had to be stopped.[20]

Facing incarceration for violating the Mann Act and federal
postal laws, he feared the humiliation that would come with a
criminal trial. The government presented him with a choice: indictment or internment. He understood that a trial would destroy
everything he loved: his career, his marriage, and Rosamond. He
knew, too, that a German accused of espionage would have no
chance of a fair trial with an American jury. So he accepted his
fate—internment.[21]

It could have been much worse for Karl Muck. His life could
have ended the way Robert Prager's did. A half-blind, German-
born coal miner with a handlebar mustache, Prager's trouble began
when he started working in a coal mine in Maryville, Illinois, a
hamlet filled with jingoists and taverns. Rumors floated through
the camp that German saboteurs had stolen dynamite and the Kaiser's agents planned to blow up the mine, though there was no
evidence that Prager was a part of any such conspiracy. In fact,
reporters later found two American flags in his home. Although
the local mining company permitted him to work at the mine,
he still had to apply for membership with the national union, the
United Mine Workers. When he learned that the local chapter of
the UMW denied his application, he became furious, suspecting

One of the most famous propaganda posters from the Great War, Harry Hopps's illustration conveyed American fears of predatory Germans encroaching on the shores of the United States and savagely abducting helpless American women. In the case of Karl Muck, federal agents viewed him as a real menace, threatening the purity of an American maiden named Rosamond Young. *(Courtesy of the Library of Congress.)*

that the union discriminated against him on account of his heritage and socialist views. An obstinate man, Prager's outbursts convinced some miners that he was an untrustworthy pro-German.[22]

Embittered, he petitioned the miners directly, posting letters throughout the camp, urging the union to accept him. "I ask in the name of humanity to examine me to find out what is the reason

I am kept out of work," he wrote, adding, "I am heart and soul for the good old USA. I am of German birth, of which accident I cannot help." Yet Prager's socialist activity infuriated a group who viewed him as a dangerous rabble-rouser intent on anarchy. It was time, they decided, to silence him.

In the evening of April 4, 1918, a sauced gang left Maryville for nearby Collinsville, where Prager lived. They stopped at a saloon along the way, where they recruited an unruly throng, and then proceeded to swarm his boarding house. The horde banged on his door, threatened him, and told him to leave town within ten minutes. Frightened, he agreed, but not before the mob dragged him down Main Street and paraded him nearly naked and barefoot with Old Glory wrapped around his waist. The crowd demanded that he sing "The Star-Spangled Banner," but he did not know the words. Soon the police arrived, seizing Prager from his tormentors and placing him in the basement of the jail. Word spread throughout Collinsville that the police had captured a real German spy.

Hundreds of angry people surrounded the jail, demanding that the police release the German. When the officers refused, the "drunken rowdies" rushed the jailhouse and dragged Prager outside where they paraded him again down the street. When his torturers could not find any hot tar to pour onto Prager's body, they decided to hang him.

He begged the mob to spare his life. He swore he was a loyal American citizen. After the United States declared war on Germany, Prager applied for naturalization, registered for the draft, and even tried to enlist in the US Navy, though he was rejected on account of his glass eye. "Brothers," he cried, "I am a loyal USA workingman!" But the angry rabble ignored his pleas and forced him to kiss the American flag. The sanguinary mob strung him up to the branch of a hackberry tree and dropped his body three times, a vigilante explained, "one for the red, one for the white, and one for the blue."[23]

The chilling news of the Prager lynching soon traveled all around the country. Although many newspaper editors denounced mob rule, others justified it as a wartime necessity, an act of patriotism in the name of national security. "In spite of excesses such as lynching," the *Washington Post* declared, "it is a healthful and wholesome awakening in the interior of the country." In Washington, politicians argued that Congress needed to pass the pending sedition bill with severe penalties for acts of disloyalty. Massachusetts senator Henry Cabot Lodge, a zealous nativist, called for the death penalty for traitors and German spies. The *New York Tribune* insisted that if the government did not "intern alien enemies, many of them will, sooner or later, fall victims to mob violence."[24]

That same argument could be heard in Boston when federal agents arrested Karl Muck. For the sake of order—and his own life—the government had no choice but to intern him. "The temper of the nation is approaching the breaking point in tolerating anti-American utterances," and Muck's arrest, the *Boston American* proclaimed, "is necessary if wholesale lynchings throughout the country are to be prevented."[25]

In Washington, on April 5, the day of the Prager lynching, two federal agents compiled a final report recommending Muck's internment. They presented the facts of the case: "He has been most intimately associated with both men and women who are decidedly pro-German. He himself has received from the German Emperor the very highest honors which can be paid to a man of his profession . . . He is, therefore, *potentially dangerous*."[26]

However, the agents acknowledged that they had not actually caught him committing espionage. "But in these times," they maintained, "it would be unwise to be over scrupulous." Muck's actions were too suspicious to overlook. He had the ability "to do much harm to the United States." Besides, the public "would be very much against setting him at liberty; the government would be criticized for taking such a stance."[27]

In the end, the decision was put to John Lord O'Brian, the special assistant to the attorney general, who had previously stated that he had no objections to Muck's passport application. But weighing all the evidence, he now decided to intern Muck, a decision made easier by the German conductor's willingness to accept the order without protest. O'Brian authorized the district attorney to prepare Muck's transport to Fort Oglethorpe, Georgia. On April 6, US Marshals escorted him outside the East Cambridge jail, where a car and his distressed wife awaited. Dabbing tears from her cheeks, Anita wept as she kissed him goodbye and watched the vehicle carrying her husband disappear from her sight, not knowing when she would see him again.[28]

9

The Season of Doubt

A SHARP WIND SWEPT ACROSS THE BACK BAY STATION PLATFORM as the Red Sox passenger car, the Twentieth Century Limited, halted on the tracks, belching smoke and sounding a shrill whistle. A snowstorm blanketed the Atlantic Coast, following the team east from Buffalo, and by the time the train arrived in Boston in the early afternoon of Friday, April 12, sleet pelted the Hub. Cautiously stepping onto the slush-covered platform, the players grimaced and shivered, many of them coatless since they had already shipped their outerwear home with the equipment trunks. Clutching their derbies and bowlers, the men trudged against thirty-five-mile-per-hour gusts. The howling winds blew across the bay, bending tree branches and swinging creaky overhead signs. The men scattered like leaves, disappearing into the gray streets. Knowing the Babe, before he returned home to his apartment on Commonwealth Avenue, he probably visited a local watering hole to warm up with a few shots of whiskey.[1]

The bleak weather spelled doom on the eve of opening day. On Sunday, April 14, the *Boston American* gloomily announced, SNOW SHOVEL BRIGADE AT FENWAY. The groundskeepers worked furiously to remove snow from the field and the grandstands. When reporters met with Harry Frazee, they found him in the doldrums, his office colder than an icebox. It seemed that the water pipes had frozen in the bowels of Fenway Park. In Cambridge, across the frigid Charles River, the players practiced indoors for two hours in the Harvard baseball cage, hoping that the sun would break through the clouds and melt away the snow by the next day. After four days of inaction, the restless players "raced around the cage like a lot of colts let out to pasture."[2]

"A season of doubt starts for the big leaguers of baseball tomorrow," Boston scribe Burt Whitman wrote. He questioned whether the sport could prosper during the war while the government continued to call the draft numbers of ballplayers and fans alike. In a few days, the War Department would draft more than fifteen thousand men from New England to serve in the 76th Division. American sacrifices had only just begun, James Morgan wrote in the *Boston Globe*. "Now comes the year of test for our country. Not merely for our brothers in khaki and our chiefs in office, but for you and me and for all of us," he declared. "The year behind us has been only a rehearsal for our part . . . The supreme test is at hand. We must not, will not fail."[3]

Even on opening day, April 15, Boston fans could not ignore the war. Casualty lists published in the *Globe* reminded them that while they enjoyed the comfort of spring baseball, soldiers from New England were dying on the Western Front. The fans congregating on Jersey Street outside of Fenway Park could see a military flag flapping near the main entrance. It featured thirteen yellow stars— one for every Red Sox player serving in the armed forces.[4]

Jersey Street bustled with excitement. "It was the perfect day for the opening," Whitman wrote. In the last twenty-four hours the cold weather had broken. The snow and chilly air had disappeared beneath the sunshine. Clear, blue skies and a cool breeze greeted the crowd outside of Fenway Park, a redbrick building that from the Jersey Street facade looked more like a New England textile factory than a baseball stadium. Built in 1912 during the sport's first stadium boom, the steel-and-concrete park was an expression of the team's centrality to cultural life in the city. A sports cathedral, it was one of the few sacred spaces where patricians and plebeians,

Irish Catholics and Yankee Protestants assembled. United by civic loyalty and their love for the Red Sox, baseball fans from every corner of Boston claimed Fenway for their own.[5]

The fans came from all over, packing electric streetcars destined for the Fens. The noisiest group, the Royal Rooters, a platoon of Boston's most devoted "cranks," invaded the streets surrounding Fenway Park. Marching to the stadium from Michael McGreevey's Third Base Saloon at the corner of Tremont and Ruggles—"the last stop before home"—the inebriated patrons paraded wearing suits, carrying megaphones, drums, and noisemakers. Loyal Democrats, a contingent of mostly Irish sportsmen, gamblers, and politicians, the Royal Rooters had campaigned years earlier for the club's most famous leader—John Francis Fitzgerald, the former mayor and maternal grandfather of future president John F. Kennedy. Appearing frequently at Red Sox games, the charming politician from the North End surrounded himself with lobbyists, contractors, salesmen, and office-seekers. Promising "A Bigger, Better, and Busier Boston," he toured the streets and wharves "like the experienced monsignor of a large parish," William Shannon wrote, "able to greet constituents by name and tell where this one's father worked and what county in Ireland that one's mother came from." In 1914, at the height of his political career, after Fitzgerald announced his run for reelection, his ruthless opponent, James Michael Curley, threatened to expose his dalliance with Elizabeth "Toodles" Ryan, "a cigarette girl," unless he dropped out of the race. Clearing a path for Curley's victory, Honey Fitz withdrew from the campaign but remained the most prominent member of the Royal Rooters.[6]

The opening day ceremonies began with two brass bands playing patriotic numbers while the Royal Rooters carried placards across the soggy field. Hardly seven thousand paying customers—three thousand fewer than the year before—filed into the park, though Harry Frazee admitted a few thousand servicemen for free. Around 2:45, after "Pop" Connelly announced the starting lineups for the Red Sox and the Philadelphia Athletics, both teams assembled along the foul lines and marched in procession toward the flagpole in center field. Although the American League owners had decided that the players would no longer conduct military drills before games, Frazee embraced the government's Liberty Bond campaign, staging the first of many promotions at the park. Following the stream of players, one of the young batboys, dressed in a Red Sox uniform, waved a flag inscribed BUY LIBERTY BONDS. Even the players urged the fans to open up their wallets for Uncle Sam. In 1918, attending a game at a ballpark was as much about supporting the war effort and proving one's devotion to the cause as it was about the game itself.[7]

When the team captains, Boston's Dick Hoblitzell and Philadelphia's Rube Oldring, reached center field, they raised Old Glory. As a gentle breeze flapped the flag, the players removed their caps, and the band aroused the crowd with a booming rendition of "The Star-Spangled Banner." Every man, woman, and child sang along with pride.[8]

The marriage between baseball and the anthem dates back to the Civil War when military bands first began playing the song before games. By 1916, when President Wilson issued an executive order designating it as the national song for military events, the Red Sox established the tradition of performing the anthem on opening day. But it was the Great War that made "The Star-Spangled Banner" an integral part of professional sports. It transformed baseball games into spectacles of patriotism, public displays where Americans glorified competition, perseverance, and winning. Linking the flag to war, the entire practice became to many Americans an act of honoring troops, a ceremony of remembrance.[9]

Andrew Peters recognized the political opportunities of throwing out the ceremonial first pitch. Following the examples of John Fitzgerald and James Michael Curley, the new mayor, a Yankee Democrat of Puritan descent, appeared at Fenway Park shaking hands with politicians and constituents, Harry Frazee and the players. A Harvard graduate, four-term congressman, and former assistant secretary of the Treasury, Peters belonged to the aristocracy, a powerful group of WASP elites, merchants and financiers who married into what Oliver Wendell Holmes described as the "caste of New England." Peters inhabited "good old Boston," where, as

John Collins Bossidy once wrote, "the Lowells talk only to the Cabots, and the Cabots talk only to God." Like any good Brahmin, he joined the most exclusive clubs: the Somerset, the Exchange, the Eastern Yacht, the Tennis and Racquet, and the New York Harvard Club, among others. Backed by the "Goo-Goos," the Yankee property owners, bankers, lawyers, and real estate investors who made up the Good Government Association, his 1917 campaign promised to sweep the Irish out of office and clean up City Hall. Accusing Curley, the incumbent, of graft and disloyalty for his vocal support of Irish nationalists and German-Americans, the election reflected the intense ethnic-religious divide in the city during the war. "A vote for Peters," wrote the editor of an Irish weekly, "is a vote for the anti-Catholic, anti-Irish combination."[10]

Although the Irish Catholic members of the Royal Rooters did not vote for Peters, on opening day they cheered when he delivered a short speech near home plate praising the Red Sox. Standing in front of the crowd and a bevy of photographers, the mayor appealed to the bipartisan support of baseball fans, presenting himself as a man of the people, a champion of the great American game. In the final act of the opening ceremonies, he tossed the ball to Hoblitzell. His strong throw, opined one writer, indicated that he would make "a fine mayor."[11]

With that he waved to the crowd. It was time to hand over the ball to the Babe.

"There is no other city," sportswriter James Crusinberry wrote of Boston, where gambling "is allowed to flourish so openly." Notorious for its action at Fenway Park and Braves Field, the Hub developed a reputation as the most "infested" gambling town in professional baseball. A horde of bettors congregated in Fenway's right-field pavilion, placing wagers during every game. They made countless "do they or don't they" bets—risking money not only on the outcome, but on nearly every situation of a game: Would the umpire call a ball or a strike? Would the batter reach first base? Would the runner steal second? Would the Sox score this inning? It was no secret that gamblers operated in the stands along the first base line, shouting bets and exchanging cash. "Any one present," Crusinberry wrote, "can see the transactions and hear them plainly."[12]

For years baseball owners denied the pervasiveness of gambling throughout their stadiums. In 1915, American League president Ban Johnson claimed that he had swept gamblers out of Fenway Park. The truth, however, was that Joseph "Sport" Sullivan and his gambling syndicate continued making bets from the stands. On June 16, 1917, during a contest between the White Sox and Red Sox, a light rain muddied the infield and a throng began chanting, "Call the game!" By the middle of the fifth inning, with Chicago leading 2–0, the cries grew louder, echoing across the field. "It seemed as if every man in the bleachers was shouting," the *Boston Globe* reported. If the umpires cancelled the game before the fifth inning ended, the frantic sportsmen could nullify their bets as if they never placed them. After Babe Ruth quickly retired two Chicago batters, a swarm of gamblers leaped onto the field, covering the turf like an army of ants. Stalling for time, they stood around, praying for thunderstorms. The umpires scanned the grandstands for police officers, but none rushed the field. After Red Sox manager Jack Barry persuaded the gang to return to their seats, a mob of three hundred men descended onto the field just moments before the game was about to resume. This time a brawl erupted between the gamblers and ballplayers. It took more than thirty minutes for policemen on horseback to clear the field. Eventually, play commenced and the White Sox won, 7–2.[13]

When Johnson heard the news, he immediately launched a crusade against Boston gamblers, suspecting that Frazee had not done enough to evict them from Fenway. Fuming, he boomed, "Either the gamblers go or Frazee goes!" The Red Sox owner resented Johnson's threats, knowing that other owners had not been rebuked for gambling in their ballparks. Yet there was little incentive for the other magnates to discourage bettors from attending games. Gamblers were paying customers, and publicizing any hint of corruption would only threaten profits. Everyone connected with the sport knew that the cozy relationship between athletes and bookies made it easy to bribe a ballplayer to fix a game. Gambling sharks bragged about how they could handicap a baseball game as easily as a horse race. Some quietly kept ballplayers on their payroll.[14]

In the summer of 1917, acting on behalf of the National Commission, Johnson hired Pinkerton detectives who infiltrated Braves Field and Fenway Park. The investigators observed a betting ring in the pavilion at Braves Field. One detective in Fenway noticed "Sport" Sullivan—the "King of Boston gamblers"—warning fellow bettors not to draw too much attention to their activities. Instead of yelling wagers, the hustlers passed notes and used sign language; a nod and wink could seal a deal. But the Pinkertons easily identified them, providing police and the local district attorney with a list of names, Sullivan's at the very top. Cooperating with police, both Boston ball clubs barred known gamblers from entering their stadiums. Police arrested a few men who were fined $20, but the gambling culture at Fenway Park continued. In August, the *Boston American* published a headline that must have outraged Johnson: GAMBLERS ACTIVE AS USUAL AT FENWAY PARK.[15]

When the Red Sox opened the gates at Fenway on opening day 1918, gamblers noticed new signs posted on the outfield fence and on the back wall of the grandstand, warning, NO BETTING PERMITTED and NO GAMBLING ALLOWED. But the gamblers understood that the signs offered only an illusion that authorities were cracking down on them. Nothing had really changed at Fenway Park—a fact that inflamed Johnson's animosity toward Frazee.

The men sitting in the right-field grandstands knew, too, that the smart money was on the Red Sox. The Boston club may have had a practically new team—of the eight fielders in the opening day lineup, only two had played for the Sox in 1917—but with Babe Ruth pitching, victory seemed certain. Reporters noted his intimidating presence on the mound, his size and power. Ruth, F. C. Lane wrote in *Baseball Magazine*, "is a man of huge bulk, tremendous strength, iron endurance, and quenchless enthusiasm." Babe devastated batters with two pitches: a violent fastball and a curve that cut like a razor. It was a nasty combination that few "twirlers" could match.[16]

Babe rarely altered his approach on the mound and gave little thought to strategy. One time, before a game with the Detroit Tigers, former Sox manager Bill Carrigan asked him how he planned to attack each batter.

"Bush . . ."

"Fastball up and inside. Curveball, low and away."

"Vitt . . ."

"Fastball up and inside. Curveball, low and away."

"Cobb . . ."

"Fastball up and inside. Curveball, low and away."

"Crawford . . ."

"Fastball up and inside. Curveball, low and away."

He didn't care who came to the plate or how they had performed against him earlier. If he threw the ball fast enough, it did not matter who stood in the batter's box. The Babe threw a baseball the same way that he swung a bat: *hard*.[17]

Facing the Athletics on opening day, Ruth dominated the batters for most of the afternoon, allowing just four hits and one run in a complete game. In the second inning, batting ninth in the lineup, he gave the Red Sox a 2–1 lead when he ripped a single right over the first baseman's head, nearly separating George Burns "from his cap as it breezed past him." The Red Sox pounded Philadelphia's starting pitcher Elmer Myers, winning 7–1. It was just the beginning of a remarkable first month.[18]

In April, the Sox started the season 11–2, good for first place in the American League. Frazee recognized that the team's greatest strength was its four starting pitchers—Ruth, Carl Mays, Joe Bush, and Dutch Leonard. "We have the best quartet in the American League," he declared. Last season, he said, the Red Sox struggled scoring runs. He thought that he had addressed the team's offensive woes, trading for three talented hitters. Still, he had not found a productive batter to replace Duffy Lewis, who had left to serve in the navy. And with the War Department plucking ballplayers from every roster, none of the owners were willing to part ways with a starter unless they received a quality player in return.[19]

At the end of the month Frazee announced that the war had not diminished ticket sales. In fact, he said, attendance at Fenway was twice as high as it was a year earlier, though he offered no evidence to support his claim. Unquestionably, though, fans turned out to see Ruth, the "colossal southpaw pitcher and hitter most extraordinary." Frazee knew it and so, too, did Colonel Jacob Ruppert, the prominent beer mogul and co-owner of the New York Yankees. A few months earlier, in December 1917, Congress had passed the Eighteenth Amendment, prohibiting the "manufacture, sale, or transportation of intoxicating liquors for beverage purposes." Awaiting state ratification, Ruppert feared that prohibition would soon take effect, leaving him the owner of only one business. Pinched by the law, he needed an attraction that would consistently sell out the Polo Grounds. Rumors floated in the press that he had offered Frazee $100,000 for the Babe. It was, the *Boston Herald* reported, "the greatest valuation in the history of baseball." "I might as well sell the franchise and the whole club as sell Ruth," Frazee quipped.[20]

It was widely believed that Frazee planted the story himself. Knowing that the club would travel to New York in the coming week, gossip about Ruth might generate wider interest in the Red Sox–Yankees series. Advanced publicity had always helped him promote a show. Frazee stood to benefit from the visitor's share of the gate, and the Polo Grounds seated thirty-eight thousand spectators. But before the team boarded the train for New York, Ed Barrow had become increasingly concerned about the gaping hole in the middle of the batting order. By May 2, the team's cleanup hitter, first baseman Dick Hoblitzell, had fallen into a terrible slump, batting an abysmal .080. He had hit just four singles in his first fifty at bats, forcing Barrow to drop him to sixth in the lineup. Batting cleanup, left fielder Wally Schang was not much better, barely hitting above .200. Barrow pressed Frazee for help, but the Red Sox owner explained the difficulty of acquiring a top hitter, especially one who could hit from the left side of the plate.[21]

Convinced that he had a solution to the team's problems, Harry Hooper pleaded with Barrow to make Ruth a full-time hitter. "Have you thought any more about putting Babe in the field?" he asked. Perturbed, Barrow tried to shut down the debate. "How many times are you going to bother me with that?" he asked. Ruth was a pitcher, he insisted, "and a damn good one. We need him on the mound."[22]

Hooper countered that Ruth could help the team more by playing in the field every day. As long as Barrow confined him to pitching every fourth game, the Sox would continue struggling to score runs. Besides, he added, Ruth wanted to hit.

"He *wants* to?" Barrow boomed. "I'm not going to give in to every impulse that big monkey has. Can you imagine if I put the league's best left-hander in the outfield? I'd be the laughing stock of the league. Schang can play the outfield."

Wally Schang? His name didn't exactly inspire the image of a slugger. In his first five seasons, he had never hit above .300. And he had shown no signs of breaking out in 1918, either. Wally was a fine player, Hooper said, but he was not the same hitter as Ruth. "You're begging Frazee for more hitters! Here's one who's fallen right into your lap."

Barrow wouldn't budge. "We need Ruth on the mound," he repeated.

Babe did not have to quit pitching, Hooper explained. Ruth could play the field on the days he did not pitch. His bat, Hooper insisted, "could put us over the top."

"And what if he gets hurt out there? Then what? I can't do it Harry. I don't have the nerve."

Hooper persisted. "The fans love him," he said. Knowing that Barrow had a $50,000 investment in the team, Harry reminded him that attendance ballooned whenever Ruth played and that more games with Ruth playing would mean more money in the manager's pocket. Those fans, he argued, didn't come to see Ruth pitch—they came to see him hit. They paid to see the Colossus. They even cheered when he struck out.

Suddenly, Barrow's face changed. He rubbed his chin, pondering the possibilities. Finally, he relented. "All right, Harry. We'll give it a shot."[23]

10

Welcome to The Show

APRIL 6, 1918. EXACTLY ONE YEAR HAD PASSED SINCE THE UNITED States had declared war on Imperial Germany. Now the men of the 308th Infantry Regiment lined up in the dark at 4:00 a.m., company after company, each loaded heavy with gear, and marched for their final time out of Camp Upton. Troops of the 77th Division began moving out on March 27, and by the time Captain Charles Whittlesey and the 308th departed, Camp Upton had begun to look like a ghost town. They sang gaily as they moved in the early morning sunlight toward the Yaphank Station, where they boarded a train to Long Island City. From there, they scrambled aboard ferries and sailed down the river, around the Battery, and docked at the North River piers, where they and other 77th Division units embarked their three large British transport ships—the *Lapland*, the *Cretic*, and the *Justicia*, the last of which would be torpedoed on a later voyage. The months of training were behind them. Ahead loomed the war.[1]

Their training at Camp Upton may have formed them into a cohesive unit, but even the most rigorous training could do little to prepare them for the conflict being fought in France. After almost four years of frustration and stalemate that had killed and maimed millions of soldiers, the German high command believed they had

Charles Whittlesey's ancestors had served their country in all its armed conflicts since the 1637 Pequot War. And although he did not look remotely like a warrior, Whittlesey was determined to do his part for America in the Great War. In 1918, he went to France with the 77th Division to fight the Germans. *(Courtesy of the Williams College Archives.)*

the answer to the baffling riddle of the Western Front. Since the Bolsheviks had seized power during the October Revolution behind the slogan of "Peace! Land! Bread!," Russia's participation in the war had slowed dramatically and stopped entirely on March 3 with the signing of the Treaty of Brest-Litovsk. The agreement ended Germany's two-front war and allowed chief of staff of the Imperial German Army Field Marshal Paul von Hindenburg and his first quartermaster and main strategist General Erich Ludendorff to shift troops to the French front.

Yet the German high command knew that their advantage was fleeting. The British blockade had caused severe food shortages throughout the country, the U-boat campaign had failed, and virtually every day fresh American troops landed in France. Germany could not afford to wait. They had to win the war before the American buildup was complete, before starvation led to political revolutions at home and crippled the army. Von Hindenburg and Ludendorff pushed a tactical solution for a strategic problem. New *Sturmtruppen* (stormtrooper) small-group-infiltration infantry tactics combined with Captain Erich Pulkowski's and Colonel Georg Bruchmuller's sophisticated, more precise artillery innovations had been successful on the battlefield. All he had to do, Ludendorff believed, was punch a hole in the British front, roll toward the English Channel ports, and destroy large elements of the British Expeditionary Force. Without the BEF, France would capitulate.

On March 21, 1918, while Captain Whittlesey and the rest of the 77th Division were preparing to depart Camp Upton, Ludendorff launched Operation Michael against the British in the battle-scarred region of the Somme. The offensive commenced with the largest concentration of artillery fire ever seen. Mustard, chlorine, and tear gas canisters mixed with mortars rained on the forward British trenches. In five hours, the Germans fired three and a half million shells into the BEF lines. When the guns went silent, the *Sturmtruppen* attacked through the thick gas and fog, infiltrating into and past the enemy's forward trenches. In one day, the German offensive gained as much territory as the British had captured in four months of fighting on the Somme in 1916.

Although the BEF eventually slowed the assault, panic quickly penetrated the Allies' high command. On March 26, as Germany attacked the critical junction towns of Arras and Amiens, prominent British and French military and civilian leaders—including Field Marshal Sir Douglas Haig, General Phillippe Pétain, General Ferdinand Foch, and Premier Georges Clemenceau—convened an emergency meeting near the front in the tiny town of Doullens.

Out of the conference, and several that followed, emerged the agreement to appoint Foch as the supreme Allied commander, and General John J. Pershing's decision to commit his American Expeditionary Force (AEF) to fight in British and French sectors.

Unknown to the men of the 308th Infantry Battalion as they sailed past the Statue of Liberty on April 6, the battlefields of the Western Front had become even deadlier than before. Improved weaponry, more sophisticated tactics, and a mood of heightened desperation meant that they would be tossed into the fray faster than was previously planned. Military necessity altered Pershing's plan to have Americans operate their own sector and go to war commanded by American officers. Furthermore, a French commander would play a significant role in determining where and when they fought.

Those, however, were matters for another day. First, the 77th Division had to get to the Western Front, starting with a voyage across the Atlantic through U-boat-patrolled waters. A day after slipping past the Statue of Liberty, the three transports anchored off Halifax, Nova Scotia. For the next twenty-four hours, the ships took on coal and water and rendezvoused with the rest of the fleet. The men, meanwhile, practiced lifeboat procedures, lowering the smaller vessels into the water, scampering down ropes into the crafts, and rowing aimlessly in the harbor. While they enjoyed the unseasonably fine weather, the convoy gathered. Prominent was HMS *Queen Victoria*, packed with Australian troops, already sixty-eight days at sea. And leading the procession was the US cruiser *St. Louis*. Altogether, the fleet included nine transports and a host of battleships, cruisers, and sub chasers.[2]

On April 9, the convoy steamed out of Halifax harbor for open sea. Sailing just in front of the *Lapland* aboard the *Justicia*, Captain W. Kerr Rainsford of the 307th Infantry recalled the sunshine reflecting off the thin skim of ice, the screaming of a flock of seagulls, and the Stars and Stripes flying in the windows of almost every cottage. "One felt the tingling grip of brotherhood in the great world struggle on which we were launched," he wrote.[3]

Expressing this fellowship, the band on a British battleship serenaded the American troops with such staples as "Over There" and "The Star-Spangled Banner." Other bands played "God Save the King" and "La Marseillaise." A US Marine band followed with an upbeat "There'll Be a Hot Time in the Old Town Tonight." Captain L. Wardlaw Miles, who would distinguish himself in the months ahead, eloquently recalled how the landscape contrasted with the mood aboard the ships: "Behind, in contrast to all this music and movement, stood the charred ruins left by the explosion which had razed Halifax a few months earlier, and still further back, the bleak snow-covered hills. But in front—when the breakwater had been passed and the boats had turned their noses sharply to the east—in front of us lay 'Over There,' the yet unseen and unknown land of which at that hour it was customary to sing in humorous paraphrase:

And we won't come back
When it's over, over there. "[4]

The eleven-day voyage was as uneventful as it was unpleasant. Soldiers and sailors maintained blackouts at night. Smoking on deck was strictly forbidden. Officers and soldiers drilled for emergencies that never happened. Lookouts scanned the waters for U-boats that never appeared, though a whale gave the men a scare. The air in the bowels of the transports was stuffy from lack of ventilation and overcrowded soldiers. The British mess dished out food that few Americans found palatable, let alone passable. The meals, many doughboys believed, contributed to the numbers of men draped over the rails "feeding the fishes" in spasms of vomit. The nightly entertainment was about as entertaining as "a badly mutilated piano from the depths of the hold" could provide.[5]

As the days limped by, the initial excitement of an Atlantic crossing surrendered to boredom. On April 19, the southern coast of Ireland, near Old Head, came into view. There was not much to see, but somewhere close by, at the bottom of the sea, lay the sunken *Lusitania*, the ship most associated with America's entry into the war.

After rounding the southern coast of Ireland, the convoy sailed into the Irish Sea, and past the fortress-like cliffs of Wales, where they picked up an escort of seven British destroyers. The ships prowled for U-boats, "ducking and dodging through the spume like a school of porpoises." In hours, the transports had moved into the Mersey River and anchored in Liverpool's harbor. Through fog that shrouded the city came the music of more bands, the cheering of more voices. The voyage that had begun in sunshine ended in a wet mist. "Soon," Miles wrote, "hob-nailed boots were planted on terra firma." Whittlesey and his fellow soldiers were Over There.[6]

THE RELATIVE LEISURE OF THE convoy quickly gave way to frantic activity. When those days were still fresh enough for Whittlesey to remember clearly, he said that his unit "shot through England in one day." The soldiers marched off the ships, crammed into a train, and traveled from Liverpool on the northwest coast of England to Dover in the southeast. It was bitterly cold. The cars had little heating or lighting, and the men spied only fragments of the country. Miles recalled the taste of bitter, sugarless tea and a cold fish sandwich, hardly enough to dull the ache in the stomach of a hungry man. Rainsford, however, remembered spotting "an unusually pretty girl serving coffee during a halt at Rugby" and "a clear sunrise over a country white with hoar-frost and cherry-blossoms."[7]

Besides those dabbles of beauty, Rainsford judged, "nobody liked England." From the cliffs of Dover, however, the war loomed palpably. Smoke from "innumerable destroyers" rose thickly above the English Channel, airplanes and dirigibles watched over the activity below, and the muffled blasts of distant guns signaled the ultimate destination of the Americans. After the soldiers detrained, they slogged, bone-tired and heavy-legged, through the winding streets of the darkened town until they finally reached British Rest Camp No. 2.

Dover was more welcoming in the morning. It was a beautiful Sunday—gulls filled the sky, the Channel glinted blue in the sunshine, and the smell of salty sea winds wafted through the port. The peal of church bells, beat of military bands, and jocular exchanges with British Tommies left favorable impressions, but still the war brewed. That day and the next, the new arrivals—the largest number of doughboys to reach Britain since America's entry in the war—headed to the docks once more. On their way, they witnessed the wounded being carried off hospital boats—the legless and armless, the blind, the coughing victims of gas attacks.

The trip from Dover to Calais was a voyage of only an hour or so, but now the effects of bombing were visible, and the risk of death elevated. The Germans had bombed the port city so often that its buildings resembled shell-shocked soldiers—with empty, shattered windows that looked like eyes staring vacantly out at a world gone insane. There, Whittlesey said, the soldiers of the 77th Division—the first elements of the National Army to reach France—got their first taste of the war's devastation.

Operation Michael had pulled British troops away from the port towns of Calais, Boulogne, and Dunkirk. On April 9, the Germans had launched the Georgette Offensive in a poorly defended sector in Flanders, just south of the English Channel. The Germans forced the Allies out of Armentières and off much of the Messines Ridge, threatening the whole line along the River Lys. In two days, they had pushed to within fifteen miles of the ports. "Each one of us must fight on to the end," Field Marshal Haig told the BEF. A rumor spread among the newly arrived Americans: "The Boche have broken through and the 77th is to be thrown into the gap at once."[8]

Without knowing their ultimate destination, they were hastily prepared for battle. The British replaced the Americans' Springfields with Enfield rifles and provided them with steel helmets. The troops also received gas masks and learned how to use them. "They are all good masks," a British sergeant said. "Every one of 'em's seen service. The fellows who 'ad 'em all went west some wye or t'other, and now they've been fixed up for you uns."[9]

West of everything was death. The soldiers who had worn them were dead. It was a sobering thought, yet Whittlesey also noted that the Americans appreciated the British soldiers' bluntness about the horrors of battle.

Ultimately, the Allies' resistance stiffened and the Germans lacked the reserves to exploit their success. The 77th Division was not deployed into the line. Instead, the Americans received six weeks of training, roughly three weeks near Calais and three weeks closer to the front south of Arras. The officers and their men remembered the period quite differently. The Pas-de-Calais was crowded with troops, and adequate lodging for the new arrivals did not exist. They bedded down in tents and barns on dirt floors, or wherever they could find shelter. "Washing facilities of a French barnyard are restricted," a member of the 308th explained, "and the constant intrusion of poultry and rats and the imminence of the manure pile proved unattractive features." Soon they began to experience the plague of the trenches—lice. Tortured by the "cooties," they scratched and picked and tried every known remedy to get rid of the bugs, but as the British and French troops had discovered, nothing worked very well.[10]

Making life even more miserable, they dined on British cuisine. Napoleon supposedly once observed that an army marches on its stomach, and if that is indeed the case, the American troops fed in British messes displayed an angry, slow gait. American soldiers debated the worst aspect of the rations—the meager servings, the numbing lack of variety, or the awful taste. Hardtack—with an emphasis on hard—was the basic staple. Occasionally it came with a slice of fatty bacon (breakfast), a bit of mutton stew (dinner), or a dab of jelly (dessert). Sometimes the cooks would "treat" the troops to corned beef and salmon, and perhaps a nibble of gamey cheese.

Nor did the average doughboy warm to their British instructors. The two groups got off to a rocky start. A large percentage of the men in the 77th Division were of Irish decent, and on the trip across the Atlantic, they had gazed over the rails misty-eyed when the convoy passed close to the Emerald Isle. "It could hardly be expected," Miles observed, that they "would be enthusiastic over

English methods and English instructors." In addition, although most of the US troops picked up a smattering of such English phrases as "Carry on!," "Cheerio," and "The Show," they initially complained that they could understand the French more easily than the British.[11]

Life was significantly better for the officers. Like their British counterparts behind the lines, they slept in beds, dined at dinner tables, and enjoyed sparkling conversation. Rainsford recalled those early weeks in France as "probably the pleasantest." His men of the 307th Infantry "quartered in large conical or small-shelter tents . . . along the edge of the splendid beech-woods, and if only they could have learned to like the British ration, British shoes, and British Tommy, might have been perfectly happy. But the first was too short, the second too flat, and the trouble with the last difficult to determine."[12]

Certainly, Rainsford found no cause for complaint, recounting "the frequent and astonishingly elaborate banquets" hosted by such units as the East Lancashires "with delicious food and excellent wines, with music and song and stories." He painted scenes from a Hollywood set—the British officers riding their "splendid, well-groomed horses," the gatherings under "leafy beech-woods," the laughter and music that hung "like a curtain across the distance, the steady thunder of guns." They talked, not of war but of friendship, and sang drinking songs of friendship. But behind the romantic bonhomie was the reality of the war, and the East Lancashires took a beating later that summer, causing Rainsford to wonder "how many are still left of that gay gathering."

Whittlesey also recalled that the British division headquarters were in a rustic château, but brigade headquarters were sixty feet underground in an abandoned quarry to escape the constant artillery pounding—and battalion headquarters were at the front in the mud. His picture of the 308th's time in Flanders lacked Rainsford's romance. It rained steadily, day after day, and though he was tall and long-legged, the mud was up to his knees. He didn't recall the drinking songs, but he did remember the night patrols after the 308th was relocated closer to the front. During one "quiet night," he and a British comrade went out with two noncoms. German sharpshooters hit the soldiers twenty feet from the officers, but they didn't realize it until they found their bodies. "It was pretty noisy on a quiet night, out there," he said.[13]

It was the war, not the banquets, which occupied Whittlesey's attention and time. During the day, he labored in his job as operational officer at Regimental Headquarters. There he efficiently handled the 308th's paperwork. He recalled, for example, his hospitable dealings with French peasants, complaining only about "the numerous claims for damages they filed, for every sort of thing—mostly for chickens that were missing." At night and on his free days, he ventured to Arras on "Cook's Tours" of the front. There he received military as well as social lessons. From the safe side of a hill, he observed how swiftly German artillery targeted enemy observation posts. Artillery was the great killer in the war, accounting for roughly 80 percent of combat casualties. Yet, he learned, there were methods to minimize its impact. Furthermore, war was a great social leveler. In one New Zealand battalion he saw white Kiwis and dark-skinned Maoris fighting alongside each other. It was the first black and white mixed unit he had ever seen, and it, as much as the scale of the war itself, impressed him.

Except for the Cook's Tours, Whittlesey and his regiment remained at a safe distance from The Show. They trained, observed, and learned, mastering tasks and knowledge that they had not picked up in Camp Upton. Once billeted near Arras, the sound of the guns was louder, and the proximity to the action nearer. On May 21, the unit suffered its first casualties. At La Bizique Farm, near a busy road outside of Arras, a shell from a long-range enemy gun killed Private Stanley Belen and wounded Private George Schiesser. So exceptional was the event that Colonel Nathan K. Averill, the highly respected commander of the 308th, noted it in his general orders. The casualties were not without meaning, he explained. "This Regiment has entered upon a conflict to which all its lives are pledged—a struggle for an ideal for which the sacrifice of life is just and right. And this Regiment, 'New York's Own,' does honor to Private Belen, a soldier whose example has quickened our hearts with a new devotion to the cause for which he died." Soon it would have been as impossible as it was depressing to mention the regiment's dead in a general order.[14]

If, in fact, there was a 308th Regiment to issue general orders. Early in the morning of May 27, the German high command began Operation Blücher-Yorck, their third offensive of the spring. This one hit the French in between Soissons and Reims in the Champagne sector. As usual, German troops enjoyed astounding initial success, knifing through French forces massed in forward lines and advancing thirteen miles toward the Marne River and Paris beyond before nightfall. Crisis gripped the Allies. Parisians fled the city, clogging roads and spreading panic. French Socialist deputies demanded peace, and politicians made plans to move the government to Bordeaux. To help strengthen the sagging Marne line, General Pershing committed the US 2nd Division and elements of the 3rd Division to fight under French corps and army command. Soon the American troops were struggling heroically and victoriously at Vaux and Belleau Wood.

On June 4, as the fighting in Champagne raged, orders arrived in the 308th Regimental Headquarters informing the staff that the unit would be dismantled and amalgamated into the British 2nd Division. As operations officer, Whittlesey was charged with drawing up further orders for each battalion, noted Miles, "giving the information as to place, time, and manner of relief of the front line troops." It was a shattering command, in effect dissolving the unit's identity. A year before, the soldiers had arrived at Camp Upton as strangers. Since then, they had trained together, shared the ups and downs of camp life, marched down Fifth Avenue in the snow, sailed across the Atlantic and the English Channel, forced down British food, and slept in French barnyards—always together. But now, the orders announced, all that was over. Almost from top to bottom, American units would now come under British command. Only platoons would preserve their identity. To Whittlesey and the other staff officers, it appeared that a portion of the proud Liberty Division, "New York's Own," would perish not in battle but from some bureaucratic reshuffling.[15]

Yet as in so many other matters, indecision characterized the efforts of the high command. After beginning the process of amalgamation, on June 6 Whittlesey and the other officers of the 308th learned that the order had been rescinded. Pershing had once again decreed that American troops would only fight under American officers.

11

P.O.W. 1046

On April 9, 1918, after an exhausting four-day train ride accompanied by US Marshals, Karl Muck arrived in Chattanooga. Winding farther south toward the Tennessee-Georgia line, he looked through a trolley-car window and absorbed the view of sloping hills, the jutted limestone ridges of Lookout Mountain, the lush green forests of the Chattanooga Valley, and the red clay of Chickamauga Park. Approaching the gates of Fort Oglethorpe, War Prison Barracks No. 2, a thirty-two-acre stockade enclosed by a ten-foot barbed-wire fence, Muck could see twelve elevated sentry towers, equipped with spotlights, telephones, and Gatling guns.[1]

Soldiers led him inside the guardhouse, where they inoculated, fingerprinted, and examined Muck before assigning him an identification number—1046. The guards reported the fifty-nine-year-old conductor in "good" health. For the duration of the war, he endured the barren, treeless camp, what he described as "a little city of wooden barracks, with approximately four thousand internees, Germans and Austrians." Touring the dreary compound, he saw hundreds of prisoners milling about, their somber faces reflected a sadness that he could not escape. When the guards escorted him to his own room in Camp A, he found an eight-by-five cabin with a single metal bed, mattress, pillow, linens, and blanket.[2]

Two days after entering the camp, he wired Anita, reassuring her that he was safe. "Have arrived am well and have agreeable quarters and good company. Don't consider coming to Chattanooga before receipt of my first letter from here. All my mail will be delayed 10 days. Please sign your full name and address to all correspondence with me. Please wire if and when there is something important. Best love. Dr. Karl Muck." In the bottom right corner of his telegram, a censor stamped it with heavy ink:

EXAMINED & PASSED
Hqs. War Prison Barracks
Ft. Oglethorpe, Ga.[3]

The prisoners surrendered all privacy. Twice each day the guards scoured every building and bed for contraband. They permitted the internees to write two, two-page letters per month and one postcard each week as long as they did not exceed two hundred words. The censor scrutinized every word that they wrote and often held incoming and outgoing mail for weeks. He scanned letters and telegrams for coded messages and invisible ink—any signs of espionage. If a prisoner wrote an "objectionable" letter, the censor returned it for revisions or simply redacted it with splotches of black ink, usually because the prisoner had made a casual reference to the war or to the camp. The prisoners loathed the censor. One of them described him as "one of the ugliest fellows I have ever met. A teacher of German in some college, dry and pedantic to the bone, this man considered his office a means of inflicting mental torture on the prisoners."[4]

In early May, Anita traveled to Chattanooga. Except for weekends, the prisoners' wives were allowed to visit the camp one day each week for two hours. She arrived especially distressed. A few weeks before she visited at the fort, the Swiss legation announced that it would not extend citizenship protection to Muck, a decision that left him devastated and hopeless. Desperate for help, he asked her to seek legal aid, but there was no one who could rescue him. Making matters worse, the US Custodian of Alien Property had seized their assets and cherished Boston home, though Anita later arranged to rent it and often spent long stretches of time at the Signal Mountain Hotel just outside of Chattanooga.[5]

With the help of Charles Ellis and her well-connected friends, she managed to survive, but the wives of most prisoners were not as fortunate. Many of them were dependent on their husbands, and they relied on a relief fund established by the more affluent prisoners of the camp. Some of the prisoners' families moved to Chattanooga, where they found hostile American neighbors. The wives tried enrolling their children in the local schools, but the school board denied them admission.[6]

When Anita visited her husband, she found a bitter man. The anguish on his lined face divulged a sense of loss, an emptiness that nothing could fill. He complained about sleepless nights, rheumatism, and chest pains. During their weekly visits, a guard lorded over the couple, his shadow a reminder that only English could be spoken between them.

WHEN IT RAINED, THE CAMP's red soil became sticky mud. On that same red clay, in September 1863, after the Battle at Chickamauga, thirty-four thousand casualties lay amidst the clouds of dust and gun smoke from one of the bloodiest engagements of the Civil War. That battle, fought mostly in dense forests, scarred the land for twenty years. More than three decades later, during the Spanish-American War, volunteers trained at Chickamauga Battlefield in a temporary camp before departing for Cuba. In 1902, the US government built a permanent base north of Chickamauga Park, naming it Fort Oglethorpe in honor of Georgia's founder, James Edward Oglethorpe.[7]

During the Great War, the Fort Oglethorpe Army Post, a sprawling complex of more than 1,500 buildings, included three satellite camps. At Camp Warden McLean, reserve officers trained for active duty. At Camp Forrest, a base for the Corps of Engineers, infantry, and machine gunners, six miles of trenches and rifle pits formed a makeshift training ground. The troops simulated combat conditions, practiced marksmanship, and drilled for gas attacks. At Camp Greenleaf, "the West Point of Medicine," thousands of doctors, medics, nurses, and ambulance teams prepared for the worst. Sixty thousand servicemen passed through Chickamauga Battlefield on their way to Europe.[8]

Fort Oglethorpe also served as one of four German internment camps. East of the Mississippi River, all Germans considered potentially dangerous or guilty of violating federal law were sent to Fort Oglethorpe; West of the Mississippi, civilian prisoners were taken to Fort Douglas, Utah; German naval officers and sailors were locked up at Fort McPherson, Georgia; and merchant seamen were initially imprisoned at Hot Springs, North Carolina, before they were escorted to Fort Oglethorpe or Fort Douglas. At Fort Oglethorpe, the decorated commandant, Colonel Charles W. Penrose, a slender, graying man with a handlebar mustache, came out of retirement to oversee the camp, commanding thirty-two officers and more than four hundred enlisted men from the 17th Infantry Regiment.[9]

A few days before Muck arrived at the fort, a correspondent from the *Boston Globe* interviewed Penrose. After touring the camp, the writer published a three-part series exploring how the US government treated German prisoners. He reported that the internees were "a cheerful lot as a whole," living in conditions similar to American soldiers, an indication that the United States was, in the words of Penrose, "a humane and Christian nation." According to the reporter, the prisoners said that they "would be contented and almost happy if not for 'that fence.'"[10]

Penrose divided the prisoners into three camps. Camp A—the "millionaires' compound"—housed Muck and other wealthy prisoners who were exempt from labor and could afford to pay for their servants and cooks. It had three barracks, subdivided into small rooms and a small mess hall. Although the majority of the prisoners were not millionaires, they were men of means, paying $18 per month for room, board, and privileges that ordinary internees could not afford. During dinner, the camp's prisoners—bankers, scientists, professors, writers, and musicians—enjoyed music performed on a grand piano. And yet the moment a prisoner stepped outside the mess hall he could see a barbed-wire fence that bounded the inner camp. If he dared to touch that fence, a guard would open fire.[11]

Unlike Muck's exclusive group of about two hundred prisoners, the majority occupied Camp B, a compound of more than thirteen crowded barracks, each housing about one hundred beds. In the words of the *Boston Globe* reporter, it was packed with "the most violent and vociferous agitators of the I.W.W. type, would-be-dynamiters, beer hall plotters, and propagandists and the very offscourings of the Teutonic humanity." The common prisoners were required to do hard labor, quarrying rock, breaking stone, buildings roads, digging ditches, and constructing buildings. Unlike "the millionaires," who usually wore the same clothes that they had on when they entered the camp, the laborers were made to wear denim and brown overalls. As time passed, the men in Camp B grew to resent the privileged internees for their more comfortable conditions. It was a division that Colonel Penrose invited and inflamed; separating the internees by class denied them the power of unity.[12]

Finally, Camp C housed disobedient prisoners. Hoping to prevent a mutiny, Penrose deliberately isolated the most rebellious men—the radicals and agitators who made trouble. By early June, about 10 percent of the prisoners served time in Camp C. They were confined to the main stockade without canteen privileges or access to mail, mostly because they refused to "volunteer" for work at the rock quarry. Their refusal was part of a protest over reductions in the meager pay prisoners were offered for their labor—from one dollar per day to twenty-five cents. After Swiss commissioners investigated the conditions of the camp, Penrose clarified his orders, stating that he did not intend to punish the prisoners for refusing paid labor outside the camp, but rather to punish those troublemakers who refused to do mandatory "work necessary for their comfort or the upkeep of their prison barracks."[13]

The prisoners' dull daily routine began every morning with a 5:45 a.m. reveille. By six, the prisoners were out of bed. Before their 6:30 breakfast, they cleaned their barracks and lined up for the guards to count them. After breakfast, the men walked for an hour. By 8:00 the prisoners from Camp B reported for an eight-hour workday. At noon, the bugle sounded again for mess. From one to three, the prisoners were required to remain silent. At 5:30, the guards closed the gates surrounding the camp barracks, counted the prisoners again, and then sent them to dinner. In the evening, the internees were free to do as they pleased from inside a prison camp. At 10:00, "lights out," taps sounded with the prisoners in bed. The next day they did it all over again.[14]

If it were not for the barbed-wire fence and the armed guards, Fort Oglethorpe could have been mistaken for a small German town. Prisoners passed the time reading newspapers, magazines, and mail, writing letters, watching films and plays, planting gardens, playing sports, and attending lectures at the "university." Some men played chess, pool, or pinochle, a game brought to the United States by German immigrants. Writers established a literary magazine, the *Orgelsdorfer Eulenspiegel*, while a group of singers organized a choral society. Muck enjoyed vocational pursuits, including carpentry and tinsmithing, as well as the courses given by prominent academics. But, as one prisoner explained years later, none of these activities could truly distract them from the "unbearable uncertainty as to the duration of our detention."[15]

The prisoners frequently complained about the conditions of their confinement, pleading for relief from the Swiss legation. They deplored the cruel guards, inadequate sanitation facilities, and poor medical care. The summer proved insufferable, too. The hot sun beating down on their shoulders exhausted them, especially the manual laborers. Playing baseball, basketball, and volleyball, the prisoners' shirtless bodies turned "as red as blood from the sun," wrote a Chattanooga reporter. The stifling heat and humidity turned the barracks into ovens. "The first summer," Muck wrote, "was hard to bear. There is no other protection from the scorching rays of the tropical sun than to sit <u>under</u> the barracks, as every tree in the camp has been cut down and no shady spot is available. The barracks, covered with black tar paper, are virtually hell during day time."[16]

As the months passed, his spirits flagged. With no end to the war in sight, he had no idea how long it would be until his release. Broken, he appeared "a gaunt, haggard looking, bronzed figure," a fellow prisoner observed. The misery of camp life consumed him. "It is impossible to concentrate," he wrote a friend. "There is not a minute in the day when one does not have nearby talking, noise, and unrest." The stress of confinement unnerved him, though he handled the duress far better than the prisoners who succumbed to what was called "barbed-wire disease," a combination of home-sickness, ennui, and despondency.[17]

The worst cases manifested in delusions of persecution, violence, and suicide. According to one prisoner, "dozens and dozens" of men suffered from "barbed-wire madness," and had to be transferred to St. Elizabeth's Asylum in Washington. "To be sure," German poet Erich Posselt wrote, "many of those who went there were slightly off before they had been interned. But quite as many acquired their mania in Oglethorpe." One prisoner so desperately wanted to leave the camp that he washed his hair in urine, hoping that the authorities would diagnose him with insanity. The camp physicians, however, reported that he was quite normal.[18]

Trying to escape the camp carried great risks. Two barbed-wire fences surrounded the compound. Armed with short-barreled shotguns and machine guns, sentries monitored the camp from guard towers mounted on stilts about fifteen feet above the ground. The guardhouses were spaced about fifty yards apart around the perimeter. In the evening, searchlights illuminated the camp. Flashes of light irradiated the barracks windows, making it difficult for the prisoners to sleep undisturbed. Guards warned the prisoners to stay six feet away from the inner fence—that was the "dead line." If a German stepped out of bounds or made a run for it, the guard had the authority to kill.[19]

Prisoners who tried to escape paid the ultimate price. Posselt recalled that during a "dark and silent night" two men slipped through the fence surrounding Camp B and crept downhill toward the main gate. "Then, through the open inner gate of the main fence, the first man wormed his way, inch by inch, into the space between the

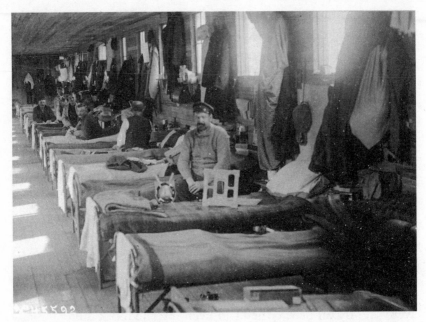

Fort Oglethorpe served as one of four German internment camps during World War I. Treated like prisoners of war, most of the approximately four thousand internees, including Karl Muck, posed no real security threat to the United States. Nonetheless, the Germans lived in barracks like the one pictured above. *(Courtesy of the National Archives.)*

two lines of barbed-wire surrounding the entire camp." The second prisoner lagged behind by about one hundred feet. Suddenly, a squad of soldiers appeared. "Hands up!" an officer shouted. The prisoners froze, jumped to their feet, and raised their hands toward the sky. Then, standing just four feet away from one of the unarmed prisoners, a lieutenant unloaded his sawed-off shotgun into the runaway's stomach. A few days later, he died in the infirmary.[20]

The lesson was clear: the prisoners had a better chance surviving the war inside the barbed-wire camp than they did trying to escape.

HENRY HIGGINSON KNEW THAT THE end had come. The Muck scandal had broken his spirit. The weathered patriarch contemplated disbanding the Boston Symphony Orchestra. Writing a friend, he acknowledged, "I tell you dear child, I never had such a painful experience in this life . . . I cannot conceive that we play another year." After thirty-seven seasons, on April 27, the eighty-three-year-old philanthropist announced his retirement. Going forward, a new board of trustees would be placed in charge, while also managing the search for a new conductor.[21]

The whole ordeal had left Higginson exhausted. He could no longer give his life to music. "The tensity [*sic*] of war-time feeling and the sorrow that came from clinging too long to the trust he had placed in one who proved unworthy of it, imposed a burden he could no longer bear," observed Higginson's friend and later biographer, Mark De Wolfe Howe.[22]

On May 4, the orchestra honored him one final time with his favorite Beethoven symphony—the Third. Mayor Andrew Peters thanked him for his philanthropy and devotion to the city. When Higginson appeared on stage, the patrons showered him with affection, rising in a standing ovation. Anticipating his farewell address, "a feeling of sorrow and great regret seemed to permeate the entire building," reported a *Boston Globe* writer. Reflecting on his career and the artistic value of the Symphony Orchestra, Higginson expressed his gratitude to the public and the musicians who made his dreams come true, though he made no mention of the most brilliant conductor he had ever known: Karl Muck.[23]

Since the maestro's arrest, Higginson had not seen him or written him. After his internment, Higginson wrote John Lord O'Brian, "Whatever the government decides is law for me." Muck's arrest forced him to consider whether the conductor had betrayed his trust and the trust of the American people. "To this day I have never known [Muck] to have done anything wrong so far as the United States is concerned," he wrote. "If I had believed that he had sinned in any way against our country, I should have dismissed him at once."[24]

The new board of trustees did something that Higginson refused to do. On June 22, it dismissed eighteen German musicians, including the assistant conductor, Ernst Schmidt. "Citizens of the United States and subjects of the allied nations only will be employed henceforth," the board announced. It replaced the Germans with French musicians, a politically expedient move that transformed an ensemble once known as a German institution.[25]

Three days later, the press reported that Anita Muck returned to the Back Bay police station where her husband was first jailed. Accompanied by Charles Ellis, her loyal confidant and acting attorney, she appeared at the Boylston Street station in a large touring car. A pack of photographers called her name and snapped pictures while Ellis tried to protect her, covering Anita's face with his hat. Standing by her side, Ellis tarnished his reputation among the Brahmin class. He'd lost many friends when he supported the German couple even as rumors persisted that the conductor had organized a plot to sabotage supply depots and railroad yards. But like Higginson, Ellis never considered Muck an enemy of the state.[26]

Earlier that spring, the Justice Department, spurred by widespread fear of spies, had decided that German and Austrian women living in the United States should register with the government. The intelligence agencies believed that the Kaiser was using the perceived innocence of women to conduct espionage on American soil. On April 19, 1918, President Wilson went even further, announcing that the alien enemy regulations would henceforth apply to German women, meaning that they would be subject to arrest and internment, though very few were ever sent to internment camps. Given the public scrutiny and media attention her husband attracted, Anita knew that she had no choice but to appear before authorities to register herself under the new rules.[27]

At the Back Bay police station, a crowd gathered outside, blocking the street. Inside the building, police officers questioned Anita and took her fingerprints and photographs. She was one of 163 German and Austrian women who registered that day in Boston, though hundreds more had already done so. She resented being treated like a criminal. The *Boston Globe* reported that she "protested against the registration," maintaining her husband's innocence and Swiss citizenship.[28]

Muck's situation remained as distressing as ever. However, there were bright spots. Journalists reported that, in an effort to reclaim some semblance of his old life, Muck formed an orchestra with

While Karl Muck languished in a Georgia internment camp, his wife, Anita, registered as an enemy alien at the Federal Building in Boston. Throughout Karl's internment, Anita and her attorney Charles Ellis (pictured on her right) pressed the US government to set him free. *(Courtesy of the National Archives.)*

thirty-five musicians. According to *Musical America*, "a real competition" had developed between him and Ernst Kunwald, the distinguished Austrian conductor of the Cincinnati Symphony Orchestra, who was also interned at Oglethorpe. According to one biographer, "Muck detested Kunwald as [a] man and musician." Like Muck, Kunwald had endured attacks from jingoists who protested his performances on stage. Even after he agreed to conduct the national anthem before his orchestra's concerts, special agents investigated his association with Germans, while the Daughters of the American Revolution accused him of spreading enemy propaganda. Without disclosing any evidence against him, the Justice Department had interned him under the approval of a young official named J. Edgar Hoover.[29]

Apparently, Kunwald had already organized an ensemble even before Muck's internment. Fort Oglethorpe housed musicians from impounded German luxury liners, the entire naval band from the German colony of Tsing-Tao, China, and some amateur players. *Musical America* claimed that Muck and Kunwald were "rehearsing feverishly," preparing for some kind of competition. "Dr. Muck may not find the means at his disposal as satisfactory as they were in Boston. Nevertheless, he will not be obliged to play 'The Star-Spangled Banner' before every performance, though there might be an element of poetic justice in compelling him to do it."[30]

Was Muck really conducting a makeshift symphony orchestra behind a barbed-wire fence? The last time he stood on a podium, federal agents arrested him. Embittered and angry, he'd come to despise the country that had helped make him a world-renowned conductor. Posselt, one of his fellow comrades in Camp A, recalled, "Dr. Muck swore he would never conduct again in America."[31]

In his surviving correspondence, Muck never mentioned conducting or any musical competition at Fort Oglethorpe. Yet comforting music carried beyond the camp's fence. Locals parked their cars outside the post so that they could listen to the concert. Did it come from Muck's orchestra? Perhaps. One thing is certain: he had one remarkable performance left.

12

The Great Experiment

BABE RUTH KNEW HIS WAY AROUND NEW YORK'S SALOONS AND brothels better than the way back to his team's hotel. He didn't play in the Red Sox's 2–3 loss to the Yankees on Friday, May 3, and had spent the night on the town, returning to his room shortly before sunrise. At least, that was the rumor Yankees manager Miller Huggins heard on the morning of the game. Nevertheless, Ruth was slated to pitch on that day. Assuming that the Red Sox ace was tired and hung over, Huggins devised a sound game strategy. In crucial situations, whenever possible, he planned to give his boys the bunt sign. Make the left-hander move hard to his right, bend down to field the ball, spin toward first base, and make an accurate throw across the diamond. That, Huggins thought, would be no small task for a pitcher with liquor still on his breath.[1]

The plan worked perfectly. While the Red Sox's bats were silent, the Yankees scored one in the first and second innings, and two in the third. Two Ruth errors were critical to the Yankees' success. The worst, a third inning gaffe, occurred when Ruth rumbled toward the third base line to field a Frank "Home Run" Baker bunt, falling as he reached for the ball, and then, from a sitting position, sailed a throw over the first baseman's head. Two Yankees scored as Red Sox fielders scrambled after Babe's errant toss.[2]

By the middle innings, Ruth had sobered considerably. In the seventh, with his team down 4–1, he came to the plate against spitballer Allen Russell. Perhaps overconfident after striking out Babe in three pitches earlier in the contest, Russell made a careless throw. Ruth pulled it down the right-field line, lifting it into the Polo Ground's second deck, just inches foul. The power of the blast, wrote W. J. Macbeth for the *New York Tribune*, struck "the fear of the Lord" into the Yankees.

After watching the ball land out of play, Ruth told the catcher and umpire that he would hit the next pitch to the same location, but this time inside the foul line. Then he did it, sending the ball into the upper deck and fair by a considerable margin. He finished the day by knocking in another run with a long double over the outfielder's head in the ninth inning, closing the Yankees' lead to 5–4 and giving the New York fans a few moments of doubt. Although the Yankees won the game with Ruth still on second, Babe's first home run of the season was the story of the day. Even New York fans reacted with awe at the force of his swing.

In the final game of the Red Sox–Yankees series, Ed Barrow made a significant lineup change. He had lost too many hitters to military service, and the ones remaining were not batting in runs. Of the four runs scored in the previous game against New York, Ruth had banged in three. The answer, Harry Hooper kept telling him, was obvious: Play Ruth. Pitch him in the regular rotation and send him to first base or the outfield when he was not on the mound. Finally, if for no other reason than to silence Hooper, Barrow started Ruth at first base in place of an injured Dick Hoblitzell, who had continued struggling at the plate. To Barrow, however, the change was not permanent; rather, it was a temporary move to solve an injury problem and use Ruth in a ballpark whose short right-field line favored left-handed pull hitters.[3]

With Babe playing first and batting sixth, Boston lost—badly. The Red Sox scored three runs in the fourth inning and zero in the other eight. Yankees runners touched home ten times. Yet Boston's defeat was in spite of Ruth's performance, not because of it. He went two for four at the plate, including what one reporter described as "a saucy home run, high into the attic in the grand-stand." Once again, the Red Sox slugger, not the Boston defeat, garnered the headlines. BABE RUTH IS HERO, WIELDS VICIOUS CUDGEL read the *New York Times*' story. RUTH STARTS RALLY, BUT RED SOX LOSE, countered the *Boston Globe*. It was Babe Ruth that thrilled baseball fans, taking, at least for the moment, their minds off the dreary headlines from the Western Front. It was Babe Ruth that sold newspapers during a lackluster season. Even though he wore a Boston Red Sox uniform, commented Paul Shannon, "Babe Ruth still remains the hitting idol of the Polo Grounds."[4]

The next day Barrow moved Ruth to the cleanup position against Walter "Big Train" Johnson, the most feared power pitcher in the game. Some sportswriters, looking back on the era, attributed Babe's spectacular performances at the plate with the equally spec-tacular decline in pitching over the same period. Uncle Sam, they argued, had created a batter's dream by summoning so many top-notch throwers into military service. Johnson, however, was still in his Washington Senators' uniform, and he was, statistically, the greatest pitcher of the first quarter of the twentieth century. In 1936, the Hall of Fame voters selected only two pitchers to be included in the first group of inductees to Cooperstown: Christy Mathewson and Johnson.

The first thing that batters noticed about Big Train was his unnaturally long arms. His wrists seemed to extend six inches below his cuff, and his hands hung to his knees. "He had those long arms," recalled contemporary Davy Jones, "absolutely the longest arms I ever saw. They were like whips, that's what they were. He'd just whip the ball in there." And how he'd whip the ball in there! "Did you ever see those pitching machines they have?" Detroit Tiger's great Sam Crawford asked a sportswriter. "That's what Walter Johnson always reminded me of, one of those air-compressed pitching machines. It's a peculiar thing, a lot of batters are afraid of those machines, because they can gear them up so the ball comes in there just like a bullet. It comes in there so fast that when it goes by it *swooshes*. You hardly see the ball at all. But you hear it. *Swoosh*, and it smacks into the catcher's mitt. Well, that was the kind of ball Walter Johnson pitched. He had such an easy motion it looked like he was just playing catch. That's what threw you off. He threw so nice and easy—and then *swoosh*, and it was by you!"⁵

Ty Cobb claimed that Walter Johnson's sidearm fastball didn't so much *swoosh* as *hiss*. "The first time I faced him, I watched him take that easy windup. And then something went past me that made me flinch. The thing just hissed with danger." All his life, Cobb retained a vivid memory of facing Johnson. Furthermore, the dirty ball of the era seemed to enhance the speed of his pitches. Major leaguer Jimmy Austin recalled, "On a cloudy day you couldn't see the ball half the time, it came in so fast. That's the honest-to-goodness truth."⁶

Already in May 1918, reporters had begun to compare Ruth's power at the plate with Johnson's on the mound. A batter's power and a pitcher's speed were the two irreducible elements of baseball. "The crashing, heavy hitter is a greater idol than the artistic tapper," wrote W. A. Phelon in 1915. "The crack of the bat, resounding far, draws more uproarious applause than the neatly worked base on balls . . . And the pitcher who burns them through with tremendous roaring speed is more talked about than the scienced [*sic*] wizard." Power versus speed—Ruth versus Johnson—it was a classic duel, and a test of Babe's skill.⁷

The Senators soundly defeated the Red Sox 7–2. Johnson excelled, surrendering only four hits, batting 3–3 at the plate, and driving in two runs. Throwing slow curve balls, he got Ruth out in his first two plate appearances. In the sixth inning, however, Johnson tried to throw a fastball past him. Babe "got hold of a fast one and gave it wings. It sailed on and on over the garden wall, messing up a war garden and scaring a mongrel pup half to death." The home run even pleased the Senators fans. A *Boston Herald and Journal* columnist expressed the opinion in the grandstand when he wrote, "My idea of a hard hit ball is Babe Ruth crashing into Walter Johnson's fastball for a home run."⁸

Ruth had hit homers in three straight games, but Boston had lost four in a row. Was the "great experiment"—using Babe as a pitcher and a hitter—working? Sportswriters debated the question, most suggesting that he was too valuable on the mound to risk injury or exhaustion by playing him on a daily basis. "Putting a pitcher in as an everyday man," opined the *Globe*'s Melville Webb, "no matter how he liked it or how he may hit, is not the sign of strength for a club that aspires to be a real contender." Ruth's pitching outing against Washington on May 9 underscored the problem—at least for some observers. He was magnificent at the plate. Batting fourth in the lineup, he went five for five with a single, a triple, and three doubles. Furthermore, he pitched a shutout through six innings. Then he tired, giving up three runs in the final three innings and losing the game in the tenth.[9]

The bottom line was that Babe and Boston were going in different directions. Ruth had never hit better. Near the middle of May, he was batting .500, a league-leading average. He astonished spectators wherever he played. "They all go wild for the big fellow; they all want him in every game and Barrow has felt the pulse of the fans and is giving them what they desire," wrote Burt Whitman. Yet the Red Sox were mired in a slump, dropping seven of eight contests between May 3 and 11, and Babe had lost his two pitching starts. That, Hooper thought, was baseball. Sooner or later, Ruth's hitting would begin to win games. But the losses weighed on Barrow like an anchor, making him question his decision and fret over his team. The question of how best to use his star consumed his thoughts. What he didn't consider, however, was the prospect of playing without Ruth at all.[10]

SOON THE TIDES CHANGED. ONLY now the Sox were winning and Babe was struggling at the plate. Boston swept a four-game series against Detroit, but he managed a mere three hits in fifteen official at bats. He needed a break. Seeking relaxation, on Sunday, May 19, an off date for the Red Sox and the first warm day of the year, he took his wife, Helen, to Revere Beach for an outing. Located just north of the city, it was the nation's first public beach, a working-class "people's beach" that featured amusement rides, a boardwalk, and an elaborate pier, as well as swimming facilities. Babe spent the day in the sun, eating a picnic basket full of sandwiches and drinking warm beer, swimming on a full stomach, and enjoying his own celebrity by playing a game of baseball in the sand with some locals. He couldn't have been happier.[11]

Later that night, Ruth complained of a terrible fever. His temperature climbed to 104 degrees, his body ached, he shivered with chills, and his throat throbbed. He had all the symptoms of the flu, a condition that he shared with millions of other Americans in the spring of 1918. As far as epidemiologists can tell, the initial epidemic began in late February in Haskell County, Kansas, and spread to nearby Camp Funston. From there it traveled with the troops to camps on the East Coast and in the South, and eventually to Europe. Twenty-four of America's thirty-six largest army camps experienced massive outbreaks of influenza, and city populations near them were particularly vulnerable. About forty miles northwest of Boston, Camp Devens experienced a crippling outbreak. This flu, however, received little attention compared with the deadly strain that lay in wait. Although some people died, most struck with the "Spring Flu" struggled through the aches and sweats of the fever and recovered.[12]

Ruth might have been among the lucky ones, but the Red Sox physician made matters worse. The day after his trip to the beach, Babe was scheduled to pitch. He showed up at Fenway looking like a ghost, feeling miserable, obviously ill, and in no condition to take the field, but determined to throw nonetheless. Dr. Oliver Barney "took a look at the big fellow, decided that the trouble was something more than a mere sore throat, and recommended four or five days of complete rest in bed." Barrow agreed, immediately crossed Ruth's name off of the lineup card and sent him home with the doctor, who liberally swabbed Ruth's throat with a caustic compound, silver nitrate, probably a 10 percent solution. In fact, he painted Babe's throat too liberally. Among the dangers of using the solution to treat tonsillitis, the standard *American Journal of Clinical Medicine* (1914) noted: "Caution: Great care must be exercised that no excess silver-nitrate solution oozing from the swab drops into the throat, lest serious results follow; for as we know, cases are on record in which edema [swelling] of the glottis, severe spasms of the larynx and other spastic affections of the throat, even suffocation, resulted from such accidents."[13]

The treatment hit Ruth like a line drive to the throat. He choked and gaged, writhed in pain, and finally collapsed. Immediately, he was rushed to the eye and ear ward of Massachusetts General Hospital. There a physician packed his inflamed throat in ice. Soon rumors shot through Boston that "the Colossus . . . worth more than his weight in gold" was on his deathbed.

Two days later, the news from Massachusetts General significantly improved. "Babe's great vitality and admirable physical condition have started to throw off the aggravated attack of tonsilitis [sic]," noted the *Boston Herald and Journal*. "The prophecy now is that the big lad will be out of the hospital in four or five days" and would be ready by the end of the month to travel west with his teammates.[14]

WITH RUTH LAID UP IN a hospital bed, Harry Frazee worried that he had lost his best player. Three days later, Frazee received even worse news when Provost Marshal Enoch Crowder announced that by July 3 all draft-age men with deferred classifications would have to enlist in the military or obtain work in an "essential industry." The War Department made its position clear: young, able-bodied men would either shoulder a Springfield rifle on the fields of France or manufacture them on the home front. The "work or fight" order, as it was known, meant that men like Ruth who were engaged in unproductive labor were likely to be drafted even though they had previously received a deferment.[15]

Frazee and the owners feared a mass exodus of ballplayers fleeing for farms, steel mills, and shipyards. If the players complied with the order, the Red Sox wouldn't have enough men to field a team. Panicked, baseball executives requested clarification from the government. Knowing that actors had received an exemption from the order on the grounds that they were essential to public entertainment—a ruling that kept Frazee's theaters open for business—the owners wondered if athletes might receive the same consideration. What were professional baseball players if not entertainers? The War Department, however, failed to settle the matter: "No ruling as to whether baseball players ... come under the regulations regarding idlers or nonessential pursuits will be made until a specific case has been appealed." The players, therefore, could appeal to their local draft boards just like anyone else, but it was unlikely that there would be a class exemption.[16]

Immediately after Crowder's announcement, sportswriters debated the implications of the "work or fight" order. Some suggested that the government would never interfere with the operations of the national pastime. The presence of soldiers and sailors attending Major League games, F. C. Lane noted in *Baseball Magazine*, attested to the sport's pull on the nation during the war. Furthermore, Lane argued, baseball was more than a game; it was an essential industry that contributed "its due share in taxation for the successful prosecution of the war." Other writers maintained that baseball mattered little in an age of global crisis. "There's nothing especially inspiring, anyhow, in these times, in watching a bunch of strong bodied youngsters tossing a baseball around," Nick Flatley wrote in the *Boston American*. "Those who read the casualty lists daily with fear-wracked feelings just naturally can't enthuse much about a ball game."[17]

Anticipating that the government's "work or fight" order would force the owners to close their gates, dozens of ballplayers quit their major league teams for work in the shipyards and munitions plants. Critics, like syndicated columnist Hugh Fullerton, suspected that these "shipyard heroes" were simply trying to avoid military service. Most of them, Fullerton observed, were not actually working in the factories and yards. They were simply signing up to play baseball for company teams in the steel and shipyard leagues for salaries that far exceeded those of regular workers. In Massachusetts, state legislator Calvin Page toured shipyards and found ballplayers who delivered two pails of paint to the actual painters and then spent the rest of their "work" week playing ball.[18]

Ten days before Crowder's announcement, "Shoeless" Joe Jackson, one of the game's most lethal hitters, learned that he had been reclassified 1A. After playing only seventeen games, Jackson left the White Sox for a position with the Harlan & Hollingsworth Shipbuilding Company in Wilmington, Delaware. Defending his decision, he claimed that he had to support his wife, mother, and two younger siblings, but the soapbox patriots villainized him as a "shipyard slacker," a coward shirking his duties as an American citizen. When Jackson suggested that shipbuilding was dangerous work—three men from his crew of bolters died in one day—*The Sporting News* scoffed, "Come on, Joe. Show us the blisters and calluses on your hands; let us see your pay envelope to prove that it contains only the wages of an honest plate-fitter and not a fat bonus for playing ball for the amusement of slackers high and low."[19]

About a month after delivering the "work or fight" order, Crowder reaffirmed that baseball players would not receive any special consideration from draft boards. Slackers—those contributing "nonproductive" labor—included people "engaged and occupied in games, sports, and amusements, except actual performers in legitimate concerts, operas, or theatrical performances." Without specifically mentioning baseball, Crowder's ruling threatened the season. The announcement frustrated Ban Johnson. "I do not understand Gen. Crowder's statement that baseball is nonproductive in the face of the fact that the two major leagues alone will deliver to the government in war taxes nearly $300,000." Owners, players, and league officials had helped raise more than $8 million worth of Liberty Bonds, he added, and had contributed to the Red Cross and other wartime charities. "Where," he asked, "is there another class of men earning as much per capita for the government?"[20]

WHILE THE BASEBALL TITANS WORRIED about the condition of their game, Babe Ruth rested quietly in the hospital. On May 26, he walked out of Massachusetts General "a free man," pounds lighter, still weak, but ready to go back to work. Soon, a reporter speculated, "the cave man will be out there again fighting for the glory of the crimson stockings." His physician, however, prescribed more rest, and since Boston was winning, he did not play until the final game of the month. Even then, Barrow only called on him to pinch-hit in a losing effort against Washington.[21]

On May 31, the Red Sox boarded a westbound train for Detroit, where the next day they began a four-game series against the Tigers. Before they returned to Boston on June 18, they would battle Cleveland, Chicago, and St. Louis—seventeen games in seventeen days. Physically, the stretch promised to sap the energy of all the players on the understaffed squad, but none more than Ruth. Although he was still recovering from the flu and the silver nitrate treatment, Barrow planned to call on him to pitch, hit, and help protect the team's two-game lead in the pennant race. The manager and player fully expected an exhausting half-month on the road. What they, or anyone else, didn't anticipate was that during those seventeen days, Ruth would fundamentally change the character of the game. After the western swing, players and fans alike would view baseball very differently.[22]

Detroit's Navin Field was Ty Cobb's home, the citadel of the Dead Ball Era. One of baseball's new steel-and-concrete stadiums, it had opened its doors on April 20, 1912, the same day as the first game at Fenway Park. Although it took the name of its owner, Frank Navin, Cobb's oversized personality gave the park its character. Baseball as Cobb and the players of his era knew it was a sport of aggressive, often vicious, incremental advances. For the man dubbed the Georgia Peach, a singularly inappropriate moniker, baseball was like combat. It was meant to be ferocious. "Baseball," he wrote in his autobiography, "is a red-blooded sport for red-blooded men. It's no pink tea, and mollycoddles had better stay out."[23]

Since every aspect of the sport was warfare in microcosm, Cobb planned each engagement as carefully as a military campaign. Navin Field showed his concern for detail. The length of the grass, the consistency of the dirt, even the nature of the batter's box bore his stamp. Cobb insisted, for instance, that the Navin Field ground crew water down the dirt in front of home place, an area that became known as Cobb's Lake. The wet dirt slowed down his bunts and made them more treacherous to field. How many of Cobb's record 4,191 career hits resulted from fielders slipping in the lake while they scrambled after one of his bunts? Undoubtedly, the Georgia Peach could have provided a close approximation.

Babe Ruth did not care a wit about Cobb's Lake. That was for bunters, dime-a-dozen singles hitters, chop-swing ballplayers who only wanted to make it to first base. Everything about Ruth challenged Ty Cobb's approach to baseball, from the length of his swing and his disregard for striking out to his determination to hit the ball far and his glorification of the home run. Baseball was not war for Ruth; it was entertainment. Spectators did not want tiny battles of bunt and run; they desired enormous spectacles splashed against distant fences. The long ball was the essence of Babe Ruth, the centerpiece of his revolution, and nothing else on the ballfield really mattered to him. He was a man of excess—he ate too much, drank too hard, drove too fast, talked too loud, and fornicated too indiscriminately—and the home run, like Cobb's combativeness, was the essence of his style and approach.

In the second game of the Detroit series, Babe provided a demonstration of his philosophy. Back on the mound for the first time in over a week, he lacked his normal speed and control. When he came to the plate in the sixth inning, the Tigers led 4–0. In an attempt to redeem himself, noted a Boston writer, the "Cave Man" crashed a home run. It was a Ruthian four-bagger, deep into the center-field bleachers, the longest hit that season in Navin Field. The next day he crushed another homer into the center-field bleachers. And the day after that he did it again. The spree inspired the chronicler in sportswriter H. W. Lanigan: "Someone else in balldom might have did it in the long long ago, but the record book fails to show it—meaning that Battering Babe Ruth's performance of smiting out three home runs on three consecutive playing days for the second time this campaign is probably furnishing the baseball historians with some new material."[24]

Ruth's assault on the record books continued the next afternoon. Against Cleveland's Johnny Enzmann, Babe hit his fourth home run in as many days. Now there were no doubts about the singularity of his achievement. "When 'Babe' Ruth, the mighty Red Sox smiter, lifted the ball over the right-field wall for a home run at Cleveland," noted the *Boston American*, "he established a major league record."[25]

It hardly mattered if Boston won or lost. When Ruth was on the field, everyone watched him. *He* was the story. "Babe Ruth has us all aglow over his prodigious home-run hitting," gushed a Boston columnist. "Almost before the fan asks, 'How'd the Sox come out?' he edges in with 'Did Babe catch one? Was it a homer?'" In a way that Ty Cobb never had been, Ruth's emerging celebrity was larger than the game itself. What he did to a baseball was unique. Players had hit home runs before Ruth, but none had been so defined by his sheer power.[26]

As Ruth's incursion on American League fences continued and interest in him grew, sportswriters struggled over how to present him to their readers. Nothing about him fit the Christy Mathewson or Walter Johnson tradition of the clean-cut, all-American athlete. Nor did he even approximate the ultra-competitive Ty Cobb type. And most of the writers' efforts to describe his individuality badly missed the mark. A *Sporting News* reporter, for instance, commented, "Physically, George Ruth is a perfect specimen of an athlete . . . He drinks little, seldom smokes and takes care of himself." At the end of the interview, Ruth even flexed his muscles for the writer to feel his bicep. The interview—and others like it—was an attempt to domesticate Babe, an unsuccessful effort to soften his image, but his reality would outlive such legend makers.[27]

Yet Ruth's fame was not the result of his pitching or the success of the Red Sox. In truth, he was beginning to struggle on the mound, and Boston was just barely clinging to the A.L. lead. His renown rested totally on his home run production, and he knew it. "I just live to hit," he told a *Baltimore Sun* reporter. Pitching did not produce the same joy. On June 7, he pitched badly in relief against Cleveland, lasting only one-third of an inning, recording the loss, and dropping his record to 4–5. After the game, he told Barrow that he was through pitching. He only wanted to hit and play somewhere in the field. Uncharacteristically, the manager did not press Babe. When occasionally he asked his pitcher to take the mound, Ruth complained about a sore arm or wrist. Besides, the fans that came to the ballpark during the war-torn season wanted a chance to see him clobber a home run.[28]

All the while Ruth remained an intimidating presence at the plate. On several occasions, pitchers intentionally walked him. "Such a compliment had not been paid a modern slugger, not even Cobb," a Boston columnist wrote. Believing that discretion was the greater part of valor, they pitched around him. St. Louis beat writer L. C. Davis joked that even that strategy was dangerous. "Babe hits the pill so hard that the infielders duck even when he gets a base on balls."[29]

Ruth was not only dangerous to opposing players. His reckless behavior on and off the field courted injury and even death. Playing left or right field, he was a disaster waiting to happen. He charged balls hit into the gap heedless of Harry Hooper ranging in from center field, and only the experience and caution of his teammate prevented serious bodily injury to both. Hooper later recalled Ruth "galloping around that outfield without regard for life or limb, hollering all the time, running like [a] maniac after every ball." Fences, however, did not move to avoid contact, and several times Babe crashed into the barriers. Though he found it boring in the outfield—there was more action on the mound or first base—once a ball was hit anywhere near him, he pursued it with a joyful intensity, ignoring anyone or anything in his way.[30]

He drove cars with that same mindless nonchalance. Ruth regarded traditional stop signs, newly installed traffic lights, and basic driving regulations as advisory, not mandatory, precautions. This was especially true late in the evening when he had been drinking. On the night of June 21–22, he lost control of his automobile and crashed it into a telegraph pole. His cars, suggested a columnist in the *Boston Herald and Journal,* had short life expectancies. If the lords of baseball were giving automobiles to the most valuable players in each league, "it's a certainty that Babe Ruth would get the A. L. buggy. It's equally certain that there would be little left of the machine by the start of next season." Nevertheless, the writer believed that the Red Sox paid Ruth to hit, not drive. "Babe can hit telegraph poles as hard as he hits the horsehide. But we love him just the same."[31]

Ruth's irresponsible and obstinate behavior added to Barrow's problems. Left-handed starting pitcher Dutch Leonard had abandoned the Red Sox to play for a shipyard team, leaving a gaping hole in the rotation. Leonard's departure and the growing number of Major League players voluntarily leaving for the shipyard teams made Barrow and other big league managers worry that they'd lose more men in the coming weeks and months. But still, whenever Barrow nudged his problem child toward the mound, Babe complained about his aching arm or stiff wrist. Besides, he insisted, he was an outfielder now. Adding to Barrow's woes, in late June the Sox dropped three of four games in New York. As if Ruth felt it was necessary to prove his value as a hitter, he homered in Boston's only victory in the series. It was a "tornadic thump," commented a *Boston Herald and Journal* reporter. "If the right field grandstands hadn't been in the way," added a *New York Times* scribe, "the ball would have gone down to 125th Street."[32]

On June 25, despite another Ruth home run, Boston lost to Washington and dropped out of first place for the first time that season. And even though a victory the next day moved the Red Sox into a three-way tie with the Yankees and the Indians for the A.L. lead, the battle of wills between Barrow and Ruth was building. Sportswriters took sides, arguing, once again, whether Ruth was more valuable as a hitter or a pitcher. Teammates knew there was nothing wrong with Babe's wrist and questioned his commitment. With American soldiers on the Western Front ready to sacrifice their lives, some groused that Babe wasn't even prepared to pitch a baseball for the good of the team.[33]

Ruth's power, however, bolstered his status. In the final game of June, a rain-delayed contest against the Senators, he once again faced Walter Johnson. Through nine innings, the Red Sox and Senators battled, and the game was knotted 1–1. Babe was hitless. Then with one on in the tenth, Johnson delivered a fastball. Ruth threw all of his weight into his swing, connected, and drove the ball over the wall in right-center. At the time sportswriters said that it was the longest hit ever in Griffith Stadium.[34]

Between May 4 and June 30, Ruth had struck eleven home runs, more than five other American League teams would hit that year. Putting the number in perspective, in the previous fourteen American League seasons, only three other players had hit more than eleven, and each had finished with twelve. Ralph "Socks" Seybold's American League record—set in 1902—was only sixteen. Manipulating the numbers—a favorite baseball pastime—a *Boston American* sportswriter wrote that if Ruth played every game that season, he would have hit forty-four homers, a staggering figure. Playing in just forty-three of Boston's seventy-six contests, Babe had changed fans' expectations of the game.[35]

Even overseas Americans hungered for news of Ruth's exploits. Every night at eleven a wireless report went out from Arlington to navy ships at sea. It included a final score summary of the day's contests. Just the game scores—except for Boston. For the Red Sox, the wireless operator included whether or not Babe had clouted another home run. In an odd twist of fate and wartime circumstances, the wayward kid from Baltimore, the son of a German-American saloonkeeper, had become a hero even to sailors and soldiers fighting to make the world safe for democracy.[36]

13

Slackers and Shipyards

During May and June of 1918, the months when Babe Ruth altered the strategy and tempo of the national game, American troops had their first taste of sustained warfare on the Western Front. They were still arriving in France that spring, hundreds of thousands of soldiers dressed in khaki facing daunting logistical problems, lacking practical military training, and confronting their own fears of going into battle on foreign soil. But there was no time for leisurely preparation; the German offensives that spring and summer would determine the American timetable. The Allies needed the American Expeditionary Force to fill holes made by the German assault.

With their minimal training, the US soldiers were forced to learn on the job. The price they paid for experience was thousands of lives and limbs. Although their French and British allies were initially skeptical of the professionalism and ability of the American troops, they soon began praising their courage and élan. The US 1st Division's struggle to retake the town of Cantigny, the US 2nd and 3rd Divisions' efforts to reinforce the sagging lines at the Marne, and the heroic stands by American soldiers and Marines at Vaux and Belleau Wood—all testified to the tenacity, determination, and grit of the doughboys. And as they fought, others disembarked from ships in Brest and Bordeaux. In March, only three hundred thousand poorly trained US soldiers had set foot in France. By June, there were 1.2 million, many with a better idea of the realities of warfare on the Western Front.

Manpower and firepower, Americans soon learned, were what mattered in industrialized warfare. They grew to appreciate that power on the battlefield, just as sports reporters were exploring the meaning of Ruth's impact on baseball. By the end of June, journalists had begun to compare American fighting forces in France with Babe's performances in America. "The story of Babe Ruth's mighty hitting, his Homeric smashes, kindles a glow in the hearts of all those who know baseball," commented a *Boston Herald and Journal* columnist. "In Italy, in Normandy, in Alsace, and in a hundred camps along the firing line, men meet and ask for the latest news of the gifted hitter of home runs. The story of each succeeding circuit clout is received with acclaim. It lightens and breaks the dangerous tension of a soldier's duty and it's not stretching a point to say that in his own inimitable way the Colossus is contributing a worth-while gift to the morale of Uncle Sam's fighting men both in the new and the old world. He is the hero of all present day baseball."[1]

Increasingly, Ruth's power at the plate became a metaphor for America's power in the war. As his reputation ascended, his ethnic heritage vanished into the mist of the past. Reporters molded Ruth into an emblem for all that was good in America. This ballplayer who "only lightly brushed by the social veneer we call civilization" was transformed, as Harry Hooper dimly said, "into something pretty close to a god." And it started to happen during the Great War.[2]

Of course, the creation story depended on some modicum of cooperation from Ruth himself. While the shipyard leagues tempted some ballplayers, he fulfilled his patriotic duty, bringing joy to Americans seeking refuge from the stresses of war.

ON JULY 2, 1918, BABE Ruth declared his Independence Day. That afternoon in Washington, DC, he left a game against the Senators after striking out in the sixth inning, complaining of a stomach-ache. At least that's what Barrow told reporters. But the truth was that Ruth didn't return to the field because he couldn't stand hearing his manager snap at him one more time. Trailing by three runs, Barrow implored the free-swinging Ruth to exhibit more patience at the plate, but Babe had never exhibited self-restraint in anything he did. He insisted on doing things his own way. After striking out on three consecutive pitches, he retreated to the dugout where the skipper blasted him for swinging at every pitch, swinging so hard that he twisted his body and nearly toppled over.

"That was a bum play," the manager barked.

"Don't call me a bum," Ruth shouted. Exchanging insults, Babe threatened to punch Barrow in the nose.

Fuming, Barrow retaliated, warning Ruth that his disobedience would cost him $500.

"The hell it will!" Ruth shouted. "I quit!"

He stormed out of the dugout and bolted for the clubhouse. When the inning ended, a teammate found him sitting glumly on a bench, his jersey unbuttoned. "I've had it with that bastard and I've had it with this whole goddam team," he groused. Ruth changed clothes and then found a seat in the stands where he watched the last three innings of the game before disappearing.[3]

Without a word, he left town, abandoning the team just before Barrow and the others boarded a train for Philadelphia. Later that night, Ruth surprised his father when he showed up at his Baltimore saloon on South Eutaw Street. Talking to a reporter, he vowed never to play for Barrow again. Knowing that there were industrial teams that would pay top dollar for his services, he sent a telegram to Frank Miller, manager of the Chester Shipbuilding Company team. Throughout the season scouts from the Bethlehem Steel League had offered financial inducements to the best professional ballplayers. Other leagues had shown interest, as well. The Red Sox had already lost star pitcher Dutch Leonard to the Fore River team in Quincy, a club run by Joseph P. Kennedy. And sportswriters reported that Ruth had signed a contract to play for the Chester Shipyard.[4]

Rumors circulated in the press that Babe Ruth—the biggest star in baseball—had quit the Red Sox. Barrow could not believe it. He told reporters that he expected Babe to return to the team the next day. Yet Frazee was clearly concerned. "Where is this shipyard?" he asked a writer. "Who's in charge of the team?" Frazee threatened a lawsuit against Ruth and Miller. He'd pay the top lawyers to get an injunction against the Chester Shipbuilding Company. Babe was under contract, he argued, and if he jumped to a shipyard team, then he was in clear violation of their agreement. "Ruth won't get away with it," he said. "I won't stand it and you can make that as strong as you like."[5]

In Baltimore, a local writer interviewed Ruth, asking about his plans. Babe admitted that he intended to play for the shipyard team, but only for a day, contradicting reports out of Chester that Frank Miller had signed him for the remainder of the season. Miller had already started advertising Ruth's appearance with the squad. Still furious with Barrow, he admitted that he was "too mad to control myself." He insisted that he had not actually quit playing for the Red Sox, though he had no intention of paying any fine. When would he return to the Boston club? "Just say I don't know what I'll do," he answered.[6]

Fans and writers wondered if he had deserted the Red Sox because the "work or fight" order had taken effect the day before he left. Yet Ruth maintained that Crowder's edict had no influence on him. Like many of his teammates, he belonged to a unit in the Massachusetts Home Guard. He was a loyal American, prepared to serve his country. "I've been deferred because I'm married," he said, "but we've all signed up anyway to do our bit after the season is over. Any time they want me, all they have to do is call on me and I'll go."[7]

Ruth and the "camouflage ship workers" outraged many Americans, particularly troops overseas. Lieutenant Harry McCormick told the *Baltimore Sun* that soldiers had become disillusioned with professional baseball because too many athletes had evaded the military. Serving as the sports editor of *Stars and Stripes*, the armed forces newspaper, Lieutenant Grantland Rice encountered doughboys who had become "bitter against star ball players, fight-ers, and motion picture actors who had remained behind." They were slackers, a scourge on America that should be blacklisted from the game, *The Sporting News* charged. The editors of *Stars and Stripes* declared, "Sport as a spectacle, sport as an entertainment for the sideliners, has passed on and out. Its glamour in a competitive way has faded." Therefore, after July 26, the editors discontinued the sports page. Professional athletes no longer deserved publicity; the real heroes were the soldiers, courageous young men making real sacrifices on the Western Front. "There is no space left for the Cobbs [and] the Ruths . . . when the Ryans, the Smiths . . . and others are charging machine guns and plugging along through shrapnel or grinding out 12-hour details 200 miles in the rear."[8]

Ruth's protest may not have had anything to do with the "work or fight" order, but it revealed his politics. Asserting his indepen-dence, Babe defied management. It was not the first time, either. On the eve of the 1917 season, after the owners agreed to salary reductions and freezes, Dave Fultz, the head of the Players' Fra-ternity, had called for a strike and applied for a charter with the American Federation of Labor. At a time when many Americans feared labor radicals disrupting industry, sportswriter John B. Foster smeared the Players' Fraternity, labeling the union "foreign, hostile, and injurious to sport." Team owners condemned the sympathetic strikers, branding them "anarchists" and "weak-kneed pacifists." Fultz, however, struggled to unify the players, especially after Ban Johnson threatened to lock them out and impose a standard wage scale, effectively ending a star system that benefitted the best play-ers. As a result, few players supported the strike, though one young star in Boston had pledged a commitment to Fultz's cause: Babe Ruth.[9]

In the aftermath of the players' failed strike, the owners refused to deal with Fultz, and the Players' Fraternity basically dissolved. By the time the United States entered the Great War, the players held no collective bargaining power. Yet as Ruth's fame grew, so did his value. In the summer of 1918, Babe was *the franchise*, an espe-cially valuable commodity in a time when attendance lagged across baseball by as much as 40 percent. "He knows, too," wrote the sympathetic Edward Martin, "that he could fix his own price in normal times. He is not a stuck up man, is patriotic and willing to do his bit for Uncle Sam." But did Ruth really accept less money than he was worth? Did he really put aside his own self-interest for the good of the game and the country?[10]

At least one observer, C. Starr Matthews, a reporter with the *Baltimore Sun*, suspected that Babe's mid-season holdout was designed to pressure Frazee into offering him "a little boost in salary." The competitive propositions from the shipyard teams gave Ruth leverage. In early June, Frazee had offered him a $1,000 bonus if he won thirty games as a pitcher. But since he had all but given up pitching and now earned his salary as a slugger, Matthews surmised that he was seeking added compensation for swinging "the good old hickory." In any case, Barrow soon dispatched Ruth's confidant Charles "Heinie" Wagner to Baltimore, with strict orders: bring home the Babe.[11]

Nobody knows exactly what Wagner said that persuaded Ruth to rejoin the Red Sox, but in about a week's time, Frazee sent Ruth a signed letter that amended the terms of his original bonus. Frazee now agreed to pay him $1,000 immediately, plus Ruth could earn another $1,000 if the Red Sox won the American League pennant—a sweet incentive that presumably made him abandon any notion of playing in an industrial league.[12]

On July 4, around 2:00 a.m., Ruth and Wagner arrived in Philadelphia, red-eyed and weary from a long night. Around noon, Ruth dressed, ready to play the Athletics in a doubleheader. When he discovered that Barrow had not penciled his name onto the lineup card, Babe erupted. Years later, he told writer Bob Considine that Barrow had called the entire team together and reprimanded him. "He threatened to knock my block off if I ever left the club again without permission," Ruth said. Standing in the middle of the clubhouse, Babe ripped off his uniform and threatened to quit the Red Sox for good. Harry Hooper and a few teammates intervened, and eventually managed to talk him down. Mediating the rift, Hooper persuaded both Barrow and Ruth to talk through their disagreements. Babe apologized and agreed that he'd remain open to pitching again.[13]

Later that day, in the second half of the doubleheader, Ruth returned to the lineup, hitting a meaningless single in the team's 2–1 loss. But the outcome didn't make the lede in the *Boston American*. There was a bigger story than the game itself. The following morning, the newspaper published a bold headline, one that brought great relief to the city: BABE RUTH BACK WITH RED SOX. About a week later, writing for the *American*, Nick Flatley observed that there was a time "when the score of the game was the thing. The man in the street, the fan on the car, the person on the other end of the phone would ask interestedly, 'Who won?' But no more. Every Tom, Dick, and Harry . . . inquire first what Ruth did." In Boston, Flatley noted, "the force of his individuality" and "the sensation of his lusty war club" captivated the city. Babe Ruth swinging a baseball bat had become an event itself.[14]

ON JULY 5, RUTH TOOK the mound against the Philadelphia Athletics. It was the first time he had started a game as a pitcher since June 2. Although he displayed great endurance—pitching ten innings—he lacked command of the ball. Ruth allowed only three earned runs, but gave up seven hits, walked four batters, and hit two more. Yet once again he proved his value as a hitter. In the tenth inning, Athletics' pitcher Bob Geary cautiously threw around him. With the game tied 3–3, Geary conceded a base on balls. It seemed wise to walk Ruth. The next batter, Stuffy McInnis, ripped a triple down the right-field line, sending Babe home for the winning run. Despite the thrilling victory, the *Boston Post*'s Paul Shannon lamented that the Red Sox—now only a half game out of first place—remained troubled by a roster depleted by the war. Without Dutch Leonard, Ed Barrow might as well flip a coin to decide who would pitch every fourth day. Using language from the battlefront to describe the condition of the Red Sox, Shannon wrote, "The pitching staff is fairly shot to pieces, the infield is badly crippled and there is no help in sight." Who could rescue the Red Sox?[15]

When the team returned to Boston for a seventeen-game home stand, a sparse afternoon crowd of 5,251 showed up at Fenway for the opening game in a series against the first-place Cleveland Indians. The Boston faithful expected to see Ruth, but he started the game riding the pine. Inning after inning fans yelled his name in vain. Finally, he appeared in the sixth, marching to the plate as a pinch-hitter, carrying "two sawed-off bats." The sight of mighty Babe Ruth, swinging his weapons in a long arc, sparked a roar from the crowd, turning Cleveland's pitcher "white around the gills." The spectators' ovation escalated into "hero worship," Burt Whitman wrote. Standing and shouting, men waved their hats, smiling like schoolboys who had come to see their idol. They sensed a promise to come, a display of irrepressible power, a flash of brilliance that left ordinary men awestruck.[16]

At that moment, with the Red Sox trailing 4–2, no outs, and men on the corners, Ruth selected his cudgel. Suddenly the game changed when he hammered a triple down the right-field line. Rounding third, he headed home when Cleveland's second baseman fired the relay throw into the visiting dugout. Ultimately, his triple turned the game into a 5–4 victory, catapulting the Red Sox into first place.[17]

His summer hitting tear was only beginning. In the next game against Cleveland, he came to the plate in the tenth inning of a scoreless contest with Amos Strunk on first. Ruth clobbered a fastball, depositing it into the right-field bleachers. It should have been his twelfth home run of the season, but the official scorers of the day counted it as a triple since Strunk scored the game-winning run before Ruth could cross home plate. Two days later, on July 10, Ruth tripled again, smacking a ball deep into center field, driving two runs home. After the fifth inning, when rain clouds rolled in, the umpires called the game, a 2–0 victory for the Red Sox.[18]

The stage belonged to Babe. He was the sport's preeminent showman, "unquestionably one of the greatest attractions baseball has ever known." The legend of Babe Ruth grew with every vicious swing. "His name is on every lip these days," Edward Martin wrote. Ruth's outrageous feats turned into tall tales, shared among men sitting in the grandstands and on barstools. Pictures of Ruth published in newspapers—close-ups of his pug face, his massive hands gripping a baseball, his body uncoiled with a bat wrapped around his back—etched his image into the public consciousness.[19]

As long as he kept hitting, the Red Sox continued winning. Between July 6 and July 22, the Red Sox won fourteen games and lost only three. During that span, Ruth batted .364 with seven triples, six doubles, and nine RBIs. Pitching only once throughout that stretch, Babe mostly played the field, though he failed to hit an official home run. In fact, he had not hit one since June 30. Still, sportswriters expected him to break "Socks" Seybold's single season American League record. Some writers suggested that he might even have a shot at breaking more obscure records established during the Gilded Age. Playing in a matchbox in 1884, the White Stockings' Ned Williamson hit twenty-seven, benefitting from a Chicago ballpark with fences less than two hundred feet from home plate. Other reporters considered Williamson's record invalid and credited Washington Senators right fielder Buck Freeman's twenty-five home runs in 1899 as the more legitimate achievement.[20]

Nonetheless, Ruth needed just six more dingers to break Seybold's record. It seemed well within reach. His power surge appeared even more remarkable during a season when Major League hitters notched the fewest home runs per at bat in nearly a decade. Compared with Ruth, other batters were mere mortals. "The more I see of Babe and his heroic hitting," Burt Whitman wrote, "the more he seems a figure out of mythology or from the fairyland of more modern writers."[21]

One factor in Ruth's sustained home run drought may have been the new, inferior baseballs introduced around that time throughout the American League. In May, the government had commandeered all supplies of horsehide for the war effort so that manufacturers could produce leather boots, jackets, and gloves for the troops. The horsehide restrictions combined with wool shortages meant that baseballs produced by A.J. Reach were made with inferior materials. Initially, there seemed no appreciable difference in the balls. By the end of June, however, after Ban Johnson instructed American League clubs to conserve the number of baseballs used during each game, the dead balls contributed to the steady decline in home runs. As baseball historian Glenn Stout noted, 59 of the 95 homers hit by all American League hitters occurred during the first half of the season, when, presumably, teams were still using baseballs made before the season began.[22]

If Ruth noticed a difference in the baseballs, he did not say much about it. But he did suggest that hitting home runs proved more challenging later in the year because pitchers approached him with more vigilance. "They don't throw me very many good balls," he told Edward Martin. "Now and then, they'll slip the first one over, and if I get them in the hole, they have to pitch, but most of the time I have to make the best of what they give me." Increasingly he saw more curveballs. Testing his batting eye, Ruth struggled, waiting for a good pitch to hit. Sometimes he swung from his shoestrings, golfing for balls that grazed the dirt. He just couldn't resist.[23]

ANY HOPES THAT RUTH MIGHT break home run records that season were dashed after Secretary of War Newton Baker ruled against Washington Senators catcher Eddie Ainsmith's draft appeal. At least, that's what most sportswriters concluded. On July 19, Baker announced that every draft-eligible ballplayer was subject to the "work or fight" order. Although he acknowledged the entertainment value of the sport, he argued that the military could not forgo the services of healthy young athletes. "Baseball," he said, "along with other peace-time industries, which have been compelled to cease activities during the war, must bear its share of the burden."[24]

The baseball brass expected that most professional ballplayers would now be lost to the war. Fourteen of the twenty players on the Red Sox roster, including Ruth, were subject to Baker's order. Harry Frazee could not maintain a professional club with just six players. He still hoped that the owners could request a compliance extension that would allow the season to end after two more weeks. Such a reprieve would give the teams an opportunity to play a total of one hundred games and the World Series. Assuming that Baker's decision was final, however, Ban Johnson, without consulting the magnates, declared that all American League clubs would close their gates after the July 21 games.[25]

Not so fast, Frazee thought. Baker's ruling did not explicitly instruct the National Commission, baseball's governing body, to cancel the season. Furthermore, Frazee insisted, Johnson had overstepped his authority. "No one has the right to take the dictatorial stand that the A.L. will close its ball parks at such and such date," he fumed. Frazee would not lock the gates at Fenway Park until it was "absolutely necessary to do so." He couldn't pay the mortgage unless there were players on the field. He assured his players that the games would go on and that they would get paid, but many of them were uncertain what to do. Some considered boarding trains and heading home, whereas others thought it might be best to report for duty immediately. Frazee figured that he knew the players better than they knew themselves. "The boys will stand in line until the last ditch," he told a reporter. Ruth had already heard from numerous shipbuilding companies. It seemed only a matter of time before he would play baseball wearing a uniform that didn't represent Boston.[26]

ON JULY 22, THE DAY after a German submarine threatened the coast of Cape Cod, a sweltering heat wave drove thousands of Bostonians to Revere Beach, where vacationers cooled their bodies in the ocean, splashing and frolicking beneath the blistering sun. On the Boston Common picnickers found comfort under the cool shade of elm trees. Throughout the city, an ice shortage frustrated "hundreds of mothers" who had "stood in line" waiting for relief. The *Boston Globe* reported numerous cases of men and women hospitalized from heat exhaustion. Despite afternoon temperatures climbing into the nineties, more than ten thousand loyal fans turned out at Fenway Park for a doubleheader against

Detroit, anticipating what many believed would be the last games of the season. With the sun beating down their backs, the Red Sox endured the heat wearing their thick wool uniforms, sweeping the Tigers in two shutouts, 1–0 and 3–0. The victories gave Boston its largest lead yet in the pennant race—six and a half games over second-place Cleveland.[27]

Then, the following day, the Red Sox boarded a train for Chicago, where they would meet the White Sox in a four-game series. While a group of baseball officials and owners, including Frazee, planned to meet with Provost Marshal Crowder in Washington on July 24, both the National League and American League clubs had decided that they would continue playing. Competing in front of only two thousand fans, the Red Sox lost the series opener in Chicago, 4–2. One writer noted that it was "as quiet as ever on the South Side grounds."[28]

Perhaps the small crowd indicated that Chicagoans feared another slacker raid like the one that had taken place two weeks earlier at the Cubs' Weeghman Park. On July 11, after the first game of a doubleheader, federal agents had locked the gates at the ballpark, searching for slackers and unregistered aliens. Government operatives blocked every exit before detaining more than five hundred spectators who failed to produce their registration cards. It was part of a larger effort throughout the city in which agents targeted any place where crowds gathered: vaudeville theaters, movie houses, bars, dance halls, poolrooms, restaurants, and railroad stations. In just a few days, government officials had interrogated ten thousand men.[29]

The government crackdown against slackers demonstrated that Secretary Baker would show no leniency for ballplayers seeking deferments. But the owners were no longer asking the government to exempt athletes as "essential" laborers in the war. Instead, when they met with Crowder, the owners simply asked for an extension until October 15 so that the clubs could fulfill their financial obligations. Baker contemplated the petition and agreed to give the leagues a reprieve—but only until September 1. That meant shortening the season by about five weeks and thirty games.[30]

The new deadline, meanwhile, left unanswered questions: Did the owners have to conclude the World Series before September 1, or could they finish the regular season by that date and then schedule the championships? Or should they call off the Series altogether? The magnates were not entirely sure how to proceed. But Ed Barrow planned on winning the pennant with Babe Ruth back on the mound.

14

Brothers In Arms

THERE WERE NOT MANY LEFT BEHIND FOR THE COMMENCEMENT ceremony. More than seven hundred students had begun their first year at Harvard College in the fall semester of 1914. At the time, the war in Europe seemed little more than a distant echo for most Americans. Yet during the summer, a handful of Harvard men on vacation in France, Britain, or Germany enlisted in foreign armies. Sincere convictions of right and wrong motivated some; desire for a rousing adventure attracted others. For instance, Edward Mandell Stone, class of 1908, was living in France that summer and immediately joined the French Foreign Legion. On February 15, 1915, he suffered a shrapnel wound and died twelve days later. "He had a lot of grit, poor chap," commented a Legion surgeon.[1]

As the war crept closer to America, the number of Harvard men in uniform swelled, eventually reaching more than eleven thousand alumni, undergraduates, and faculty. In the popular phrase of the day, Elisha Whittlesey "did his part" before the United States entered the conflict, returning home suffering from the effects of poison gas and too physically debilitated to return to Europe for combat. Instead, he resumed his studies and completed his degree, "greatly to his credit I think," wrote his mother, Anna, to the editor of the *Harvard Alumni Bulletin*. Nevertheless, his relative inactivity compared with the sacrifices of other Harvard men gnawed at him. During his final year in Cambridge, his mother commented, "he was earnestly trying to enter again into active service—and each time disappointed." Still determined to do his share, he got a job with the Atlantic Corporation shipyard in Portsmouth, New Hampshire. "In reality he is still in the *service of our country*, doing his 'bit' just as faithfully as when he was driving his camion in France. Don't you think so?" Anna pleaded to her correspondent.[2]

On June 18, 1918, Elisha was one of only fifty seniors attending the graduation service in Appleton Chapel. At the Class Day ceremony in Sanders Theatre, the marshal announced that no ode would be delivered because the odist was in France. And Ralph G. Brown read the class poem in place of the student who wrote it, Lieutenant Thacher Nelson. Altogether, more than 150 of Elisha's former classmates were fighting in France, and almost 500 more were in training for combat.[3]

News of the war hung heavy over every part of the day-long ceremony. In France, American Marines and soldiers were blocking the German drive toward Paris at Belleau Wood, enduring an appalling number of casualties, including more than 1,800 killed. Lists of wounded and killed filled columns in Boston newspapers. Against this backdrop, class orator Hallowell Davis made the war the centerpiece of his address. "In all our dreams for the future, in all our plans and calculations for the present, as the first axiom stands the proposition, 'The war must be won.'"[4]

There was also a current of bitterness running through the day's events. As the list of Harvard men maimed or killed during the fighting grew, a determination seized the others as they prepared to serve their nation and to exact vengeance. Harvard professor Charles Copeland kept a number of war letters that his students sent him. One wrote about his twin brother, Copey—a Yale student. "You can take my word on it . . . that you don't meet a man of his ability and kindness in every day's journey you make . . . He was closer to me than anybody else, and I loved him as my best friend and brother." A German killed Copey, and a rage consumed his brother. Lacking President Wilson's idealistic vision, he desired an Old Testament eye for an eye. "My chief concern now is to get abroad, and when I get there to do my damnedest to avenge my brother's death. I won't stand for anything less than the complete conquering of the devils who let this hell on earth loose."[5]

Elisha, author of the 1918 Baccalaureate Hymn, agreed with the necessity to extinguish Imperial Germany's aggression, though a melancholy strain ran through his thoughts. The 1918 Harvard yearbook contains brief snippets of his poetry. One rings like a death knell for happier times:

> *They met, on college field, with other men*
> *In common discipline that guided true.*
> *Of tested temper, they will meet again*
> *Where Strong men rendezvous.*

Another brushes closer to his present concerns. With Charles in France and his brother Malzer training in San Antonio as a pilot, Elisha mused about duty, death, and the fragility of life:

> *A voice is summoning beyond the sea*
> *And many have responded from these halls:*
> *True sons of older college-ancestry*
> *Whose service waited no repeated calls.*
> *Many a man, by trial proved, will learn*
> *To travel paths his feet have never trod,*
> *And some, departed, never will return—*
> *'T is such as these that win Thy mercy, God.*[6]

IN MID-JUNE 1918, CAPTAIN CHARLES Whittlesey had recently completed the last weeks of his military training. His 308th Infantry Regiment had survived the amalgamation controversy but its future was still murky. Nor did Whittlesey have a much better grasp of the role he would play in the regiment. Looking back, he seems to have erased his past. Few letters survive that mention him, no newspaper articles detail his activities, and what military records remain give only the most perfunctory facts of his service. His image resembles the soldiers in an early reel of film—a grainy ghost in black and white, hardly distinguishable from any of the others around him. Yet as the 77th Division moved ever closer to the action, Whittlesey starts to come into clearer focus. Even before he entered into battle, he could feel the war all around him. The pungent, overripe smell of gas was in the ground, small doses mixing with the water in puddles, layering the soil into a greasy concoction, covering the soldiers' hands and faces, adding to the stains on their clothes. When the men of the 77th Division arrived at the Baccarat front in mid-June, relieving the 42nd "Rainbow" Division, they got their first true taste of the war. Captain W. Kerr Rainsford vividly recalled the battle zone near the city famous for its lace and crystal. The impact of artillery shells had churned and pockmarked the ground "into something like the surface of a sponge," and, "on misty nights, reeked with the sickish acid smell of gas." It was a nightmarish landscape. "Little half-ruined villages of roofless walls and tumbled masonry, like empty sea shells upon some desolate coast, lined the high-water mark of early invasion— and in the center of each rose the skeleton of some beautiful old church, its tower pierced with shell-holes and its entrance blocked by the fallen chimes."[7]

The Germans greeted the soldiers of the 307th and 308th Regiments of the 154th Brigade to their new post in the dark early hours of June 24. It began suddenly at 3:00 a.m. when the sky began to rain shells. Lieutenant L. Wardlaw Miles recalled the stunning arrival of the artillery assault. "It did not begin with a pattering of shells, an interlude gradually working up to the fortissimo of drum fire. It began all at once—as if at one moment an organist had pulled out all the stops, pressed down all the keys, and stepped hard on the pedals."[8]

The shells tumbled village walls, blocked streets with debris, and transformed fields into lunar landscapes. The German gunners targeted vital positions. Charles Whittlesey, stationed in the Regimental Headquarters, struggled to follow the battle as the shells destroyed communication lines. The Pink Château that had become

Battalion Headquarters took several direct hits, and throughout the shelling two planes circled the stately home, peppering it with machine gun fire. The heavy barrages wreaked havoc with communications to the trench system as well as to French, Regimental, and Divisional Headquarters. Because one of the shells contained poison gas, the staff inside the Pink Château scurried about in masks, removing them only to shout a brief message into a phone. Soon, however, there was no reason to take off their masks. The assault had cut the wires and ended communications with the front and rear.[9]

Throughout the war, phosgene and mustard gas shells had an even more dramatic impact on the men in the trenches. Many soldiers thought phosgene smelled like moldy hay. It drifted stealthily in colorless waves, often completing its deadly mission before its victims knew they had breathed a fatal dose. A day or two later their lungs would fill with fluids, leading to an agonizing death by drowning. The sharp smell of mustard gas announced its presence. Some thought it reeked of garlic; others thought it smelled more like gasoline, burnt rubber, or dead horses. As with phosgene, its effects unfolded slowly. Hours after exposure victims' eyes became bloodshot and began to water. They said it felt like they had small cinder shards in their eyes and suffered temporary blindness. Making matters worse, the moist skin of their armpits and genitals blistered, popped, and became infected. Mustard gas killed fewer soldiers than phosgene gas, but caused more casualties.[10]

When the shelling stopped, the Germans attacked. The predawn darkness burst alive with the sound of machine guns, the percussion of hand grenades, and flamethrowers' arching streams of fire. The primordial screams and grunts of soldiers as they charged and defended, battled with bayonets and bare hands, were the age-old language of warfare. Lieutenant John Flood's platoon, a crack unit composed of "Irish, Italians, East Side Jews, Russians, Scandinavians, and even a few native Americans," faced overwhelming numbers. Yet they moved to their firing trenches still wearing gas masks, opening up with rifles and Chauchats until Germans infiltrated their lines. Then the fight devolved into a hand-to-hand affair—"German potato mashers against American bayonets in the shell holes and battered trenches," wrote Miles.[11]

The fighting continued until dawn. Then at some prearranged signal, the Germans pulled back. As they retreated, their pilots flew nearer to the American lines, strafing the weary troops with machine gun fire. By the time the planes disappeared behind the German lines, more than one hundred Americans and French lay dead or wounded, and almost twice that number suffered from gassing. It was a painful introduction to the Lorraine front, but the units of the 77th that had engaged the enemy had fought well. They had made a few tactical errors, but no one could fault their courage.

The action of June 24 saw the most serious fighting the 154th Brigade faced during their five-week stay in the Baccarat area, although of course they didn't know it, and therefore stayed on full alert. Only in retrospect would Miles recall that Lorraine "was, as sectors go, a pleasant one—a rather sleepy old lion who showed his deadly teeth but once, and at other times afforded fine instruction for unpracticed hunters in the field of war." Shelling and periodic raids, furthermore, continued to claim victims. In one such random shelling, shrapnel struck the major commanding the 1st Battalion of the 308th Infantry, and although his wound was not serious, it required hospitalization. Before his replacement arrived, Captain Whittlesey commanded the 1st Battalion. His command lasted only a few weeks and did not involve any frontline action, but the fate of the entire 77th Division was about to change. On August 1, the 37th Division replaced the 77th in the Lorraine sector, and the Liberty boys moved out, destined for what one soldier described as "the Hell-hole Valley of the Vesle."[12]

After the failure of their desperate Marne offensive in July, German forces retreated to the high ground north of the Vesle River. There they dug in on the slopes, determined to make their stand. The Vesle itself was not a formidable barrier. On average about thirty feet wide and ten feet deep, the sluggish, muddy stream runs through a modest valley with sloping hills on either side. "As a river, it little deserves the name," noted the official history of the 77th Division, "but as an obstacle to the passage of our troops, it proved more valuable to the Germans than a hundred dozen tons of barbed wire." German engineers destroyed bridges across the Vesle, filled it full of treacherous barbed wire, and positioned their guns to retard movement in the valley. As the men of the 77th rushed into battle, they entered a killing zone, the likes of which they had not encountered. "Lorraine was only a boxing match," noted an officer in the 77th, "Vesle was a real fist-fight."[13]

Except it was worse than any fist-fight. "Here and there, bodies caught in the wire bobbed slowly in the current," wrote historian Alan D. Gaff. "It was here the New Yorkers had their first whiff of a real battlefield, a gagging combination of excrement, powder, stale gas, blood, decaying flesh, and sheer rot." Carrion birds circled in the sky, dipping down occasionally to rip off a piece of flesh. Swarms of black flies hovered above wounded men and competed with yellow wasps for every dish or bowl of food. "At night," recalled Rainsford, "they hung in black masses . . . noisily propagating their species through the hours of darkness, and every crashing discharge of the 155s overhead would bring down an avalanche of chalk and flies."[14]

For more than a month, the 77th Division fought mostly small-action engagements, grimly determined to push across the Vesle and up the slopes. Although American and French forces eventually drove the Germans back to their Aisne River defensive line, every yard gained came at an awful price. The fighting lacked the drama of a major offensive, but the day-to-day struggle, the hand-to-hand combat in frontline trenches and muddy, shell-worn bottomland, exacted a heavy toll. The 3rd Battalion, 308th Regiment suffered staggering losses, and the 2nd Battalion did not fare much better. Those who survived the misery of the summer learned the same lessons the French and British soldiers had grasped in 1914 and 1915—dig in when under heavy fire, keep your head down, and trust the man next to you. There was nothing romantic about battles; teamwork and firepower, not individuals, won them.[15]

The heavy losses fighting along the Vesle led to personnel changes in the 77th Division. The commander of the American Expeditionary Force decided the most significant ones. The damn-the-casualties-push-forward determination of the US effort began at the top. General John J. "Black Jack" Pershing single-mindedly pursued the goal of American greatness, and that objective largely determined his strategic and tactical decisions. Fate, it sometimes seemed to Pershing, had put him in the right place at the right time to fulfill his country's ascendency. Leaving a farm in Missouri to attend West Point, campaigning against the Apache in New Mexico and the Spanish in Cuba, commanding troops during the suppression of rebellious Moro tribesmen in the Philippines and the hunt for Pancho Villa in Mexico—Pershing had served on the frontier of the American empire, following the flag and enacting what many believed was the nation's manifest destiny. Even presidents recognized his unique talents. In an era when seniority normally determined advancement, Theodore Roosevelt jumped him over 835 senior officers for promotion to brigadier general. And at a time when Woodrow Wilson ignored anyone who had TR's blessing, he placed Pershing in charge of US armed forces in the Great War. Through it all, rigid as steel and given to occasional violent flashes of temper, Pershing moved in front of the rest as if he were to the manner born.

In the fight against Germany, he had a single, overriding concern: Britain and France would not swallow American forces and amalgamate them into their armies. Instead, wherever possible, US troops would campaign in their own sector, fighting as a distinct unit and be commanded by American officers. Not only was it a matter of national pride, it was a practical issue. Language separated the American doughboys from the French *poilus*, and culture all too often estranged them from the British Tommies. Even more important, there were vital geopolitical chips on the table. President Wilson, Secretary of War Newton D. Baker, and General Pershing agreed that if their country was going to play a leading role in the postwar era, if American diplomats would help shape the peace settlement, the AEF had to win battles, and, if possible, play the leading role in the final one.[16]

Given these lofty aims, digging in and holding one's ground was unacceptable. Stalemate was not in Pershing's military vocabulary. Advancing across open space, overcoming obstacles, taking enemy positions—these were the phrases he wanted to hear. The fighting against the Germans near the Vesle frustrated the general, undermining his confidence in his officers' leadership. This was particularly true for the 77th Division. It was, after all, America's test case, the first division of the new National Army to reach France and intended to prove to America's British and French allies that enlisted men and conscripts could fight as well as soldiers from the Regular Army. With the 77th stalled along the Vesle, Pershing ordered a change in command. In late August, he replaced Major General George B. Duncan—a veteran of the Spanish-American War and the Philippine Insurrection, as well as the General Staff—with Major General Robert Alexander. Duncan had been liked and admired by his men and fellow officers, considered by one observer "a good, rough soldier, a good general, fearless, aggressive and self-reliant." Alexander's reputation was not as straightforward.[17]

He had risen through the ranks—and he looked it. Hard eyes, trimmed mustache, and bulldog chin, he had the appearance of a man who laughed seldom and regarded everyone with suspicion. No one could question his tenacity. After preparing for a career in the law and being admitted to the Maryland bar, in his early twenties he enlisted in the army as a private, a less than auspicious platform to launch a military career. Yet he advanced steadily and rapidly. He was soon a sergeant, then a second lieutenant. As he moved up the ranks, he served in domestic and foreign altercations—battling the Sioux in the west and striking Pullman workers in Chicago, fighting the Spanish in Puerto Rico and rebellious Filipinos across the Pacific. In the Philippines he had been cut by a bolo; in Mexico he had searched for Pancho Villa with General Pershing. In November 1917 he shipped to France as a colonel, was promoted to brigadier general, and in the summer fighting in the Second Battle of the Marne received his second star.[18]

General Alexander walked into the 77th Division HQ with a brick-sized chip on his shoulder. He was not a West Pointer, and he chafed at what he perceived as their old boys club. Though respected by the enlisted soldiers in his division, he won no personality contests with the officers. Many on his staff believed that he displayed a tendency to curry favor with Pershing and senior officers, take full credit for victories large and small, and shift blame to subordinates for any failures. All of this may have been true. Yet he unfailingly drove his officers, ruthlessly demanded results, and stoically accepted high casualties. These were the very characteristics that Pershing demanded. Even more important, he got results. Under Alexander, the 77th advanced beyond the Vesle to the Aisne, and during the weeks and months ahead liberated more occupied French territory than any of Pershing's other divisional commanders.[19]

As crucial as it was, the arrival of General Alexander was not the only change in the 77th Division. The losses the division suffered inevitably depleted its ranks and altered its character. It badly needed replacements. On September 20, the army transferred some four thousand soldiers from the 40th "Sunshine" Division to the 77th. They came from western states, including the National Guards of Arizona, California, Colorado, Nevada, New Mexico, and Utah. The transfers seemed like bit players from cowboy movies, a collection of ranchers, wranglers, and miners who spoke in clipped accents and had long, lean bodies. To the Italian, Irish, and Jewish soldiers in the ethnically diverse Liberty Division, these new men looked and sounded alike. Other replacements arrived from North Dakota, South Dakota, and Minnesota. Many of the new men had received only minimal training.[20]

About 1,250 of the replacements landed in the 308th Infantry, and 900 in the 307th. Some had never held a weapon. For hundreds of the new arrivals, the use of hand grenades and machine guns was completely foreign. Furthermore, although many had grown up shooting pistols and rifles, they knew nothing of military formations or tactics. "They were brave and loyal, and willing to do anything they could," noted Colonel Cromwell Stacey of the 308th. "The only trouble was that they didn't know how to do anything." Yet during the next month, the experienced officers and noncoms of the 77th integrated the replacements into platoons and companies, gave them a crash course in equipment and procedure, and readied them for battle.[21]

The 77th needed replacements at every rank. Officers fell in battle with alarming frequency. In many cases, their replacements came from junior ranks or staff positions. At the end of August, for instance, Captain Lucien Breckenridge, a temporary replacement in command of 1st Battalion, 308th Infantry, was wounded. The 77th staff pegged Captain Charles Whittlesey of Regimental Headquarters as his replacement, promoting him to major with seniority back-dated to August 13. A fine replacement, he had commanded in the field earlier, and had displayed an aptitude for leadership. He possessed unquestioned bravery. Arthur McKeogh, one of his lieutenants, noted that Whittlesey was "absolutely indifferent" in the heat of battle. It was not so much that he was "wantonly courageous," just "seemingly oblivious of the danger."[22]

Whittlesey was similarly indifferent about achieving military honors or promotions. Even after being promoted to major, he continued to wear his captain's bars rather than replacing them with gold oak leaves. The new insignia of rank, he said, could wait. Other than getting him better treatment in a hospital, he did not seem to feel that it was that important. What mattered far more to him was carefully preparing for combat, following orders, and getting the job done. Once he was in command, he pored over maps and went on patrols to frontline trenches, familiarizing himself with the terrain and German positions. He seemed to feel that sleep, like attaching gold oak leaves to his uniform, was something that he could take care of later. In the meantime, there were more important matters.[23]

Unfortunately, Major Whittlesey also evinced a complete disregard for his own health. By mid-September, if not before, he was visibly ill. The brutal fighting during the advance toward the Aisne had taken its toll on him as well as his battalion. He suffered from dysentery and a severe cold. He coughed chronically, and Miles recalled that "he could hardly speak above a whisper." Quite likely, Whittlesey also showed the lingering effects of frequent poison gas attacks. Historian Robert Laplander speculates that he had been gassed "rather severely" but never reported it. If he had reported it, he would have been pulled off the line and at least sent to a field hospital. Given his sense of duty, that was intolerable. Instead, he stayed and fought, coughed and suffered, unconcerned with any consequences down the line.[24]

Perhaps Whittlesey thought that his problems paled next to what he witnessed daily. Everywhere on the Aisne front, men were dying. On August 21, Whittlesey's friend Captain Belvidere Brooks, a 1910 graduate of Williams College and commander of Company D, 308th Infantry, was killed instantly when a shell exploded near him. Other men in the 308th had their arms and legs and faces blown off. Whittlesey could still see the enemy, could still march forward and fight. Going to a hospital in search of treatment for exposure to gas—a constant for every soldier on the battlefield— was, as he saw it, akin to seeking medical aid for a paper cut.[25]

Such valor was by no means uncommon. On September 14, near the Aisne Canal, Whittlesey's friend and comrade Captain L. Wardlaw Miles volunteered to lead a company on a hazardous attack against a German trench. Wire cutters in hand, he led the first wave assault, opening a passage through enemy wire. He was hit five times, bullets fracturing both his legs and one of his arms. Rather than leave the field, he ordered stretcher-bearers to carry him forward where for two hours he encouraged his men and directed the attack on the German trench. Only after his company had taken the position and he had lost consciousness did the stretcher-bearers carry him to an aid station, where a physician amputated one of his legs.[26]

Miles departed the 308th just a few weeks before the unit was trapped in the Argonne Forest and Americans first began to hear about the Lost Battalion and Charles Whittlesey—even so, he vividly recalled the tall, gaunt figure of his friend. Miles had been an English professor at Princeton before the war, and in his history of the 308th Infantry, he turned to the poetry of William

Wordsworth to describe his brother in arms. "Whittlesey was by nature a student," he wrote,

> *yet he was one*
> *"Who, doomed to go in company with pain*
> *And fear, and bloodshed, miserable train!*
> *Turns his necessity to glorious gain."* [27]

PART THREE

THE FLOOD

15

A Death in Pig Town

NOT KNOWN FOR SUBTLETY OR TACT, TO SAY NOTHING OF HAT-in-hand servility, Ed Barrow approached Babe Ruth with an un-usual deference. After his "wobbly" pitching staff dropped three of four games in Chicago, he needed Ruth to return to the mound. Although the Red Sox still led the American League by a com-fortable margin, and there was just over a month before the end of the shortened season, his hurlers were in trouble. Babe had only pitched twice—a total of fourteen innings—in the past two months, and Barrow had not found an adequate thrower to fill his spot in the rotation. That put added pressure on right-handers Carl Mays, "Bullet" Joe Bush, and "Sad" Sam Jones. They had done a fine job, but were sapped from overwork, and the team needed a dependable southpaw. For the good of the team, Barrow asked, would Babe return to the mound?[1]

Perhaps because Barrow was asking him as a favor, not threaten-ing him or issuing an ultimatum, Ruth agreed. The request stroked his ego, and besides, Barrow assured him that he could still play in the field on the days he was not pitching. On Monday, July 29, after playing in the outfield for four straight days against the White Sox, he returned to the mound in St. Louis versus the Browns.

It was as if he had never left. "The big boy just buzzed 'em in Catcher Mayer's glove, and in only one inning did he weaken," noted the *Boston Herald and Journal*. Even in the sixth inning, the Browns' two runs were more the result of "fluke hits" than Babe's throws. He pitched a shutout for the final three innings, finishing the contest with a 3–2 victory. Surrendering only four hits, he also contributed to the victory tripling in a run.[2]

Ruth's return to the rotation solved the Red Sox's pitching problem. Baseball's troubles, however, were more substantial. Secretary of War Newton Baker had agreed to extend the season to Labor Day. But what then? Would the players comply en masse with the "work or fight" order, or would those on the winning pennant teams get a two-week reprieve to play in the World Series? On August 3, the American League owners met in Cleveland and in a statement to the press affirmed their belief that Secretary Baker had not specifically ruled out a Series; in fact, they had every reason to believe that he would not. Therefore, they planned to move forward with preparations for a September championship series, regardless of contrary statements by Ban Johnson. The owners, not Johnson, would now speak for the American League.[3]

With no word from Washington, the lords of the game were reduced to reading tea leaves. Less than three weeks from the proposed start of the Series, Red Sox catcher Sam Agnew, outfielder Amos Strunk, and Ruth all received notices from their draft boards to find "essential occupations" by September 1. The message "put an additional crimp" in the World Series talk. Did it mean that the three would not be available for the fall classic? Had the government decided to end all player deferments on Labor Day? Would Babe Ruth be MIA? Again, it was a web of speculations, predictions, and sheer guesswork.[4]

Sportswriters ventured cautiously into the tangled mess. Politics and baseball, war and entertainment, they concluded, did not mix. For some baseball had become a distraction from more important matters. Writing for *The Sporting News*, Burt Whitman confessed, "It is difficult to figure out how a World's Series under present conditions can be anything but a joke, anything but a boomerang, a black eye to the memory of the game during the months, or years, that it is laid on the shelf. The Series lacks the approbation of a big portion on the press and the fans absolutely refuse to talk about the interleague clash. The best judgment is, then, that the Series should be abandoned."[5]

Making matters worse, by mid-August American troops in France were in the thick of the fighting. News of American soldiers' successful support of French troops in the Second Battle of the Marne and the appearance of the American Expeditionary Force as a cohesive fighting unit in the Aisne-Marne counteroffensive filled the nation's newspapers and magazines. The sacrifices of the servicemen in khaki made the wrangling over the World Series seem petty and churlish, even unpatriotic. Who cared if a handful of ballplayers received permission to play a few games before fulfilling the "work or fight" order? What did it matter if the baseball owners even held a World Series? "In one way, the present condition . . . is amusing," commented a sportswriter, "and, perhaps, when the war is over and all regain a normal attitude, we can have a good laugh over the commotion that has been caused over such a trivial thing as to whether 50 ordinary—very ordinary—day laborers should have been permitted six or eight days of grace in quitting one job and taking another." Ordinary day laborers? National heroes like Walter Johnson and Babe Ruth? Such was the impact of the war on the game.[6]

Finally, for anyone who was still interested, the War Department issued a final decision. Less than two weeks before the end of the season, Baker announced that the players on the National and American League championship teams would not have to comply with the "work or fight" order until September 15, allowing them time to compete in the World Series. Washington Senators manager and part owner Clark Griffith assured everyone that the Series was never in jeopardy, and that Baker and especially President Woodrow Wilson were baseball men through and through. "All this talk about the government wanting baseball shut down is bunk," he claimed. "It just about tore their hearts out when they gave the order that baseball was non-essential. We will play right up to September 2 and then we'll play a World Series—bank all you have on that."[7]

AS THE FORTUNES OF THE sport improved, Ruth's got worse—much worse.

Comfortably in the lead for the American League pennant, and beginning to plan for what had recently become a "legal, moral and virtuous" World Series against the Chicago Cubs, the Red Sox hosted the St. Louis Browns. Saturday, August 24, was Ruth's day to take the mound, but that was not where the troubles began. Instead, it was on the base paths. In the second inning, he reached first on a walk. Then on a long hit he streaked to third, and while confusion reigned, broke for home. Contorting his body to touch the plate as he avoided the catcher's tag, Babe tweaked his knee. He collapsed to the ground, writhing in pain.[8]

Concerned fans groaned from the grandstands, "There goes Boston's chances in the World's Series." Babe fell flat on his back and then began rolling over and over, grimacing in pain. As team-mates assisted him to the dugout, Carl Mays got up in the bullpen and began to warm up.

Ruth was hurt, but he was not through for the day. A head-line in the *Boston Sunday Advertiser and American* told the tale: BABE WRENCHED HIS KNEE; BUT QUIT THE HILL—NOT HE! In the third inning, he limped out to the mound, showered with applause meant only for a hero, and continued pitching. "Although partly crippled," wrote Francis Eaton, "Ruth was able to field his position cleverly while pitching effectively." He threw a complete game, winning the contest 3–1.

His idea of rehabilitation was a relaxing Sunday in the surf off Revere Beach. Early the next morning, however, he learned that his father had died after some sort of late-night saloon scuffle. From a confused report in the *Boston Herald and Journal*, Ruth gathered that Benjamin Sipes, his father's brother-in-law, had committed the deed. Everything else about the event was murky.[9]

George Herman Ruth Sr.'s demise was more convoluted than most Byzantine murder stories. Martha Sipes, George's second wife, had a brother and a sister: Benjamin Sipes and Nellie Beefelt. The family's primary problem, it appears, was Nellie's husband, Oliver Beefelt, who was almost as unfaithful as Babe was to Helen. In 1917, he took up with a fifteen-year-old named Emma Stopford, and continued the affair even after her parents demanded that he break it off. It was during this period of domestic discord that Nellie left him and moved in with her sister above Ruth's saloon on the corner of Eutaw and Lombard Streets.[10]

On the night of August 25, the Sipeses and the Beefelts were in the same place at the same time. Upstairs, Nellie complained to Martha and Benjamin about how poorly her husband treated her. Downstairs in the bar, George Ruth served beers, and Oliver Beefelt drank his share. Eventually, Benjamin and Oliver met downstairs and fell into a loud disagreement, which ended when Sipes departed the saloon for a cigar shop across the street.

For some reason—perhaps it was something Benjamin had said about how George treated Martha, maybe it was some other festering resentment—George followed his brother-in-law outside and struck him in his face. The forty-five-year-old bartender hit Sipes again, knocking him down and kicking him. Back on his feet, Sipes fought back, landing a solid punch that sent Ruth sprawling to the pavement, where his head banged hard against a curb, cracking his skull. Several spectators carried him back into the saloon. They tried to revive him and finally took him to University Hospital, where he died early in the morning. After a brief investigation, the police forgot about the whole Pig Town incident.

Babe did show up for the wake and the funeral of the father who so long ago had dropped him off at St. Mary's. When they laid the man to rest, his son cried. A relative said he had never seen Babe in tears before.

Finally, he was an orphan. The death of his father severed his last ties to Baltimore, ending his association with the Germans in

Pig Town and a family that had never really been much of a family. Throughout the war-threatened season, he had repeatedly returned home, spending time in his father's saloon, perhaps searching for some roots in his increasingly rootless existence.

No longer. Now he was just Babe Ruth, and he belonged to Boston. The city's newspapers, like papers across the country, provided grim reading—stories of sufferings on the Western Front, censored battle reports, and long lists of boys from New England who had been killed or maimed. For the Fenway faithful, Ruth provided grist for celebration—his pitching success and game-winning swings offered clear indications of progress toward the pennant—something lacking in the news from the battlefront. They needed him and so did his teammates. The day of the funeral a teammate reportedly quipped, "The Ball Club did not get back today, but he'll be in there tomorrow."[11]

BABE MISSED THREE GAMES, BUT was back in Boston on August 30 feeling well enough to play left field in a Friday doubleheader against the Athletics. The Red Sox won the first game 12–0 and the second 4–1, with Ruth collecting two hits for the day. The next afternoon he took the mound, giving up only three hits in a 6–1 victory over Philadelphia. His last pitching start of the regular season, the win clinched the pennant for the Red Sox, finishing two and a half games ahead of Cleveland. Since returning full time to the pitching rotation, he had performed spectacularly, reclaiming his standing as Boston's ace and the finest southpaw in the American League. He had completed eight of nine starts, and had won nine of his last eleven games. During that stretch, his ERA was under 2.00. Altogether, he posted a 13–7 record for the season, and his .650 winning percentage was second best in the American League.[12]

Even more remarkably, on many of the days he did not pitch he played in the outfield. Although in the last part of the season he cooled off at the plate, hitting only .282 with six extra base hits during August, he finished the campaign with a .300 average. For both leagues that year, he finished first in slugging percentage and extra base hits, and tied for first in home runs. In 1918, there was no Most Valuable Player award, but had there been one, Babe would have won it as surely as he disturbed the repose of the alligators back in Arkansas.

No baseball player is a one-man team, but in 1918 Ruth came as close as any in major league history. So much so that as the Red Sox prepared to meet the Chicago Cubs in the World Series, sportswriters framed the event as Babe versus the Cubs. RED SOX HOPE LIES IN RUTH, SAYS EXPERTS, blared a *Chicago Tribune* headline. BASEBALL FANS DECLARE THE RED SOX ONE-MAN TEAM, agreed the *Baltimore Sun*. Reporters blasted Boston as the "weakest of flag winners," scoffing at their anemic hitting and inconsistent fielding. They posed the question: Could mighty Babe Ruth overcome his team's myriad and obvious flaws? Cubs manager Fred Mitchell thought not. "We will outhit the Sox and outfight them," he said, "and I believe . . . our pitching will be able to stop Ruth's batting. The Sox are a one-man team and his name is Ruth. But we have studied his ways and his mental processes so much this season that we will spike his guns."[13]

BY THE TIME THE RED SOX arrived in Chicago on September 3, ships anchored at Boston's Commonwealth Pier carried a lethal virus. The same virus had cropped up in late August in three widely separated locations throughout the world—all of which were highly trafficked hubs of wartime travel and activity. In Brest, France, whose deepwater port was packed with men going to and coming from the war, the grippe had returned. The grippe that had caused so many problems earlier that year, in the spring, had been less deadly. This strain of the flu, however, killed in great numbers. Because 40 percent of American troops landed at Brest, the outbreak portended catastrophe. As early as August 19, the *New York Times* observed, "A considerable number of American negroes, who have gone to France on horse transports, have contracted Spanish Influenza on shore and died in French hospitals of pneumonia." The report did not seem to indicate that the outbreak was of deep concern—but that would soon change as the epidemic wracked the French harbor.[14]

A second outbreak developed in Freeport, Sierra Leone, where ships and crews traveling to and from Europe, South America, and Asia met and mingled. On August 24, two Sierra Leonean stevedores died of pneumonia, and many more were afflicted with chilly sweats, uncontrollable vomiting, and pounding headaches. By August 27, five hundred of the six hundred laborers of the Sierra Leone Coaling Company failed to show up for work. Those who did mixed and labored alongside the crews of the HMS *Africa*, HMS *Chepstow Castle*, and *Tahiti*. Hundreds of the crewmen died as result. Thousands—soon many thousands—of Africans suffered the same fate.

On August 27, the affliction stretched across the Atlantic and reached Commonwealth Pier in Boston. That day two sailors reported to the receiving ship's sick bay with chills, fever, sore throat, and coughing—the usual symptoms of influenza. The next day, 8 more checked into the infirmary; the following day, 58; and by the end of the week, there was an average of 150 a day. The receiving ship—a massive floating barracks where the sailors slept and ate as they waited to depart—was "grossly overcrowded," a petri dish for the spread of the disease. Soon the outbreak overwhelmed the medical facilities of Commonwealth Pier, and patients were transferred to Chelsea Naval Hospital, just north of Charlestown.[15]

In less than a week, the killer had snuck past the guards at Commonwealth Pier and made its way into the neighborhoods of Boston. On September 3, the first civilian struck by the flu had entered Boston City Hospital. That same day, four thousand men, including one thousand sailors from Commonwealth Pier, marched the streets of Boston in a "Win the War for Freedom" parade. The sailors' contact with civilians and shipyard workers helped spread the calamity. Soon residents of Cambridge, the North End, the Back Bay, Roxbury, and other sections of the city were admitted to a new emergency hospital. Complaining of weakness, sore muscles, and backaches, many of the patients said that they felt as if they "had been beaten all over with a club."[16]

On September 5, Dr. John S. Hitchcock, head of the communicable disease section of the Massachusetts State Department of Health, warned Boston officials about the developing crisis: "Unless precautions are taken the disease in all probability will spread to the civilian population of the city."[17]

But by that time, it was already too late.

16

The Shadow of War

"THE MIGHTY SHADOW OF BABE RUTH FALLS ATHWART CHICAGO tonight like a menace," Burt Whitman declared. "The Colossus of Clouters" would be "the difference between defeat and victory" for the Red Sox. And he was not the only sportswriter to predict that Ruth's bat would determine the championship battle between the Boston Red Sox and the Chicago Cubs. At the height of public fervor over the war, everyone waited anxiously for the next draft call, scheduled to begin the week after the Series began. Baseball's promoters hyped Babe as the antidote to waning enthusiasm for the national pastime. While syndicated columnist Hugh Fullerton noted "interest is lukewarm in all parts of the city," Edward Martin, one of Ruth's most influential mythmakers, suggested that Babe was "the magnet that will draw thousands of fans to the Series." It didn't matter that Ruth had not hit a home run in more than two months. If anyone could resuscitate the game, Martin believed, it was Ruth, "the fence breaker." Surely fans would turn out to see him. "Everybody and their relatives," Martin wrote, "are just going to sit back and wait for Babe to bust one."[1]

Ruth couldn't wait to play. "I'd pitch the whole series, every game if they'd let me," he told one writer. "I hope I don't have to sit on the bench a single inning." On September 3, a day before

Game One, Ed Barrow indicated that Ruth would play left field and probably wouldn't pitch during the Series, a surprising revelation considering how well he had thrown in the weeks leading up to it. But the next morning, the players woke to cool winds and gray skies. Before long, thick rain clouds emptied on the city, soaking the outfield at Comiskey Park. Even if the rain ceased by midday, there was no chance that the Red Sox and Cubs would be able to play.[2]

That morning, notices were posted throughout the city informing the public that the first game of the Series had been postponed until the next day. Staying at the Metropole Hotel, on Twenty-third Street and Michigan Avenue, the Red Sox filled their time playing poker and reading about the Germans' retreat to the Hindenburg Line. Some made a trip to the movie theater. Several players joined thousands of spectators at the War Exposition in Grant Park, where men dressed as soldiers reenacted battles, demonstrated hand-to-hand combat, and scooped limp bodies off the ground as if they were saving lives at the Belleau Wood. Miles of trenches and barbed wire stretched across the park; visitors saw real warplanes and met soldiers who had recently returned home from France.[3]

Then, shortly after 3:00 p.m., word spread throughout the city: the war had come to Chicago.

ACROSS TOWN, ON THE EIGHTH floor of the Federal Building, William "Big Bill" Haywood, a burly one-eyed man with "a face like a scarred mountain," sat in the "cage room" of the US Marshal's Office, dictating a letter to his personal secretary. Under heavy guard, Haywood awaited transfer to the Leavenworth Penitentiary. One of the founders of the Industrial Workers of the World (IWW)—the "Wobblies"—a radical union of unskilled laborers trying to wrestle power away from capitalist robber barons, Haywood had instructed his followers to disrupt the "rich man's war" by any means necessary. "It is better to be a traitor to your country than to your class," he declared. Five days prior, in the Federal Building's sixth-floor courtroom, Judge Kenesaw Mountain Landis had sentenced Haywood and fourteen of his comrades from the IWW—"the Bolsheviki of America"—to twenty years in prison for violating the Espionage Act. Based on insubstantial evidence, the government prosecuted and convicted a total of more than one hundred Wobblies during the same trial. Each of them was charged with over one hundred separate crimes related to sedition, subversion, and sabotage.[4]

In the American consciousness, the fight against the Wobblies was part of the domestic theater of the Great War, pitting Haywood and his fellow revolutionaries—"Imperial Wilhelm's Warriors"— against Landis, a zealous patriot who had no sympathy for pacifists, slackers, or anarchists. Known for a harsh ruling against Standard Oil and for protecting Major League Baseball owners from the Federal League's antitrust suit, Landis, the most famous judge in America, who would go on to become the commissioner of Major League Baseball, cut an imperious figure on the federal bench. A tobacco-chewing bourbon drinker with a hatchet face, "parchment skin," and a shock of white hair, the judge looked, as journalist John Reed put it, like "Andrew Jackson three years dead."[5]

During the war, Landis embodied the country's jingoism, campaigning as one of the most prominent of the Four-Minute Men in Chicago, a group that delivered four-minute speeches in movie theaters, preaching the gospel of 100 percent Americanism and the evils of Germany. "Damn the Kaiser and his sons," Landis declared. A longtime Republican who had denounced union leaders and radicals from the bench, he managed to conduct the IWW trial with unusual restraint. But when he announced the sentences against Haywood and the other defendants, he made clear that he was motivated by a patriotic duty to punish them to the furthest extent of the law. "When the country is at peace," he said, "it is a legal right of free speech to oppose going to war and to oppose preparation for war. But when once war is declared that right ceases."[6]

In the days after the sentencing, the trial remained on the minds of everyone who worked at the Federal Building. While US Marshals kept a close watch on Haywood, a sixteen-year-old substitute mail carrier named Walt Disney, an aspiring cartoonist, worked in the basement post office sorting letters and packages. On September 4, shortly after 3:00 p.m., as Chicago's baseball fans cursed the rain, Disney finished his mail run, walked through the Federal Building lobby, and headed toward the West Adams Street exit.[7]

Suddenly, a frightening blast shook the ground beneath his feet. He later recalled hearing a thunderous "WHOOOM!!!!"—a deafening explosion that left him disoriented. A bomb had erupted, cutting a massive hole out of the Federal Building wall. A fog of black smoke, flames, and dust clouded the lobby. Rubble and glass covered the marble floors. Hurled to the ground, Disney heard panicked voices crying for help. On the eighth floor, Haywood felt the building tremble. The force of the blast was so powerful that across the street, workers in the Marquette and Edison Buildings were thrown from their chairs, many of them cut by glass shards and splinters. Crowds ran in every direction as police officers and federal agents rushed to the scene. Wounded men and women sprawled across the pavement, lying in pools of blood. The bomb injured more than thirty people and killed four, including one of Disney's fellow mail carriers.[8]

Conflicting accounts from witnesses made it difficult for authorities to identify the bomber. A few postal workers recalled seeing two suspicious men lingering outside the Adams Street entrance just before the explosion. Another witness claimed a red Stutz with two men "who looked like Italians," one of them sporting a fedora, the other wearing a brown felt hat, pulled up to the Adams Street entrance. Then one of the "Italians" darted in and out of the building, returned to the car, and sped off with the getaway driver. A woman told investigators that a man wearing a tan raincoat entered the lobby holding a cigar box under his arm, dropped it, looked around, and kicked it under the radiator before hurrying out the door.[9]

Immediately, federal agents, US Marshals, police officers, and vigilante volunteers raided the IWW headquarters on Madison Street. Authorities detained one hundred men, about half of them Wobblies. None of the apprehended, however, was ever charged with any crime. In fact, it remained unsolved. Although Judge

Landis was away on vacation during the attack, Bill Haywood emerged from the Federal Building unscathed, confronted by a rabble shouting, "Hang him!"[10]

The night before the World Series, Chicago inched toward chaos. It seemed that America was losing the war against enemies at home. Fear gripped the city. Throughout the war, the American Protective League, an army of thousands of volunteer spies working with the Bureau of Investigation, surveilled and slandered Americans all in the name of national security. Yet "the firm hand of repression," wielded by Wilson's government, did not make Americans feel any safer.

In a time of heightened distress over violence and anarchy, even attending a baseball game came with risks. The games played on, but the terrorist attack reminded America that there was no escaping "the shadow of the war."[11]

On the eve of Game One of the 1918 World Series, terrorists bombed the Federal Building in Chicago. The following day federal agents and Chicago police combed the city, searching for the bombers while the Cubs and Red Sox played baseball at Comiskey Park. (*Courtesy of the National Archives.*)

"THE EFFECT OF THE WAR was everywhere," observed a *Boston Globe* writer. Looking out at the sparse gathering at Comiskey Park, the reporter noted that the 19,274 fans in attendance constituted "one of the smallest crowds which ever turned out for a World's Series opening." Compared with Game One of the 1917 Series, which was also played at Comiskey, about thirteen thousand fewer fans attended the opener of the Cubs–Red Sox championship. It seemed that the Cubs business manager had grossly miscalculated the demand for tickets when he decided to move the team's home games—the first three contests of the Series—from Weeghman Park to the more spacious stadium of the White Sox. Entire sections of seats remained empty. Suggesting that inflation and war taxes discouraged fans from buying tickets, the *Globe* writer failed to note that the three-game box seat packages that sold for $15 in 1917 cost only $9 in 1918.[12]

Before the game began, Ruth entertained the crowd during batting practice. He transformed meaningless warmup swings into a show, an awesome display of his power. Even during batting practice the sight of the Colossus clubbing a ball over the fence could intimidate opposing teams. A fierce wind blew across the diamond as Ruth gripped his bat. When the pitcher grooved the ball right into his sweet spot, he swatted the ball with ease, depositing it over a right-field wall sign that read BUY WAR SAVINGS STAMPS AND DO IT NOW.[13]

Perhaps the Cubs manager had seen Ruth punish the ball during batting practice. Or maybe Fred Mitchell knew well enough already that Babe's bat could dictate the course of a game. Either way, the Cubs skipper decided that he would start southpaw Jim "Hippo" Vaughn, knowing that Ruth fared worse at the plate against lefties. Although Ed Barrow had indicated before the Series that Ruth would play the field every day, he decided right before the first game that Babe would pitch and bat ninth. Usually when Ruth was on the mound, Barrow had him hit third or fourth in the lineup. Batting the most dangerous hitter in the game ninth, however, was a questionable choice.

When Ruth threw the opening pitch, he showed no outward signs of a late night. According to *New York American* reporter Gene Fowler, the previous evening, Babe had imbibed with a group of "sports writers, gamblers, and other students of human nature" in a hotel room. Babe nevertheless appeared "fresh as a cornflower, although he had taken aboard many helpings of the sauce." When the writer asked him if he would have the nerve to pitch the next afternoon, the "hale young man gave me a bone-rattling slap on the back. 'I'll pitch 'em all if they say the word!'" Then, Babe announced that he had a date with "someone who wore skirts."[14]

Even in Chicago, the partisan crowd cheered as loudly for Babe as they did any Cub. The game however, turned out to be largely uneventful. "There was no cheering during the contest, nor was there anything like the usual umpire baiting," noted one Boston writer. Nothing aroused the crowd more than when a twelve-piece brass band interrupted the yawns and idle chat with a vigorous rendition of "The Star-Spangled Banner." During the seventh-inning stretch, the players removed their caps and faced the flag atop the right-field pole. Standing at attention, Boston's third baseman Fred Thomas, a sailor on leave from the Great Lakes Naval Station, saluted Old Glory. As the band played, the crowd swelled with pride, singing louder and louder. "When the final notes came," observed a writer, "a great volume of melody rolled across the field." It seemed so important that the *New York Times* led its coverage of the game with the anthem story. Throughout the season, when the owners were charged with avarice and players endured accusations of slacking, performing the anthem on baseball's greatest stage helped protect the magnates' business interests as much as it advanced their political agenda. So moved, Harry Frazee elected for a band to play the anthem before every Series game in Boston.[15]

Ruth dominated the Cubs' batters, retiring ten straight in the final three innings to clinch the first game, 1–0. Praising Ruth, the *Boston Post*'s Paul Shannon opined that Babe "twirled a game that will go down into history as one of the most brilliantly twirled battles in the annals of postseason encounters." Dating back to his last World Series appearance in 1916, Ruth's six-hit shutout against the Cubs now gave him twenty-two consecutive scoreless innings. Of course, his victory would not have been possible without the incredible defense of George Whiteman, who preserved Ruth's shutout with three remarkable catches. But headlines about some thirty-five-year-old journeyman named Whiteman didn't sell newspapers. "Superman" did. The real story, Hugh Fullerton wrote, was Ruth, the "super-human." "Another bomb exploded in Chicago when Babe Ruth . . . single-handedly won the first game of the World's Series."[16]

In Game Two, Superman was nowhere to be found. Recognizing that Ruth and his teammates struggled against left-handed pitchers, Mitchell started George "Lefty" Tyler, a master of change-ups and curveballs. Despite Ruth's power, Ed Barrow had little faith that he could hit Tyler. In a curious move, Barrow benched Ruth. Boston's legion of sportswriters was baffled by Barrow's decision. After the Red Sox lost 3–1, the Hub's reporters wanted to know, "Where was Ruth?" Even in the ninth inning, when Boston threatened a late rally, flustering Tyler with back-to-back triples, Barrow refused to send Ruth to the plate as a pinch-hitter. After the game, Eddie Hurley of the *Boston Evening Record* excoriated the Boston manager as "an inglorious hunk of poor judgment." Benching Ruth for the entire game was "nothing but criminal."[17]

Barrow's decision played right into Fred Mitchell's strategy. For Game Three, the Cubs manager brought back Hippo Vaughn, the same lefty that had struck out Ruth twice in the first contest. Mitchell could have started one of his well-rested righties, but he was convinced pitching Vaughn would neutralize Ruth. "A right hander would have had Ruth coming up to hit," Mitchell explained, "and if he got hold of one, good night." Again, Ruth sat on the bench.[18]

In a pitcher's duel, Boston's Carl Mays confounded the Chicago batters with his "submarine" style, rearing back like a bowler, dropping his hand down to his shoelaces, and releasing the ball close to the ground, his knuckles nearly grazing the dirt. Mays, *Baseball Magazine* noted, "shoots the ball in at the batter at such unexpected angles that his delivery is hard to find, generally until along about 5 o'clock, when the hitters get accustomed to it—and when the game is about over." By the time Game Three ended, the scoreboard showed a Red Sox 2–1 victory, matching their lead in the Series.[19]

If Boston fans wondered when Ruth would play again, they did not have to wait very long for an answer. Ed Barrow had already decided that Babe would pitch in the opener at the Fens.

A "PALE BLUE HAZE" FILLED the Michigan Central train cars as the locomotive carrying ballplayers and reporters chugged eastward toward Massachusetts. From the time the train departed the LaSalle Street Station until sunrise, men gambled and drank, and the smell of cigars wafted in the air. The constant noise—the roaring sound of laughter, singing, and arguing—made sleep nearly impossible. Racing through the aisles like adolescents, hooting and hollering, Babe Ruth and Walt Kinney, a mediocre pitcher from Texas, found great amusement snatching men's straw boaters. Smashing their fists through the tops of the hats, Ruth and Kinney chortled, placing them back on the heads of passengers. For Babe, it was all in good fun. What else could he do to pass the time?[20]

Ruth and Kinney were known for their hijinks, pranks, wrestling, and boxing. But the rough play nearly cost the Red Sox their starting pitcher. Reporters' accounts differed, but it seems that during the train ride, Ruth and Kinney's grappling ended in an accident. Supposedly, Ruth lunged or swung his left fist at Kinney, but when the train lurched Babe's pitching hand smacked an immovable object: the hard steel wall of the car or a window. One writer reported, "The heavy glass shattered and fell, clattering inside and outside." The middle knuckle on his left hand swelled and turned red. Writers described it as "bent," "broken," and "cut."[21]

Barrow snapped. "You damn fool! You know I've picked you to pitch the fourth game and you go and bust up your hand that way. Don't you want to win this Series?"[22]

Babe insisted that he was fine. Nothing could stop him from pitching—except maybe a rebellion.

At some point during the night, the players started reviewing the paltry gate receipts from the first three games. Before the Series began, the National Commission had sent them documents explaining how potential bonus payouts to both teams would work, but the players had hardly paid them any attention. The complex formula for dividing World Series shares among the two pennant winners paid the players 60 percent of the gate from the first four games. The owners did not pay them any money for playing more than four games, fearing that the players might intentionally extend the Series for a greater windfall. However, the players now realized that a new rule established before the season began required the World Series clubs to split the pot with players on the second-, third-, and fourth-place teams in their respective leagues. Plus, the Commission had announced that 10 percent of the revenue would be donated to war charities. Making matters worse, the owners capped the bonus payouts for every player at $2,000 per winner and $1,400 for the losers. But as the train rolled on, the players did the math: poor attendance and reduced ticket prices meant that they were unlikely to make even that much. The winners and losers were more likely to receive $1,200 and $800, respectively, the lowest payouts ever for a World Series.[23]

Fueled by whiskey and rage, the players' anger turned into action. Something had to be done. Although the players no longer had any type of union, they began organizing. Two representatives from each team—Harry Hooper and Dave Shean from the Red Sox, and Les Mann and Bill Killefer from the Cubs—planned to confront the three-man National Commission when the train arrived in Boston. If the Commission refused to hear them out or objected to their demand for larger bonuses, then they would borrow a page from the Wobblies' manifesto—and strike.

17

In God's Hands

THE NEWS FROM BOSTON SPELLED DISAPPOINTMENT FOR BASE-
ball fans. "No World's Series game will be played here today unless
the National Commission comes to some agreement with a committee of players from the Boston and Chicago clubs," reported
the *New York Times*. On the morning of Game Four, September
9, players from the Red Sox and Cubs pressed the commissioners
for a meeting, but the executives refused to convene until after
the contest at Fenway Park. August Herrmann, president of the
National Commission, maintained that the three-man council did
not have the authority to make any changes to the bonus system
without authorization from all sixteen owners. Reluctantly, the
players conceded to meeting them again after Game Four, but they
remained disgruntled. Later that afternoon, the *Boston American*
assured its readers: "Rumors of a strike among the Red Sox and
Cubs were killed early today."[1]

More than twenty-two thousand spectators showed up at
Fenway, a disappointing turnout considering that the park could
hold about thirty-five thousand fans and it was the first World
Series game played at Fenway since 1912. Throughout the sta-
dium, empty patches of seats checkered the stands. Even the Royal
Rooters, Boston's vaunted fan club, hardly made themselves heard.

About thirty minutes before the first pitch, around 2:00, the crowd rose to its feet when fifty-four wounded soldiers dressed in blue and khaki uniforms, many of them hobbling on crutches, some missing limbs, appeared in the grandstands. Fans greeted the servicemen with gratitude and handshakes. The scene was a stark reminder that the disabled and disfigured soldiers who'd returned home would live with the war for the rest of their lives.[2]

But those veterans came to Fenway to forget the war, at least for a moment. Although Boston fans doubted whether Babe could play with a lacerated finger on his throwing hand, Ruth convinced Ed Barrow that he could pitch through the pain. Standing on the mound, he gripped the ball, his swollen finger stained yellow with iodine. Barrow watched him intently, studying every ball that he threw. Ruth's tender middle finger made it difficult to spin a curveball and command his pitches. He struggled early on, though his teammates' defense bailed him out and prevented Chicago from scoring.[3]

Batting in the fourth inning, Babe rewarded Barrow's faith in him with one mighty swing. Facing Lefty Tyler with two men on base and two outs, Ruth cocked his bat as he watched three straight balls pass low and outside the plate. Then, hankering for a fastball, he whiffed at a slow curve. On the next pitch, when Tyler threw what Ruth thought was ball four, Babe tossed his bat and began jogging toward first, but the umpire called it a strike. Ruth picked up the bat and kicked the dirt in frustration. The count was full. This time Tyler fired a fastball right in Ruth's wheelhouse. Babe stung the ball with his bat, launching it deep into right field and over the head of Cubs outfielder Max Flack. The ball bounded past Flack and rolled all the way to the fence. Ruth's two-run triple gave "the Hubmen" a 2–0 lead. He proved that even against a lefty, he could hit. "Giving Babe Ruth a fast, straight ball, letter high and exactly over the plate is not a mite more dangerous than tickling the roof of a man-eating tiger's mouth with your little finger," Burt Whitman wrote.[4]

Pitching with the lead, Ruth labored on the mound, holding the Cubs scoreless for seven straight innings. But in the eighth, he unraveled and surrendered two runs to Chicago. Reporters noted that he had set a new World Series record for consecutive scoreless innings pitched (twenty-nine), breaking Christy Mathewson's previous mark by one inning. Later in the eighth, however, Boston managed to score the go-ahead run. Ruth returned to the mound in the ninth, the Red Sox leading 3–2, but after giving up a single and a walk to the first two batters, Barrow replaced him with Joe Bush and sent Babe to left field. Bush quelled the Cubs' rally and the Red Sox won, taking a 3–1 lead in the Series.[5]

Once again, writers fixated on Ruth's batting power, celebrating his only hit as the deciding play of the game. "Big Babe Ruth's mighty bat wrote another page in the annals of World Series championships yesterday," Paul Shannon wrote. Ruth's triple, added another a writer, "will take its place among the prodigious blows in baseball history." These accounts, of course, exaggerated the significance of the hit—but Ruth was the most interesting player on the field, and the writers knew his story would sell newspapers.[6]

The following morning, around 10:00 a.m., more than four hours before Game Five, Harry Hooper and Dave Shean of Boston, and Les Mann and Bill Killefer of Chicago arrived at the Copley Plaza Hotel, seeking a meeting with the National Commission. Hooper argued that the players on the World Series teams shouldn't have to divide their bonuses with clubs that did not win their respective pennants. The players were now willing to accept reduced shares—$1,500 for the winners and $1,000 for the losers—but the Commission reiterated that they could not reapportion the payouts without consulting all of the owners. August Herrmann promised that they would meet again after the game, but the players knew that if the Red Sox won, then the Series was over and they would lose all leverage. Without any guarantees, the players left the hotel in a fury.[7]

Earlier that day, the morning newspapers had dismissed rumors of a players' revolt. The *Boston Globe* reported, "There is nothing approaching a strike or a walkout." Yet around two o'clock, only thirty minutes before the opening pitch, after more than twenty-four thousand spectators settled into their seats, the crowd grew restless. Curiously, there were no players from either team warming up on the field or taking batting practice. The dugouts were empty, too. Running out of patience, a fan yelled, "Where are the players?"[8]

Searching for answers, reporters scurried around the team clubhouses. Soon, the news leaked outside of Fenway. On the streets of Boston newsboys from the *American* waved papers hot off the press, shouting a bold headline: RED SOX–CUBS ON STRIKE. On the front page, two columns below the masthead, the *American* reported a story even more disturbing than the players' rebellion. Two Boston men had died from the "Spanish influenza." Local physicians were fairly certain that the grippe had spread from Commonwealth Pier, and that there might be more deaths to come if the city did not act swiftly.[9]

WHILE BOSTON FANS WAITED FOR the players to appear on the field, Ban Johnson and August Herrmann stumbled into the Red Sox clubhouse, totally loaded after drinking for hours at the Copley Plaza bar. They were in no shape to handle a crisis. Johnson was a notorious drunk. One time, after a long night of hard drinking, he teetered back to a hotel, glassy-eyed, and found a man sleeping in his bed. Confused, Johnson knew that he had the right room number, but he was standing in the wrong hotel. When he staggered into the Boston locker room, he pushed Herrmann aside and pontificated about everything he had done to make the World Series possible. Beating his chest, he told Harry Hooper, "I went to Washington and had the stamp of approval put on this World's Series." Slurring his words, he repeated, "I made it possible. I did. I made it possible, Harry."[10]

When Hooper tried negotiating with the commissioners, Johnson stopped him. Wrapping his arm around Hooper, Johnson told him that nothing could be done about the bonuses. There was simply not enough revenue to pay the players more money. Hooper insisted that the players were prepared to strike, but Johnson knew that if they didn't take the field the fans would blame them for ruining the game. Reminding Hooper about the soldiers sitting in the stands, he appealed to patriotism. "With a war going on and fellows fighting in France, what do you think the public will think of you ballplayers striking for more money?"[11]

Fearing a riot at the ballpark, a police sergeant called for reinforcements and dispatched four mounted policemen onto the field. Distracting the crowd, a band played, "Tessie," "Over There," "Keep the Home Fires Burning," and other patriotic tunes. The crowd roared as a group of wounded soldiers and sailors found their seats. "These mighty heroes of the real game," a local reporter noted, "must have made everyone within hearing of that tribute think a mite."[12]

The presence of soldiers and sailors weighed on the players. They had no choice. A strike would stain the game. In the bowels of the stadium, the players could hear the rowdy crowd becoming increasingly agitated. Hooper convinced the players on both teams that they couldn't turn their backs on the very people who had supported them throughout the season. After a private discussion in the umpires' quarters, Hooper informed the commissioners that they would play as long as they could make a public statement before the game and Johnson swore there would be no retribution.[13]

Shortly thereafter, while the players dressed, John "Honey" Fitzgerald, carrying a megaphone, strode toward home plate. The charming former mayor and most prominent member of the Royal Rooters faced the stands. Raising the megaphone to his mouth, he twisted and turned in every direction so that all corners of the park could hear him. Then he made an announcement that reverberated throughout the quiet ballpark: the teams "have agreed to play for the sake of the public and the wounded soldiers in the stands."[14]

When the players took the field, a chorus of boos drowned out the cheers. Taunting them, the hecklers shouted, "Bolsheviki," "slackers," and "a lot of other names that would not look nice in print." From the perspective of angry fans, the players' threats to strike represented everything that was wrong with the country. "Baseball," Arthur Duffey declared in the Boston Post, "is dead . . . The game has been dying for two years, killed by the greed of players and owners." The entire scene, he added, was "a disgusting spectacle."[15]

The Red Sox lost Game Five, 3–0. Again, Barrow had benched Ruth against another Cubs lefty. Disillusioned by the players' greed, the following day an unforgiving crowd of about fifteen thousand fans showed up at Fenway for Game Six. Although Ruth only played two innings as a substitute left fielder, the Sox clinched the championship in a 2–1 victory over the Cubs. It was Boston's fourth championship in the last seven seasons. Yet there were no parades or wild celebrations on the streets of Boston. It was hard for many citizens to celebrate a team of perceived "slackers" who seemed to reject the country's wartime values of sacrifice and loyalty.

In retrospect, we can see that the anticlimactic Series marked an end of an era. Barrow's benching of Babe Ruth against lefties, his slavish devotion to the dictates of "scientific baseball," signaled the last gasp of the Dead Ball Era. The manager had taken the bat out of Ruth's hands. He had benched the most sensational long-ball hitter in the game out of his fidelity to the demands of a "small ball" age. That would not happen again. The future belonged to the Babe.

On September 11, the same day that the Sox won the Series, the Boston newspapers reported that five hundred bilious sailors at Commonwealth Pier had contracted the grippe. The next day, ninety-six thousand Bostonians stood in line to register for the draft—sneezing, coughing, and breathing on one another in crammed registration halls. In a matter of days the plague spread as fast as the fear of death.[16]

THIRTY MILES WEST OF BOSTON, an epidemic tore through Camp Devens, where forty-five thousand soldiers trained. The virulent flu strain devastated the camp. In the packed mess halls and cramped barracks, sick men eating, sleeping, and showering together spread the disease. Waves of infected soldiers flooded the hospital. The camp's chief nurse recalled, "One day fifty were admitted; the next day 300, then the daily average became 500; into a 2,000 bed hospital 6,000 patients crowded." On a single night, one person remembered, "the men were dying like flies." By the end of the month, about 28 percent of the entire camp had the grippe—more than fourteen thousand cases—and 757 people had died. The crisis became so dire that the hospital refused to admit new patients, no matter how sick.[17]

The outbreak overwhelmed the camp's medical staff. Ordinarily, Devens had twenty-five doctors, but now more than 250 physicians were treating patients. There were hardly enough nurses to keep up with the number of soldiers admitted to the hospital. The camp's sickbay overflowed with young men lying on cots soaked with sweat, suffering from cyanosis, their lungs packed with gelatinous fluid. Blue-faced with purple lips, the soldiers drowned when blood, foam, and mucus swamped their lungs. Writing a colleague, one doctor observed how rapidly "death comes." The patients developed "Mahogany spots over the cheek bones, and a few hours later you can begin to see the Cyanosis extending from their ears and spreading all over the face, until it is hard to distinguish the coloured men from the white."[18]

Patients often complained of violent pains, as if someone was stabbing them. They screamed in agony, tormented by severe earaches, headaches, and stomachaches. Some flinched at the mere touch of their skin. Others lost their vision or their sense of smell. Blood poured from everywhere: the mouth, ears, eyes, and nose, a disturbing sight for even the most experienced physicians.[19]

In Boston, the death rate escalated rapidly, day-by-day, hour-by-hour. On September 18, the city's health commissioner, Dr. William Woodward, estimated that there were at least three thousand cases of influenza. He also reported forty deaths in the past twenty-four hours. The public didn't know what to do, especially since the newspapers offered conflicting accounts about the severity of the crisis. That day, when the *Evening Transcript* reported, GRIP DEATHS INCREASE, the *Post* claimed, SPANISH GRIP ON THE WANE.[20]

But it would only get worse. The mutant virus had already contaminated every corner of the city, permeating the tenements in the North End, ripping through the flats and row houses in South Boston, infiltrating the brownstones and mansions in the Back Bay, and coursing through the saloons and shipyards in Charlestown. It afflicted passengers riding ferries, trollies, and subway cars. It infected the patrons of dance halls, theaters, nickelodeons, and Fenway Park.

Undoubtedly, crowded public events—three World Series games, parades, rallies, and the draft registration drive on September 12—helped spread the plague. Woodward advised the public to avoid unnecessary travel on streetcars, subways, and trains, but there were no laws prohibiting people from leaving their homes.

Rumors fed widespread panic. One story passing on the streets claimed that a German sub had penetrated Boston Harbor, rose out of the ocean, and emitted a deathly gray gas that drifted ashore, poisoning the city with germs. With German U-boats prowling the Atlantic Coast, some military officers circulated a theory that the Huns had unleashed a toxic germ in Europe that killed enemy soldiers and had now infiltrated American cities and military camps. Others speculated that traitorous doctors and nurses injected soldiers and sailors with the deathly virus. Blaming "*Germ*-any" for the pandemic, the *New York Times* declared, "Let the curse be called the German plague."[21]

There was no cure for influenza—no medication, no vaccination, no antibiotics, no miracle drug. Yet charlatans preyed on desperate people, selling all sorts of creams, balms, pills, and serums that promised to ward off the grippe. Even Mayor Andrew Peters received such an inoculation. Searching for an antidote, people inhaled turpentine fumes, sniffed Vaseline, rubbed poultices of garlic on their bodies, swallowed red peppers, and drank tea spiked with whiskey. One Boston physician recommended nudity. Doctors, nurses, coroners, policemen, firemen, and ambulance drivers wore gauze masks. Newspaper advertisements screamed: WEAR A MASK AND SAVE YOUR LIFE! But wearing a gauze mask was about as helpful as using a chicken-wire screen door to keep a dust storm from blowing dirt into a house.[22]

The streets emptied as hysteria paralyzed the city. With hundreds of victims dead, patrolmen stacked decomposing corpses wrapped in white sheets on the sidewalks, waiting for the meat wagons to scoop them up. The stench of putrefying bodies poisoned the air. The Boston newspapers published daily tallies of the deceased. The city morgue couldn't keep pace with the influx of corpses. Undertakers ran out of coffins.[23]

The shadow of death frightened children, especially. The grippe turned many young boys and girls into orphans. Looking back on the autumn of 1918, when he was eleven years old, Kenneth Crotty remembered the terror he felt when the virus contaminated his block in Framingham, Massachusetts. "It was scary because every morning when you got up, you asked, 'Who died during the night?'" Francis Russell recalled that when he was only seven years old, growing up in Dorchester, the pandemic and the continuous horse-drawn funeral processions made him aware of the passage of time. Horse hooves clopping along the streets; grim-faced coachmen driving black carriages; coffins piling up at the local cemetery; gravediggers shoveling dirt beneath the rain—the scenes taught him "that life was not a perpetual present, and that even tomorrow would be part of the past, and that for all of my days and years to come I too must one day die."[24]

Saving lives meant taking every precaution possible. With thousands of civilians carrying the virus, the Boston Health Department reported on September 25 that nearly seven hundred citizens had died from influenza and pneumonia. After a conference with state officials and Health Commissioner Woodward, Governor Samuel McCall issued a proclamation urging everyone with medical training to help fight the epidemic. Effective immediately, all public schools were closed. The next day, Mayor Peters closed all movie houses, theaters, concert halls, and dance halls. Public meetings were also prohibited, which meant that the city's Liberty Loan Committee could not hold parades or campaign for subscriptions. Desperate for help, Lieutenant Governor Calvin Coolidge wired President Wilson, the governors of Vermont, Maine, and Rhode Island, as well as the mayor of Toronto, requesting that they dispatch doctors and nurses to Massachusetts. By that time, state officials estimated that more than fifty thousand people suffered from the grippe.[25]

At the end of September, influenza had infiltrated nearly every state in the country. The virus spread from eastern port cities— Boston, Baltimore, Philadelphia, and New York—and traveled along the rail and river lines into the interior of America, reaching New Orleans and Chicago's Great Lakes Training Station. It even appeared on the West Coast in Seattle, San Francisco, and Los Angeles. The contagion polluted factories and farms, shipyards and schools. The grippe wiped out thousands of sturdy young men training in military and naval bases. Even with General Pershing calling for reinforcements, the situation had grown so dire that Provost Marshal Crowder cancelled an October draft call for 142,000 men.[26]

In early October, Anita Muck planned to visit her husband at Fort Oglethorpe. But news of an outbreak in Chattanooga scared her from heading south. Concerned for her safety, Karl sent a telegram to Charles Ellis, warning him that Anita should avoid traveling. Half of the camp's prisoners were sick. Though he felt well enough, he wrote, "the Camp is quarantined." One of Muck's fellow prisoners later recalled, "The weeks during the influenza epidemic were perhaps the most ghastly of them all; day and night ambulances rushed through the camp; day and night patient after patient was transported to the hospital. And time and again we received word that another friend had died." In all, forty-six prisoners died from the flu at Fort Oglethorpe.[27]

Back in Boston, the only reminder of Muck's internment was a front-page story in the *Post* announcing Parisian Henri Rabaud had been appointed the new director of the BSO. Not that anyone in the city planned on attending a concert anytime soon. That same day, October 5, with no signs of the epidemic relenting, Health Commissioner Woodward expanded the closure order. All saloons, soda fountains, billiard halls, auction houses, and "other public gathering places" were officially closed. The mayor even asked ministers and priests to turn away parishioners.[28]

At that moment nearly everyone in Boston believed that the fate of the city rested in God's hands.

FINALLY, THE GERMANS WERE READY to surrender. At least, that was the story Americans read in newspapers throughout the country on October 9, 1918. By then, there was chaos in Germany, and the Kaiser's position was threatened. After the Allies broke the Hindenburg Line, capturing thousands of prisoners, Supreme

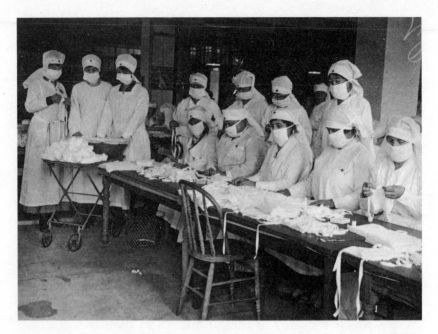

At the height of Boston's flu crisis, Red Cross advertisements urged WEAR A MASK AND SAVE YOUR LIFE! In this picture volunteers make "flu masks" that the Red Cross claimed were "99.9% proof against influenza." However, the masks were worthless against microbes that could easily penetrate the gauze. *(Courtesy of the National Archives.)*

Commander Erich Ludendorff lost all confidence in the Imperial German Army. On October 4, German chancellor Maximilian von Baden sent Woodrow Wilson a secret note, calling for an armistice based on the president's Fourteen Points—a "peace without victory." But Wilson refused to negotiate a peace settlement until Germany evacuated the conquered territory it still controlled and agreed to an unconditional surrender.[29]

On the same day that Americans read about the Germans' willingness to surrender, newspapers published stories about a rescue mission in the Argonne Forest involving a "Lost Battalion" surrounded by German forces. For the past week, stories had been appearing in the news about a number of companies from the 77th Division that were trapped in the "Argonne Jungle."

On October 2, a cold, damp day, Major Charles Whittlesey led roughly seven hundred men into what turned out to be a death trap. He was weak from a hacking cough and dysentery, and few of his men were much better. They were short on sleep, low on rations, light on ammunition, and almost entirely in the fog about what was in front of them in the dense forests and chiseled ravines.[30]

On October 3, the *New York Herald* published one of the first stories about the Lost Battalion, headlined DESPERATE FIGHTING BY WHITTLESEY UNIT. The following day, *New York Tribune* scribe Wilbur Forrest published a dramatic account about troops from Camp Upton fighting their way through "thick belts of man-made barbed-wire and nature's underbrush." Fighting in the dark forest made it "impossible to see ten feet ahead." Under a barrage of German fire and explosive mines planted deep into the forest and along the roads, the Americans launched grenades and mortars at their enemies. Desperate, Whittlesey's men were in the middle of an old fashioned dogfight, a battle against nature and the Germans.[31]

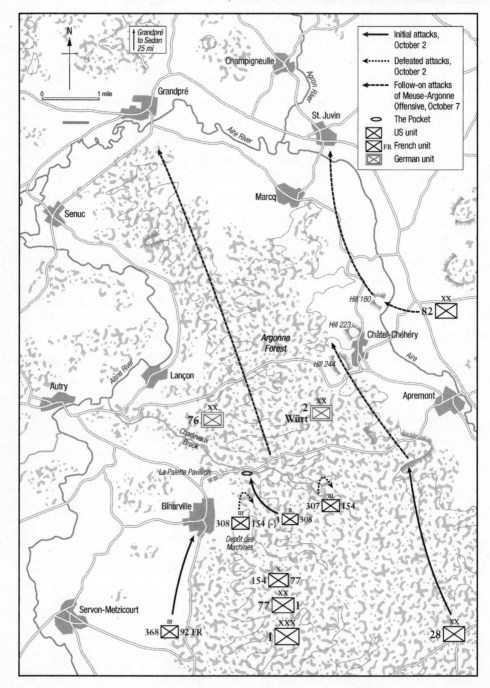

The Argonne Forest sector of the Meuse-Argonne Offensive. *(Credit: Bounford Studios.)*

18

"Whether You'll Hear
from Me Again I Don't Know"

By the end of September, the Allies' forward momentum had stalled, and trouble like a river was flowing downstream. At the headwaters stood Supreme Allied Commander Marshal Ferdinand Foch, the leader who had designed a four-pronged *en echelon* grand offensive to defeat the Germans by the end of 1918. It was a broad offensive, stretching along the Western Front from Verdun in the south to Ypres and the English Channel in the north. The linchpin in the plan was the Meuse-Argonne Offensive, a primarily US operation with French support, commanded by General "Black Jack" Pershing and staffed by the troops in the American Expeditionary Force. Pershing had two primary goals. The first was territorial. His army would attack north into the German position between the Argonne Forest in the west and the Meuse River in the east, drive toward Sedan, and interdict the Sedan-Mezières rail network that was critical to supplying German forces along the Western Front. The offensive's second aim was strategic. Knowing the importance of the Meuse-Argonne to the German war effort, General Pershing reasoned that a successful Allied assault into the area would force Field Marshal Paul von Hindenburg and General

Erich Ludendorff to commit their strategic reserves to the region rather than shifting them to stop the British and Belgian offensives in the north. Simply put, American success in the Meuse-Argonne combined with British, French, and Belgian assaults elsewhere on the Western Front would stretch Germany's resources to the breaking point, opening up the Hindenburg Line, the Rhine River, and Germany itself.[1]

In any case, that was the plan, one that placed an initial force of six hundred thousand troops at the center of the action. Before dawn on the morning of September 26, the rain stopped and the dark clouds that had hung low for days parted. Soldiers looking toward the sky caught a glimpse of the moon. Then almost on cue, across the front, at 2:30 a.m. American and French artillery crews, operating 2,773 guns, opened fire. Rapid-firing French 75s and slower-firing but more powerful 105mm and 155mm howitzers pounded the enemy in the north. They targeted Germany's front-line trenches and defenses, as well as barracks, roads, headquarters, artillery positions, and ammunition depots. For one gunner, it seemed as if "Hell was loose . . . and tons of shells were screaming over the hill toward No Man's Land." Captain Harry Truman of the 129th Field Artillery estimated that his gunners fired three thousand rounds from their 75s in four hours, rendering him "deaf as a post." It was an awesome display of raw power—exceeding all the ammunition the Union army fired in the entire Civil War—a thunderclap of noise and fireworks that crushed buildings, felled trees, and churned land into a muddy quagmire.[2]

As barrages go, it was relatively brief. In the Meuse-Argonne Offensive, Foch and Pershing depended on the element of surprise and would often follow a truncated artillery barrage with a combined infantry, armor, and air assault. At 5:45 a.m., after the shelling had come to an end, Major Charles Whittlesey shouted, "Let's go!" He pushed Lieutenant Edwin Lewis out of their trench, and in turn was pulled out by him. Moving into the Argonne Forest, Lewis, a newspaperman before the war, was struck by "the weirdest panorama of mist and mystery." No Man's Land "was shrouded in a thick, white fog . . . Beyond and through the fog the flashes of bursting shells flickered." He felt lost, isolated in a bubble, "in one chilly breath" separated from companies on his right and left. "All the carefully planned instructions in regard to liaison" disappeared in the mist and fog.[3]

Lewis was overwhelmed. His "ear was confused by the muffled echoes of friendly artillery," he wrote, while his "eye was confused by the haze." "It was almost as though the infantry was asked to go over the top blindfolded." Yet the most daunting challenge was the forest itself. "The dank breath of the Argonne, saturated . . . with the odor of stagnant, muddy pools, hiding treacherous carpets of tangled wire grass" brought "to the nostrils of the new crusaders" reminders of past slaughters. Despite all their training—and the new men in the 308th had not even been adequately trained—very few of the soldiers in Whittlesey's unit were prepared for the battle ahead.

The carefully hatched plans for the Meuse-Argonne Offensive began to fall apart as soon as the soldiers' boots hit the ground. The German defenses created an immediate obstacle. For most of the four years of the war, Germany controlled the region's high ground. Three imposing hills dominated the twenty-four-mile front between the Argonne Forest and the Meuse—Hill 285, Vauquois, and Montfaucon. From their commanding heights the Germans could track and shell American and French positions. There was simply no way for the offense to succeed unless the Allies took those hills.

Yet the path to the high grounds was treacherous, especially through the Argonne Forest along the left (west) flank. Pershing tasked General Hunter Liggett's I Corps with taking the territory, and placed General Alexander's 77th Division on the extreme left where the US First Army abutted against the French Fourth Army. There was a good reason the Germans occupied the Argonne early in the war. There was an equally sound reason why they held it. It was an area of dark forests that reduced visibility to yards and feet. Thick, vine-laden undergrowth that caught and tripped un-wary infantrymen combined with steep gullies made coordinated movement difficult even at the squad level. On top of it all, there were few roads—and those that did exist could hardly be called anything more than paths. Well-positioned hills, rugged terrain, swampy ground near the rivers—no wonder that armies since at least the time of Caesar had chosen to go around the Argonne rather than fight in it.

Lieutenant Arthur McKeogh, one of Whittlesey's most trusted officers, had never experienced anything as rugged as the Argonne. "I know the Adirondacks and the Berkshires," he wrote, "and I have read of the Civil War field of the Wilderness. But compared with the Argonne Forest they are as polo fields." Everywhere danger lurked. "Vines clasped your neck and roots entwined your feet till you were a prisoner of untamed Nature." All the while, fog and smoke made it nearly impossible to see the enemy in front of you or fellow soldiers beside you.[4]

Further strengthening the enemy's position was the enemy himself. The Germans had taken the defensive advantages of the region and improved upon them by constructing a series of trenches, blockhouses, pillboxes, and machine gun nests, all well camouflaged to increase their deadly effectiveness. Adding to all the natural and manmade advantages was the quality of the German soldiers in the sector. They were tough and dependable—experienced, proud, and committed to their cause. The 2nd Landwehr Division from Wurttemberg, for instance, had spent much of the last four years in the Argonne. Many called it their second home. They knew the slope of the hills and the pitch of the ravines, the bend in the paths and twists in the streams. Although outnumbered by the Allied forces, the Germans would assuredly not shrink from a barrage of guns and a charge of khaki-uniformed Americans.[5]

When the Americans attacked that morning, they made some initial gains, though they took none of their important objectives. The Germans followed a tried and true formula: they fell back from their lightly held forward trenches, sought the safety of their rear defenses, and when the artillery subsided, launched counterattacks and leveraged their command of the high ground to pound the Americans. Soon they had stopped the AEF's initial thrust and had begun to inflict significant casualties. Inexperienced soldiers failed before the hills of Vauquois and Montfaucon, though they often fought bravely. More-experienced troops in the 77th and 28th Divisions had little more luck in the Argonne. September 26 ended with few tangible accomplishments, and most of the next few days were devoted to reappraisal and recrimination. The entire Western Front offensive depended on success in the Meuse-Argonne. The questions became: Who's to blame? And what could be done?

FOCH HAD READY ANSWERS. HE believed that Pershing was not up to the job. The American leader was too inexperienced for such a command. From the beginning, Foch thought, success in the Meuse-Argonne depended upon the sophisticated use of infantry, armor, artillery, and aircraft, but Pershing's answer for everything was to send in more ground forces in a sledgehammer frontal assault. To remedy the problem, the supreme Allied commander decided to put the American soldiers under the command of experienced French generals. Initially Pershing agreed, but upon reflection changed his mind.[6]

For the sake of the alliance, Foch backed down. "In order to satisfy him I agreed to maintain the organization of the command as it was," he later wrote, "provided the American attacks should be resumed and once started, continue without pause." In essence, Foch and Pershing had reached a qualified truce. Pershing could keep his command, but only if he achieved results—immediately. If his American army did not break through the Argonne and force the Germans to deploy their tactical reserves, Foch left no doubt that he would go through with his planned changes.

The urgency for results—and especially the "get it done or you're done" ethos—made its way down the command structure. Pershing ordered 1st Corps commander General Liggett to resume the offensive, take territory from the Germans, and once in control of a piece of land to hold it. No more withdrawals when the enemy counterattacked. Liggett sent his aide-de-camp to General Robert Alexander, whose 77th was the only division wholly committed to the Argonne Forest. Alexander reacted with his usual aggression, claiming that his men were attacking, had not given up any ground they had taken, and that he had already "canned" subordinates "showing incompetency, timidity, or neurasthenia." In truth, units in the 77th had surrendered territory because of counterattacks, but in arguments, Alexander, like Pershing, preferred the offensive. Also similar to Pershing, Alexander sometimes canned officers under his command to shift any blame from himself.[7]

Now Liggett's chief of staff told Alexander that there could be no excuses. Failure was not an option. As Pershing had emphasized, "the attack should not concern itself with the flanks or losses, but should instead push ahead as far and as rapidly as possible." Alarmed about pushing too far in front of the French forces on his left and the Americans on his right, Alexander was told, "Flanks will be taken care of by our own people." That was enough for him. He was not about to be the weakest link in Foch's Grand Offensive.[8]

So it continued down the command chain. Alexander immediately telephoned General Evan M. Johnson, commander of the 154th Brigade (307th and 308th Regiments) and an experienced officer. Although Johnson was visiting his lines, Alexander left an unequivocal order, accusing him of holding up the French on his left and the American 153rd Brigade on his right. "The 154th Brigade must push forward to their objective [the major east-west La Viergette–Moulin de Charlevaux road and the railway paralleling it] today," read the message. "By 'Must' I mean must, and by 'today' I mean today and not next week." He later wrote, "My orders were quite positive and precise—the objective was to be gained without regard to losses and without regard to the exposed condition of the flanks."[9]

Closer to the actual fighting than Alexander, Johnson recognized the misstatements and problems presented in the order. He called Alexander, explaining that the 154th was not lagging behind, or at least no more so than the other stalled units. His superior did not want to hear talk about flanks, losses, or anything that smacked of excuses. The next day, October 2, the French and the American 28th Division would advance, and if Johnson could not keep up, Alexander "would get someone else who could." Although the question of losses concerned Johnson less than advancing in a forested terrain with unprotected flanks, an action that he thought might have catastrophic consequences, he was bound tight by the chain of command. Orders were orders. He accepted them, hoping he could think of a tactical solution to prevent disaster.

Colonel Cromwell Stacey, commander of the 308th Regiment, was even less sanguine about the orders than General Johnson. When he received his commander's call at 4:00 p.m. on October 1, he listened incredulously to the plan. Stacey knew the fragile realities of the deteriorating flanks. He worried about his men in his battalions—hungry, cold, sick, battle weary after too long on the front facing daunting odds. After some heated discussion, he told the general that his scouts believed the planned assault for the 308th was untenable.

A brief but pregnant silence followed before Johnson replied, "Are you questioning my orders, Colonel?"

"No sir," Stacey said. "But if you send them up there you will have to give me the orders in writing, and I will also write a statement to the effect that if you order me to send those men up there I will do so, but I will not be responsible."[10]

Johnson knew that Stacey was normally not subject to exaggeration or timidity. He was Regular Army, and had been part of the 3rd "Rock of the Marne" Division, earning French and American decorations for bravery. His assessment was so bleak that it shook the general, causing him to call divisional headquarters. But he was wasting his time. General Alexander had no interest in revisiting the order. It all had been decided. The next morning the push would begin, and regardless of flanks, casualties, weather, or misgivings—the Germans would be cleared out of the Argonne.

The chain-of-command path finally arrived at the tip of the arrow pointed into the heart of the foreboding forest. Resting in his bunker after a day of frustrating combat, Major Whittlesey, 1st Battalion, 308th Infantry Regiment, had just dispatched a report to Stacey. He had lost some men to German machine gun fire, and others to enemy artillery assaults. He was in an indefensible position in a ravine. "The sides are very steep; the bottom is marshy, and any solution to the problem involving an operation on both sides by one unit will be difficult." And by difficult he meant damned near impossible.[11]

Yet about 10:00 p.m. Whittlesey received his orders for the next day. He was to advance through the steep ravine, toward the area studded with German machine gun nests, under hills smoking from artillery fire, away from any flanking support. His orders demanded him to do exactly the thing that he had thus far not been able to accomplish—and to do it with fewer men and supplies.

Later that night, under the cover of fog, Whittlesey and Captain George G. McMurtry, commander of the 2nd Battalion, 308th Infantry Regiment, trekked back to regiment headquarters at Dessauer Platz to talk with Stacey. To get there, they had to follow a runner line set up to relay messages between the front and the rear command. It was so dark, the route so convoluted, that Whittlesey had to hold on to the back of the runner's cartridge belt with McMurtry clutching the back of his coat. Once he arrived, he explained again and more fully that attacking up the ravine would be an act of lunacy—the equivalent of reading a book a second time in hope of a different ending.

Colonel Stacey did not exactly disagree. Instead, he expressed his full confidence in Whittlesey and his men. When his major continued to object, he cut him off. Whittlesey had his orders—attack, push forward, reach his objective. In the end, all Stacey had to offer was the mantra passed down from the generals: Don't worry about flanks; they will be taken care of. Don't worry about losses; such are the sacrifices for victory. That was all the colonel had to say. "All right," Whittlesey supposedly said. "I'll attack, but whether you'll hear from me again I don't know."[12]

The officers departed neither satisfied nor inspired by Stacey. They slowly worked their way back to their bunker in the same manner they had left it, holding tight to the man in front of them. Whittlesey was clearly worried. On the way to his base, a signal platoon sergeant saw him and asked how much communication wire he needed for the next day. Whittlesey replied, "You haven't got enough wire to reach where I'm going."

OCTOBER 2 BEGAN WET AND foggy, and what light there was barely penetrated the forest's cover. It seemed that nature itself was conspiring against the American soldiers. About one kilometer east of "the battered piles of mortar and stone that had once been the town of Binarville," Colonel Whittlesey and his men ate breakfast in a ravine swarming with Germans soldiers. Yet the arrival of rations was something of a celebrated event. Since the Meuse-Argonne campaign began a week before, there had been constant supply problems and the 308th had been short on rations and ammunition. Most of the men had not eaten for several days, and they quickly consumed the food. Some breakfasted on bread with syrup and jam; others munched on hardtack and corned beef. They also loaded up on ammunition—two hundred rounds per rifle, five boxes of shells for each machine gun, grenades, and an assortment of entrenchment tools, flares, and messenger pigeons. Beyond those supplies, they traveled light, not expecting to be out of the reach of their base of support for more than a day or two.[13]

At 12:30 US gunners began to shell suspected German positions, and at 12:50 the general firing shifted into a rolling barrage. On cue, Whittlesey gave the order: "Let's go! Forward!" During the previous week, his 1st Battalion, 308th Infantry and Captain McMurtry's 2nd Battalion, 308th Infantry had both suffered staggering losses. Therefore, the two men combined forces, with Major Whittlesey, the senior officer, in command and McMurtry in support. The unit Whittlesey led into the German lines soon became known as the Lost Battalion, but it was not a battalion in any strict sense except for general size. It comprised six companies (A, B, C from the 1st Battalion and E, G, H from the 2nd) of wildly different sizes. During World War I, the AEF table of organization called for 250 men in a full infantry company—but by best estimates, the Lost Battalion's Lilliputian companies ranged between 18 and 101. Whittlesey also commanded headquarters, runners, and scouts from the 1st and 2nd Battalions, as well as C and D Companies from the 306th Machine Gun Battalion and a few medics. During the early morning of October 3, K Company from the 3rd Battalion, 307th Infantry Regiment would join the ragtag, undermanned unit. Perhaps as many as 700 soldiers served in the Lost Battalion.[14]

The great Allied push was well under way when Whittlesey advanced. Most of the 77th Division and French on their left had moved toward "the gates of hell" that morning. They trudged forward bravely, honorably, and in most cases disastrously. The 77th's 153rd and 154th Brigades advanced at different times, allowing the Germans to shift forces where they were most needed. Compounding the ineffectiveness of the poor timing, the attacking troops faced miles of barbed wire, well concealed machine gun nests, baffling sniper fire, and artillery barrages.

It was too much. To the east of Whittlesey's position, it was as if the 153rd Brigade had run into a wall of steel and lead. As willing as the soldiers were to fight and die, they were stopped cold by a more effectively deployed, more experienced German force. Most of the 154th Brigade—as well as the French forces on Whittlesey's left—did not fare much better. Shrouded by fog, surrounded by trees, struggling through thick undergrowth, and confused by fire coming from all directions, companies and even squads began to separate. Men lost their directions. They scurried about randomly, making easy targets for virtually invisible snipers and machine gunners. Germans killed or wounded hundreds of Americans, and captured many more. What General Pershing and his staff had planned neatly on maps back at headquarters looked very different on the battlefield.

The simple fact that war is not neat creates unseen and unanticipated opportunities for both sides. While Germans were meeting and overcoming French assaults to the left and Americans to the right of Whittlesey, the forces in front of him thinned. To be sure, the enemy troops facing his regiment had not lost their bite. Moving slowly forward on either side of a ravine below Hill 198, his men received withering fire. One American soldier recalled, "The bullets seemed to come from all directions. Even if you wanted to get behind a tree you couldn't tell which side of the tree to get on for safety."[15]

One by one Americans fell. It was slow going—a process of trial and error where a misstep or a wrong turn could cost a soldier his life. Through it all, Whittlesey kept his men moving forward. He sent his more experienced soldiers on missions to outflank machine gun nests and silence snipers, and encouraged his recent arrivals to advance. The sluggish, agonizing pace of the assault frustrated him, causing him at one point to order, "Advance until the last man drops!"[16]

And they did advance, while up and down the line other American and French forces had been stopped and even forced back by German artillery and counterattacks. Again, Whittlesey and his men were singularly fortunate. Not only had the enemy forces in front of him been depleted, the ravine he advanced along happened to be a border between two German units, a fragile seam where the enemy had not maintained a tight liaison. At great cost, Whittlesey's 308th Regiment slipped through that seam, overcoming the opposition in the forest, penetrating a kilometer behind German lines, and advancing across the Charlevaux Brook to the base of a steep hill below La Viergette-Moulin de Charlevaux road. During a day that had witnessed American and French forces struggle unsuccessfully to achieve Generals Foch and Pershing's goals, Major Whittlesey had miraculously accomplished his objective. As in Tennyson's "The Charge of the Light Brigade," he had, on the orders of his superiors, led his battalion into "the valley of Death."[17]

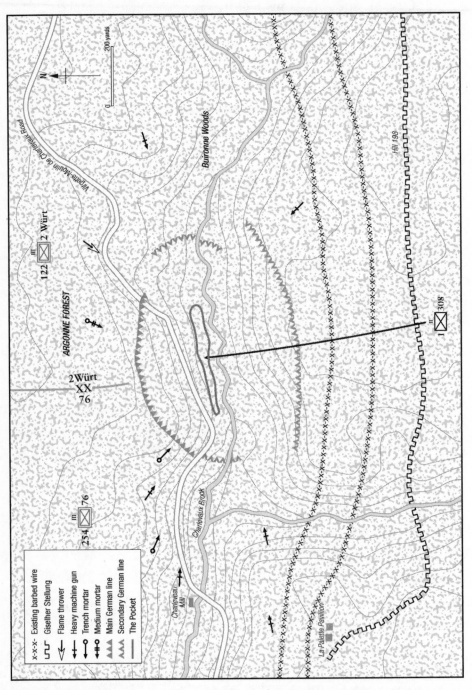

The Lost Battalion's Pocket, based on a map prepared by Captain Holderman.
(Credit: Bounford Studios.)

19

Into the Valley of Death

THE GRAY SKY WAS TURNING BLACK WHEN WHITTLESEY AND McMurtry decided to settle in for the night. They selected their terrain wisely. It was south of La Viergette–Moulin de Charlevaux road on a steep reverse slope, largely protecting them from German artillery. Although they were vulnerable to high-angle mortar, snipers, and machine gun assaults, neutralizing the Germans' deadly artillery was their primary goal. Mercifully, there was a source of water nearby, just meters from the camp. Muddy, dawdling, and weed infested, the Charlevaux Brook wasn't much, but it was better than nothing, especially to men with empty canteens and parched after a day of fear and intense combat. With safety in mind, Whittlesey told his men to spread out and set up defenses. He ordered his largest companies to protect the left and right flanks, and positioned his headquarters in the center of the outpost. The other companies filled in the rest of the site, and the men immediately began to dig protective funk holes in the rocky, root-laden ground. Most lacked entrenching equipment, but with Germans moving about on the road above them and bullets kicking up dirt around them, they dug fast using bayonets, helmets, spoons, and whatever else was at hand. When the temporary outpost was finished, it measured about three hundred feet long and sixty wide. It was there in that pocket that Charles Whittlesey and his men would earn their fame.[1]

Whittlesey strengthened "the Pocket" by placing his machine guns on the flanks, but the size of it was significant. Inside the oblong perimeter was an area roughly the size of a football field between the hash marks. With more than six hundred soldiers—and more soon to join his unit—the Lost Battalion mustered a tight defense that was difficult to penetrate. Whittlesey could throw considerable firepower in every direction, and shift troops quickly and effectively as the situation warranted. Nevertheless, the men were tightly packed, their small, hastily dug funk holes so near to one another that the doughboys could share the same toothpick. This meant that they frequently took hits from incoming mortar, machine gun, and sniper fire.[2]

The close quarters may have reflected Whittlesey's instinct to keep his men near him. By packing his companies in a tight pocket, he could move from one man to another freely—encouraging, imploring, advising, comforting. Yet as well intentioned as his care was, such ministrations more properly belonged to the junior officers and noncoms at the company, platoon, and squad level. By undertaking that work personally, Whittlesey was stretching himself thin.

Whittlesey did, however, rely on the support of his subordinates, few more so than his second in command, Captain George Gibson McMurtry Jr. He was built like a bulldog—thick, powerful, square-jawed—and absolutely fearless. The son of an Irish immigrant who embodied the rags-to-riches success story, McMurtry was a man of extremes. He possessed a warm, sympathetic nature and a violent temper. A fellow officer judged, "I don't believe that a braver or a more heroic soldier ever trod a battlefield. He was stern and determined but kind, and had a keen sense of humor. No sacrifice was too great for him to make for the comfort of his men. They all loved and honored him." Furthermore, as much as any soldier in New York's Own, he was through and through a true Son of Roosevelt.[3]

In 1898, a year before his class's graduation, he took a leave from Harvard to join TR's Rough Riders. In Cuba he fought in the Battle of Kettle Hill, but soon afterward contracted jungle fever and returned to Harvard, where he graduated with his class. After school, he plunged into Wall Street, assaulting the bond market as boldly as he had the San Juan Heights. By the age of thirty he was a millionaire, and a decade later he was ready for another challenge. Like Whittlesey, he attended the Plattsburg Camp, received a commission, and helped train the polyglot conscripts that showed up at Camp Upton. As he dropped pounds during training, he seemed to shed years. He was a boy again, radiating an infectious enthusiasm. It was an attitude he carried onto the battlefield. When he entered a room, he often announced, "Okay, I'm here. What's the dope?" He approached the Argonne with the same boundless energy.

McMurtry and Whittlesey shared a funk hole, and although the commander slept little, they both settled in on the night of October 2. It was bitter cold. When the 308th had gone into the Argonne on September 26, they had been ordered to move light and fast, discarding such niceties as blankets and overcoats. Consequently, soldiers suffered, shivering from the recurrent rainfall, their stomachs growling from hunger, and dreading noises in the brook below them and movements on the road above. Even for the bone weary, sleep came in spurts, and a firefight on the left flank didn't help matters.[4]

There was movement out in the forest, however. The Germans knew that an American force of indeterminate size had discovered an opening in the Giselher Stellung, their first main defensive line, and slipped through. Depending on the size of the task force and the ability of the Americans to reinforce it, the Lost Battalion presented a potentially catastrophic threat. Despite command problems that caused some delay, the Germans stitched tight the kilometer seam in their defensive line. At the same time, they surrounded the Pocket, positioning troops to attack the flanks, and deployed snipers, machine gunners, and trench mortars to the high ground in the front and the rear of the Lost Battalion. With the repositioning came additional troops. The *Amerikanernest* (American nest) had to be isolated, attacked, and ruthlessly eliminated.[5]

Learning of Whittlesey's success, General Johnson of the 154th Brigade became determined to protect the Lost Battalion. In a time when the Argonne offered nothing but great difficulty, somehow Whittlesey's force had reached its objective and established an island in the German sea. Johnson desperately needed to reinforce, secure, and build up the outpost. As a first step, he ordered the 307th Regiment forward toward the Pocket.

They moved several hours too late. Determined Wurttemberg troops stopped the advance, save for K Company led by Captain Nelson Holderman. That his company got through was not surprising. Holderman was a "soldier's soldier," a warrior who was born in Nebraska, enlisted as a private, and advanced through the ranks by dint of hard work, bravery, and love of army life. He was a character out of an adolescent adventure novel—a handsome, blue-eyed man, a risk-taker and joke-teller, the sort of combat soldier who inspired the poems of Rudyard Kipling. He was sick on the day he moved out for the Pocket and probably should have been under the care of a doctor—but then he would have missed out on the action, and as he told one of his officers, "he would rather die on the field than to have the men believe he was trying to avoid the heavy fighting."[6]

Company K, with acting commander Lieutenant Thomas Pool in the lead and Holderman in the rear, found one of Whittlesey's runner posts and advanced single file at a snail's pace toward the Pocket. Occasionally, out of the indigo night, they heard German voices. Yet seldom did any of the men have a clear view of anything. Still, they made it through, and by 4:00 a.m. stood on a ridge above the Charlevaux Valley. With a few hours until sunrise, Holderman gave his troops a couple hours' sleep, and then early the next morning led them into the Pocket. Company K's arrival placed some eighty additional men under Whittlesey's command.[7]

He positioned Company K on the vulnerable right flank, but more immediate concerns occupied his mind. Isolated on the side of a steep ravine, cocooned in a small, fortified pocket, he lacked the most basic military information. Where were his two companies that were supposed to be moving up the west side of the ravine? Where were the liaison units, the forces that were supposed to be on his right and left? Even more urgent, where were the Germans, and in what numbers?

On the morning of October 3, he sent units to gather information, and what they learned—only after suffering heavy casualties—was that Whittlesey's force was effectively isolated from immediate support, and that the Boche were everywhere. They controlled the hills to his north and south, and were probing flanks to the east and west. They were positioned to keep relief forces out and the 308th in. As far as the Germans were concerned, there was nothing at all "lost" about Whittlesey's battalion.

Meanwhile, the supplies were running thin. Whittlesey's men were hungry. Only some of the soldiers who had attacked on the 2nd had carried a day's rations. After sharing their meager supplies with their buddies, nothing remained. "All reserved rations had been consumed during the earlier phase of the advance," Whittlesey later wrote in his Operations Report. He also needed blankets, overcoats, and ammunition. By the early afternoon, the Germans had wiped out his carefully planted runner posts, and the only way he could communicate with divisional headquarters was via carrier pigeons. Using the one-way communication system, he requested "8,000 rounds of rifle ammunition, 7,500 chauchat, 23 boxes of machine gun ammunition, 250 offensive grenades." Meanwhile, the Germans were moving about and closing in fast.[8]

His situation was precarious and getting worse. Whittlesey did not even know if his pigeons were getting through to headquarters, and with his runners dead, wounded, or captured, he was out of touch with the generals in charge of the offensive. Furthermore, the German probing was becoming more intense—and deadlier. The Lost Battalion's position on a reverse slope meant that they were largely safe from German artillery, but enemy machine guns and *Minenwerfer* (trench mortars) were still a threat. Against this firepower, all his men could do was dig in deeper, keep their heads down, and pray.[9]

Whittlesey's options were shrinking. His only hope was relief from the outside, and although he could hear the rumble of distant American artillery, it was still far away from his forlorn ravine. Well behind the front, officers in divisional and corps headquarters were congratulating each other on Whittlesey's success, all but ignoring his immediate peril. He had gotten through, they said, and that was what mattered. He had achieved his objective. In the Pocket, however, the objective had changed. After consulting with McMurtry, the two leaders personally communicated the new goal to each company commander: "Our mission is to hold this position at all costs. No falling back. Have this understood by every man in your command."[10]

In midafternoon, "a shower of potato-masher grenades" splintered trees and exploded near the road above but close to the Lost Battalion. As the skirmish raged, Whittlesey released a carrier pigeon to divisional headquarters. "Situation on left flank very serious." But American rifle and Chauchat fire into the German position above the road silenced the grenades. About two hours later, American soldiers heard Germans near their position. A guttural voice called, "Rudolph?"

"*Hier*," came a whispered answer from the bushes near the Lost Battalion's left flank.

"Heinrich?" came another guttural call.

"*Ich bin hier.*"

The roll call continued until the commander shouted, "*Nun, alle zusammen*" (Now, all together).[11]

With that convenient warning, the Germans attacked both flanks, and more grenades rained in from the upper ridge. "The ravine rang with the echoes of machine guns, chauchats and rifles," noted one account. "Our machine guns worked splendidly and the enemy must have suffered heavy losses from this source alone." Attacked in force on both flanks, the Americans continued to fire.[12]

The fighting lasted until the deep forest began to darken. Although serious, the attack was merely one in a series of assaults as the Germans attempted to eliminate the Pocket. From October 3 through 7, they mounted eight significant assaults. All failed—for several reasons. To begin with, the fighting around the Pocket was a microcosm of the warfare on the Western Front more generally. Although the Germans surrounded the Lost Battalion, they could not destroy it with their artillery. To accomplish that mission, they had to attack an enemy adequately entrenched in rugged terrain. Many of the men in the 308th, especially those who had been part of the unit since Camp Upton, were good shots and experienced fighters. For Germans exposed during their assaults and lacking the numbers necessary, the Pocket was a tough nut to crack.[13]

Compounding the German's tactical problem was a larger operational one. The French were attacking to the west of the Pocket and the Americans to the east. Although the German artillery and infantry were repelling the Allied offensive, they needed the majority of available frontline troops and reserves to do so. The frontal assault by the 77th Division demanded the Germans' complete attention, and although potentially dangerous, the Pocket was now of secondary concern. The numbers, and perhaps even the will, needed to eliminate it were just not there. Until the end of the Lost Battalion's struggle, it remained isolated from the larger offensive but nevertheless impacted by it.[14]

There was no absence of will inside the Pocket. It was as if everything outside of their 300-by-60-foot perimeter had ceased to exist. Inside, survival was all that mattered. There was no food, except what meager morsels the men could forage, and they lacked blankets and overcoats to keep warm during the cold nights. Though they had gone into the Pocket well stocked with ammunition, the onslaught of enemy attacks had drained their supply. Soon the need for machine gun ammunition and grenades became critical. The three medical corpsmen administering to the wounded lacked virtually everything needed on a battlefield. There were no anesthetics or disinfectants, nor were there any fresh bandages; if a soldier died, a corpsmen used his soiled wraps on the next casualty. Water was also a problem. Although they camped near the Charlevaux Brook and had discovered a small spring, the Germans covered those sites with machine gunners and snipers. After a German shot one doughboy attempting to fill a canteen for a wounded comrade, Whittlesey posted a guard to prevent daytime missions to the brook.[15]

Even before the late afternoon German assault of October 3, Whittlesey called for help. Since the Lost Battalion had moved forward the day before, nine soldiers had been killed and 140 wounded, reducing their force of able-bodied soldiers by about 25 percent. The wounded, noted the regiment's history, "strove to grit the little devils of pain and anguish between their teeth, but there were moans and half suppressed cries in the dark along the hillside every night." McMurtry visited one soldier who had taken a stomach shot. "It pains like hell Captain, but I'll keep as quiet as I can," he said. Still, others could not suppress their screams of pain, and drew bursts of German machine gun fire.[16]

If any of the Americans thought it couldn't get worse, they were mistaken. Although on the morning of October 4 it appeared to Whittlesey that the Boche had withdrawn troops during the night, the status of the Lost Battalion remained critical. "Many wounded here whom we can't evacuate," he noted in his 7:45 a.m. pigeon message to headquarters. "Need rations badly." At 10:55 he sent another plea: "Men are suffering from hunger and exposure; the wounded are in very bad condition. Cannot support be sent at once?"[17]

In the afternoon, the arrival of American artillery heartened the Lost Battalion. Behind their position, American shells began to fall on a ridge, gradually increasing in intensity and creeping forward. The beleaguered Lost Battalion cheered as the shells tore into German positions on Hill 198. Then the shelling crossed the bottom of the ravine, throwing mud and water from the Charlevaux Brook into the air in geysers. Finally, amazingly, it slammed into the Lost Battalion. Whittlesey had chosen the site for his camp partially because the reverse slope offered protection against German artillery to the north. Unfortunately, it was defenseless against American artillery coming from the south.[18]

Inside the Pocket, recalled Whittlesey and McMurtry, it was "an inferno of noise, dust and confusion." Men jumped into the nearest funk hole, which in many cases collapsed under the ferocity of the shelling, burying the occupants. Holderman remembered the utter confusion, the mind-numbing terror of the moment. "When the men would endeavor to shift their positions in order to avoid the shells, enemy machine gunners and snipers would rake the position. German trench mortars threw in their shells, which added to the fury of the friendly fire." Private John W. Nell recalled, "There was absolutely nothing we could do. We had to just take what came, knowing without a doubt that it was our own artillery . . . Everyone was expecting the next shell to get him. There were many direct hits blowing men to pieces and wounding dozens more."[19]

Whittlesey did not seek cover. Instead, ranging across the hillside, running in a stooping gait, he tried to calm his men. He said that the barrage could not last much longer, that if they just held on it would be over soon. But it wasn't. A couple minutes stretched into ten, then twenty. Whittlesey had to try something. Concentrating, a small shrapnel wound causing a stream of blood to run down the side of his nose, he quickly scribbled a message:

We are along the road parallel 276.4
Our artillery is dropping a barrage directly on us.
For heaven's sake, stop it.

He gave the note to Private Omar Richards, who was in charge of the pigeons. Richards wrapped the message into a tiny aluminum tube and reached into a cage for one of the last two remaining pigeons. A shell exploded. The bird escaped Richards's grip and flew away. He grabbed the last bird, a two-year-old black and gray checkered one named Cher Ami. He fastened the message and released the pigeon into the air. But Cher Ami chose not to fly immediately home. Instead, he perched in a shrapnel-scarred tree and watched the tumult below, resisting Richards and Whittlesey's entreaties to fly. Richards shouted. He threw a stick. He scrambled out of his hole, ran toward the tree, and began to climb, finally reaching a position where he could shake Cher Ami's branch. Only then did the bird take off, circling several times to get its bearings before heading home. Although it was knocked down by an explosion, lost an eye and leg, and had a hole in its chest, Cher Ami made it back to its loft with Whittlesey's message hanging from the torn tendon of its missing leg.[20]

The shelling stopped. An artilleryman with the 152nd Field Artillery claimed they had already completed "what little shooting" they had scheduled for the day. Yet the men of the Lost Battalion credited Whittlesey and Cher Ami for ending the friendly fire. The barrage had lasted two hours, killing or wounding thirty soldiers. By then, Whittlesey had lost more than a third of his men, and during the next three days others would fall, victims of German bullets, mortars, and flamethrowers, as well as bacteria, infection, dysentery, and hunger.

Furthermore, bad luck stalked the Lost Battalion. On October 6, after the US 50th Aero Squadron located the 308th, pilots attempted something they had not done before: resupply from the air. That Sunday, the pilots dropped packages attached to parachutes near Whittlesey's position. They were full of food, ammunition, medical supplies, and even more carrier pigeons—altogether one thousand pounds of desperately needed goods.

But they did not land near enough. The pilots did their best, flying low into the German field of fire at considerable risk. Yet their drops never reached the Lost Battalion. Several reasons could account for the failure, including the small size of the Pocket, pilots misjudging the wind and their own airspeed, or an inability to determine coordinates from the air. Whatever the reasons, in a cruel twist of fate, the only beneficiaries of the drops were the Germans, who eagerly accepted the gifts. A member of the German 254th Regiment observed, "It would not be an understatement of the pure joy that we experienced as these supplies fell into our hands. We were greeted by packages of chocolate and tobacco pouches . . . these were gifts fit for a king."[21]

By October 7, Whittlesey's soldiers were near their breaking point. Lack of food had drained their energy, and too little water had compounded the problem. Some became apathetic, others moved about in confused states. Suffering from what later would be termed "battle fatigue" or "combat exhaustion," many evinced signs of psychological trauma, including anxiety and nightmares. Psychological studies of the impact of military disasters on individual soldiers maintain that as casualties rise, group cohesion declines. Yet somehow in the claustrophobic Pocket, surrounded by experienced German soldiers, harassed at every turn, unable even to fill a canteen without fear of enemy bullets—somehow the men of the Lost Battalion maintained discipline and group integrity.[22]

Leadership was the reason. As the commander, Whittlesey's consistency and calm presence held the Lost Battalion together. On one level, he continued to be the same stickler for regulations that he had been at Camp Upton. Rules were rules, even during the most trying times in the Pocket. If he saw a soldier relieving himself behind a tree, Whittlesey told him to use the latrine or face punishment, as if there were any disciplinary measure that could make life worse than it already was inside their perimeter. Throughout it all, he remained outwardly the perfect Yankee gentleman.[23]

Sometimes even his references betrayed his exceptional Williams/Harvard education, which distanced him from his men who hailed from the East Side of New York City and the mountains and plains of the West. Once, after a deadly skirmish, Whittlesey and his troops heard Chauchat fire from beyond Hill 198. It was distant and vague, but a clear sign that American troops were engaging the enemy and moving, however slowly, toward them. Listen, Whittlesey told the men near him, the sound was "like the pipes at Lucknow." The allusion to John Greenleaf Whittier's "The Pipes at Lucknow," about the lifting of a siege during the Sepoy Rebellion, was undoubtedly lost to all except perhaps McMurtry and a few other Plattsburg graduates. But the remark was typical of Whittlesey, who even surrounded by death perhaps recalled the lines:

Sweet sounds the Gaelic pibroch
O'er mountain, glen, and glade;
But the sweetest of all music
The pipes at Lucknow played![24]

By his punctiliousness, his courtly manners, his literary references, and his outwardly calm demeanor, Whittlesey remained steadfastly consistent. Certainly, he must have suffered. Although he seemed never to sleep, he did occasionally drift off late at night. One soldier who slept next to him later confided that the commander cried in his sleep. Nevertheless, because he was a stiff leader, his men initially tended to view him as nothing "more than a local tyrant, a kind of drill-sergeant with brass on his shoulders."[25]

But life and death in the Pocket, packed together in a small hell, changed the soldiers' view of Whittlesey. They discovered that beneath his chilly exterior he cared intensely about every man under his command. Morning and night, he made rounds of the camp, moving from one funk hole to the next, offering a word of encouragement and promise of relief. This was especially true during his visits with the wounded men. Even more remarkably, Whittlesey did not disappear into his funk hole during the daily mortar assaults. When soldiers lifted their heads to peek outside their holes, they often saw their long-legged major darting from position to position, giving orders and advice "like the worried president of a corporation, perfectly oblivious of the noise and death all around him." With a wry sense of understated humor, he often said to the doughboys, "Remember, there are two million Americans pushing up to relieve us."[26]

Perhaps no one appreciated Whittlesey more than McMurtry. They were ostensibly as different as tea with cream and sugar and black coffee. Whittlesey was reserved, McMurtry outgoing; Whittlesey cool, McMurtry passionate; Whittlesey a man of rules, McMurtry a rebel. Yet they both were natural leaders. Plattsburg had not *made* either one. And they had each other's back—sometimes quite literally. In one skirmish with the Germans, a potato-masher grenade exploded behind McMurtry, and its wooden handle embedded into the captain's back. Suffering pain from another wound, he didn't notice the new one until Whittlesey pulled out the shard of wood.[27]

By October 7, the fifth day in the Pocket, even Whittlesey had difficulty buoying flagging spirits. Everything save misery was in short supply or gone. Hungry men crawled outside the perimeter scavenging for bits of food from the pockets of dead Germans. Exhausted burial details had given up trying to dig graves in the rocky soil and just covered the dead with some dirt and leaves. Wounded men, many still ambulatory and in the line, reeked of gangrene. Ammunition was all but gone. More than half of their machine guns, essential in warding off enemy attacks, were out of commission. Some of the finest lieutenants and sergeants were dead. There was not much to say or do, though some soldiers wrote farewells on scraps of paper. Others rolled leaves in their yellow message paper and smoked them. One use seemed about as good as the other. Although determined to hold their ground, they knew they could not hold it much longer.[28]

In spite of the suffering and the sense of impending doom, Holderman noted that "the morale and discipline of the command was high" and many still entertained hopes for relief. Whittlesey put the effective strength of the Lost Battalion at 275 that morning, but that obviously included men like Holderman and McMurtry who were still on duty having suffered multiple wounds. The number of unwounded soldiers was about two hundred. Yet when the Germans attacked that morning, anyone who was ambulatory "dragged themselves to firing positions, and in their eagerness to hold the enemy out of position, soon forgot their wounds." Once again, they forced the Germans to retreat.[29]

That afternoon, the Germans tried a different ploy. Lieutenant Heinrich Prinz, an intelligence officer who had once lived in Spokane, Washington, advanced a peaceful solution to the problem of the Lost Battalion. First, he interrogated Private Lowell Hollingshead, a recently captured member of the Lost Battalion. Prinz was a "well dressed and handsome" man who spoke perfect English and appeared more a friend than an enemy. He had a doctor treat Hollingshead's leg wounds, fed him a hearty meal of black bread, vegetables, and meat, and offered him a gold-tipped cigarette. "We were for all the world like host and guest rather than an officer and captured enemy soldier," remembered Hollingshead.[30]

Prinz had a proposal. He prefaced it by admitting that he admired the American stand—their courage, their commitment, their steadfastness. He had witnessed their bravery, and heard the cries of their wounded. Yet it was all in vain. "The Germans felt it was absolutely suicidal for the American detachment to persist in its defense," Prinz later said. He then asked Hollingshead to take a message, a surrender request, to the Lost Battalion's commander. After some hesitation, the American agreed.

Hollingshead departed the German position blindfolded and leaning on a cane that Prinz had given him, along with two packs of cigarettes and some German bread. Guards led him to the Charlevaux road and removed his blindfold. From there, under a white flag of truce, he limped into the Pocket. It was about 4:00 p.m. when an American sentry escorted him to Whittlesey and McMurtry's funk hole. Holderman happened to be there as well. Whittlesey took the message, telling Hollingshead to go back into the American line where he belonged.

Whittlesey read the letter, typed in English on an excellent sheet of paper. It complimented Hollingshead as "an honorable fellow, doing honour to his father-land in the strictest sense of the word." More important, it requested that Whittlesey's unit surrender since "it would be quite useless to resist any more in view of the present conditions. The suffering of your wounded men can be heared [sic] over here in the German lines and we are appealing to your human sentiments." It added that "a white flag shown by one of your men will tell us that you agree with these conditions." The letter was signed, "The German Commanding Officer."

Whittlesey read the note and handed it to McMurtry. He read it and passed it to Holderman. The three looked at each other. They smiled—"for there was humor," Whittlesey later wrote, "both sardonic and typically Teutonic, in the words, 'We are appealing to your human sentiments.'" After daily savage assaults, relentless mortar and machine gun activity, snipers picking off doughboys when they tried to get a canteen full of muddy water, flamethrowers breathing on Americans like dragons, verbal jests employed as psychological weapons—after all this, the German commander thought about "human sentiments." And yes, the Lost Battalion had fought with the same grim determination to kill Germans, though they lacked the arsenal of weapons. Yet for the three American officers, what "a strange appeal it seemed from an enemy who for five days killed or wounded more than fifty per cent of our besieged command."

"Legend," Holderman later wrote, "has made famous the reply: 'Go to Hell,' which Major Whittlesey is reported to have hurled at the Germans upon reading the demand for surrender." In truth, he gave no answer, though he did order two white airplane panels used for airdrops to be immediately taken down to ensure that the Germans did not mistake them as signs for surrender. No reply, of course, was a resounding one, as eloquent as "Go to Hell."

Across the length of the Pocket, news of the letter and Whittlesey's response spread. Exhausted, starving soldiers took heart. "The men began to call out to the Germans, inviting them to come over and take the command if they wanted it," Holderman recalled.

Whittlesey did not waste time lingering over the letter. He prepared for the German response by redeploying men for an expected attack. Now desperately low on ammunition and machine guns, his soldiers began shining their bayonets in the wet dirt, expecting that hand-to-hand combat would be the final act of the siege.[31]

They came over the cliffs on the left front, supported by machine guns, snipers, and trench mortars. Americans, many wounded and barely able to stand, took positions on the firing line, aiming at the advancing soldiers. Men too weak to fire loaded rifles for their comrades. Unable to break through, the Germans assaulted the right flank with "liquid fire," throwing flames into two companies, burning the flesh off several Americans. But rather than disorganizing the men on the flank, it angered them. They rose out of their funk holes and charged, killing the Germans manning the flamethrowers. "It seemed that the enemy must come over," Holderman remembered, "but the [Germans] made one last effort and . . . fell back, never to come again."[32]

The Pocket was a small world unto itself, but that day the Meuse-Argonne Offensive began to intrude upon it. The US 82nd Division had begun an attack into the Argonne, threatening the German position around the Lost Battalion. If the Germans remained above the Charlevaux road, they might find themselves encircled and cut off—exactly the same fate that the Lost Battalion had suffered. Following orders, they fell back, allowing units of the 77th Division to finally reach and relieve the 308th.[33]

It was dark and cold in the Pocket on the night of October 7. "The hopeless seriousness of the situation was beginning to penetrate even the stoutest hearts," Whittlesey and McMurtry wrote in a classic understatement. "It [looked] as if the Battalion was abandoned to its fate."[34]

As the Lost Battalion prepared for another night, First Lieutenant Frederick Tillman of the 307th and a couple of scouts stumbled into the outer reaches of the Pocket. He was overwhelmed by the stench. It smelled like a glue factory. There were dead and decomposing soldiers everywhere, though it was too dark to get a good look. He tripped into a shell hole. A man "cried at him like a puppy," and his comrade lunged at Tillman with his bayonet. Tillman saw that they were Americans. "I'm looking for Major Whittlesey," he said.[35]

"I don't give a damn who you are and what you want," the man replied. "You just step on my buddy again and I'll kill you."

About the same time, Whittlesey and McMurtry were sitting in their funk hole talking quietly. A runner approached, breathless after scrambling down the steep right flank. An American officer was nearby, the runner reported—"He says that he wants to see the commanding officer."

Whittlesey met with Tillman, and learned that relief had finally arrived. Dressed in a clean uniform, Tillman gave the hungry commander a sandwich. Soon after, McMurtry arrived. "For God's sake, give me a bite of that!" he cried.

20

"Please Don't Write About Me"

THE SCENE AT THE POCKET LOOKED LIKE SOMETHING OUT OF THE Seventh Circle of Dante's *Inferno*, on the banks of the river of boiling blood where patrols shoot arrows at anyone who attempts to escape. Except it was worse than that—and it was not imagined or allegorical.

Before the soldiers of the relief party reached the Pocket, they could smell it. "The stench was unbearable," recalled an officer. Even medics, long accustomed to the odors of war, held handkerchiefs over their mouths and noses. Corpses in various stages of decomposition covered the ground. The ones just outside the Pocket were German, too close to American positions for their comrades to retrieve and bury. Then came the Americans, some partially stripped because their clothes were needed for bandages, others buried in pathetically shallow graves. Flames had charred some beyond recognition; artillery and mortar shells had done the same to others. Many in Major Whittlesey's command literally had been blown to bits, and fragments of hands, arms, legs, and other body parts lay scattered about. Mixed with the smell of death was the odor of vomit and excrement from soldiers racked by dysentery, as well as the sharp sulfur smell of fired cartridges—"My God! It was pitiable," said a rescuer.[1]

After all the booming chaos of the previous days, the Pocket seemed eerily quiet, save for some distant German artillery fire. Rain dripped off leaves. Wounded men moaned lowly. Some gave muffled cries for help. They were so weak from dehydration and starvation that most could not muster the energy to make much of a racket. Well-fed members of the relief party were louder, stomping through the brush, slipping in the steep terrain, coughing from the overpowering smell of the place as they spread out and began to examine and triage the wounded.

While they worked, Whittlesey's men looked on numbly. "The men sat and stared with drawn faces," commented one of the rescuers, "burning eyes, tense jaws, but with the idea of resistance fixed in their minds." Many were too weak to crawl out of their funk holes, which in many cases they shared with a dead comrade. Traumatized, soldiers seemed to gaze without seeing, and to watch without understanding. A member of the relief unit accidently stepped on a wounded man. "He merely looked at me and asked for a cigarette—his face was tense and drawn."[2]

Whittlesey took charge. Up before the others, he made his way to the creek where he shaved and washed, struggling to clean his face and uniform in the cold water. Then he started to move from one of his men to the next, distributing corn willie and hardtack like communion wafers, mumbling a few words like a warrior priest delivering a benediction, giving comfort where he could. Yet he was fragile himself—and tightly wound. Someone offered him a sip of brandy, but the glass flask slipped from his shaking hands and broke on the rocky ground—a small accident, but nevertheless Whittlesey apologized profusely.[3]

Soon General Robert Alexander, commander of the 77th Division, made his way by car and foot to the Pocket, wandering across the shelled and bloody battlefield searching for Whittlesey. Before the major could raise his hand to salute, the general grabbed it. "How do you do? From now on you are Lieutenant-Colonel Whittlesey," he erupted.[4]

Hardly looking at the general, Whittlesey mumbled a few words of thanks. An awkward pause followed. In the silence, Alexander looked at the terrain—trees scarred and splintered but still providing a thick cover. "Well," he finally said, "I can certainly see why the airplanes couldn't find this place."[5]

"Well, General, the artillery certainly found it, sir," commented Private Philip Cepaglia.

"Oh no," Alexander wrongly answered. "That was French artillery."

Clearly, the clean-shaved general in a spotless uniform was unable to engage directly with soldiers who had been through the worst conditions of the war. Whittlesey lacked the words to bridge the chasm. Instead, he mentioned the German's surrender request, then retrieved the letter and handed it to Alexander. The general read it but made no comment.

Despite the sense of relief at the rescue of the Lost Battalion, the Meuse-Argonne Offensive was not going well. Instead of a rapid breakthrough, it had devolved into a bloody meat grinder. Yet sometime during his meeting with Whittlesey or soon afterward, Alexander had an inspired thought. As he moved about the Pocket, talking with soldiers, learning more about their commander, he concluded that Whittlesey was an extraordinary man. A hero, he must have thought, or at least as close to one as he had seen in the conflict. Wars demanded heroes. Americans needed heroes. The army and Congress had designed Distinguished Service Crosses and Medals of Honor with such men in mind. It did not take him long to become convinced that publicizing Whittlesey's heroics would advance America's mission in the war.[6]

Medals, however, held no interest for Whittlesey. He fretted about his men. Along with Captains McMurtry and Holderman, he slogged through the muddy patch at the bottom of the hill, helping the wounded and directing their evacuation. McMurtry had taken a bullet through his knee and limped painfully, and the hole in his back was open and bleeding; Holderman had sustained seven separate wounds, most of which had become infected, and he leaned heavily on crutches made from two broken rifles. Both, however, refused to leave. They remained alongside Whittlesey, administering comfort to their men, until the final dead soldier had been buried and the last injured one had been hauled from the field. Occasionally, for the first time in days, a patch of sun penetrated the primordial gloom of the deep pocket. McMurtry later claimed that during a pause, Whittlesey murmured to him, "We will never again be in finer company than we are right now."[7]

By 3:00 in the afternoon, the most severely wounded had left the Pocket. Now Whittlesey followed, leading 193 officers and men back out of "the jaws of death," returning to a place where they could get a cup of coffee, a smoke, a plate of food, a shower, and a night's sleep. One authority estimated that there had been 694 men in the ravine when the assault commenced at 7:00 a.m. on October 3. By 3:00 p.m. on October 8, 456 had been killed or wounded, or were missing in action, or too gravely ill to walk. Robert J. Laplander put the casualty rate at 66 percent; in his *Memories of the World War*, General Alexander said 60 percent; and other scholars have put the number above 70 percent. The exact figures are irretrievable, but the casualties exceeded even those described in Tennyson's "Charge of the Light Brigade."[8]

WHILE WHITTLESEY MARCHED HIS COLUMN to the Depôt des Machines, past Signal Corps photographers and cinematographers and weeping soldiers, General Alexander entertained a bevy of reporters who had been following the Lost Battalion story. Damon Runyon, a former sports reporter now working as the *New York American* war correspondent, led a pack that also included Thomas M. Johnson of the *New York Sun* and Will Irwin of the *Saturday Evening Post*. They had seldom seen Alexander in such a friendly, talkative mood. He compared the Lost Battalion's stand favorably with the Alamo, and even showed the reporters the German commanding officer's letter pleading with Whittlesey to surrender. After reading it carefully, Johnson asked the pertinent question: "And what did Whittlesey tell them?"

"What *would* he tell 'em?" the general answered. "He told 'em to go to hell."[9]

The New York reporters had the biggest American story in the war—and it was a New York story. Soldiers in New York's own 77th Division, surrounded by overwhelming German forces, had dug in, confronted artillery shells, machine gun fire, snipers, and flamethrowers—and refused to surrender. Running short on ammunition, suffering crippling losses, shot up, half-starved, nearly dying of thirst, they had battled on, refusing to surrender, ready like the Texans at the Alamo to give their last courageous drop of blood for the dream of a finer world. And who were these men? Italians, Irishmen, and Jews from the Lower East Side, the Bowery, and the Bronx, along with some farm boys from farther west, commanded by a Harvard-educated former Rough Rider and a Wall Street lawyer dubbed "Go to Hell" Whittlesey.

That was surely an irresistible story. Thomas Johnson wrote years later, "Millions of Americans were throwing down their newspapers to give three rousing cheers for 'Go-To-Hell Whittlesey' and the 'Lost Battalion.' . . . Whoever invented that story was a genius at wartime propaganda. He could have put into the mouth of the New England lawyer no words that would more endear him and his men to average Americans—or more inflame their spirit."[10]

The journalists had all but written their stories by the time they met Whittlesey later that afternoon. He was in the open air, resting, but got to his feet when he saw them approaching. Runyon thought he looked every bit the lawyer that he was—"a tall, lean-flanked fellow, around forty years old. He had a funny little smile." Immediately he held up a hand and made a simple request: "Please do not write about me. Write about these men."[11]

With that, he began answering questions, deflecting ones about his experiences and dwelling on the sacrifices of his soldiers. When a reporter asked whether he had really said, "Go to Hell," Whittlesey denied that he had. Yet, Runyon wrote, "he smiled [a] little smile" when he answered. It was the smile of a reluctant hero, the sort of leader who did what circumstances demanded, never seeking glory and never wanting it. What he did not realize, of course, was that his very reluctance to take credit was his most appealing trait. The more he tried to deflect and escape, the more he could not.[12]

Whittlesey's reticence, his steadfast refusal to talk about himself, made it easier for journalists to fill in the empty spaces. A reporter for the *New York Sun*, for instance, wrote that on the fourth day in the Pocket, "long foodless and almost wholly without ammunition and . . . weak from exhaustion," the surrender note arrived. "Whittlesey did not hesitate a fraction of a second," the writer noted. "'Go to Hell!' he almost shouted," as his beleaguered men cheered in response. Journalists introduced *this* Charles Whittlesey to American readers only a few days after the return of the Lost Battalion. It was the language of Davy Crockett and Teddy Roosevelt. Loud. Defiant. A swashbuckling tribute to American manhood.[13]

There was an element of bravado in the initial stories about Whittlesey, but it was balanced by his proper New England manners. He was "as quiet as a mouse," said Mrs. G. Sullivan, who ran the New York boarding house where he lived, affirming, "He never was a swearing man. Not a single oath did I hear out of him in the seven years he was there, and I've seen him looking for a collar button at that." In her opinion, his response to the German officer's note was not exactly swearing. "It was just what I would call very good advice."[14]

Whittlesey's makeshift battalion added to the allure of his story. Although he never used the name Lost Battalion, Whittlesey emphasized their diverse composition, feeding the narrative that the reporters wanted. "The one-time counter jumpers, brokers' clerks, gangsters, newsboys, truck drivers, collegians, peddlars and what not . . . ," Runyon wrote with considerable exaggeration, "served as the anchor of the whole advance." The *New York Globe* labeled the 77th Division "an eastside division, and to be even more explicit a Yiddish division," and the *American Hebrew* praised "the spiritual stuff of which the erstwhile needleworkers, peddlars, and ghetto dreamers are made." For Runyon and the other journalists, the Lost Battalion affirmed the tenacity of the nation's melting pot

Men of the Lost Battalion, 308th Infantry, 77th Division, resting near Apremont. Almost all of them received only a brief break before returning to frontline action in the Meuse-Argonne Offensive. Whittlesey would soon return to America, but most of his men would stay in France for the duration of the war. *(Courtesy of the National Archives.)*

army. All the better, thought many of the journalists, that "a true son of Roosevelt" commanded the battalion of brash immigrants.[15]

The Meuse-Argonne Offensive rolled on. The action in the Charlevaux Valley was little more than a pinprick in the massive battle. Several days after the 308th and the other components of the Lost Battalion came out of the line, General Alexander sent many of them back to the front. But without Whittlesey. His fighting had ended on that swampy, sunken patch of French soil. The 77th Division Headquarters reassigned their new lieutenant colonel to help reorganize their reserves. Sent to a "charming little ravine" shaded by greenwoods, where he enjoyed "real fresh beef, and marmalade and coffee," Whittlesey wrote that "the war practically ended for me."[16]

Soon he received orders to return to Regimental Headquarters "to do some regular lieutenant coloneling," and after bouncing from one comfortable village to another, on October 31 he was told that he was heading home to help organize and train a new regiment. On November 4, aboard the USS *Plattsburg*, he sailed for America. On November 14, he arrived in Hoboken. It was while he was at sea, nearing Newfoundland, that he learned of the signing of an armistice that ended the war. What he still did not know was that his own story had become a national sensation.[17]

Reporters waiting for "Go to Hell" Whittlesey at the dock anticipated more war stories punctuated by memorable quotes. They were disappointed. Without a hint of swagger or bluster, he relayed the broad outline of his story. His battalion advanced to their designated spot, faced staggering enemy machine gun and mortar fire, and found themselves surrounded. Out of food and short on ammunition at that point, he said, "it was simply a matter of sticking there"—an odd, understated phrase for their terrible and heroic stand. He did not elaborate much on his memorable response, saying only, "We didn't send back a message at all. We simply told the messenger to go to hell. Perhaps he went. I don't know."[18]

With his factual recounting of the battle, he undoubtedly thought, his story would end, swallowed by the more important news of November 11, 1918. What he failed to take into account, however, was the American public's appetite for a story like his.

21

Armistice

THE BAND MIGHT AS WELL HAVE PLAYED TAPS AS THE BALLPLAY-
ers left the field at Fenway Park. After the World Series, a Boston writer declared baseball dead "until universal peace shall have
been imposed upon the world and the unspeakable Hun put down
where he belongs"—reflecting a broad consensus among the
sporting press. Harry Frazee, hoping to win over Americans who
denounced slacker ballplayers and greedy owners, proposed entertaining the troops overseas with another series between the Red
Sox and Cubs, but Ban Johnson and the government rejected the
idea. Publicly, he expressed confidence that his club would open
the gates at Fenway the following spring, but in reality neither he
nor any of the other owners knew whether it would be possible to
field teams, given the government's "work or fight" order.[1]

A day after the Series ended, grumbling Boston players col-
lected their playoff checks and scattered to the wind. Harry Hooper
boarded a westbound train for his ranch in California. Carl Mays
got married and awaited his draft call. Fred Thomas returned
to the navy. George Whiteman found work in ground aviation.
Joe Bush, Wally Schang, Amos Strunk, and Wally Mayer began
touring New England as the "Red Sox," organizing exhibitions

that helped them recover their reduced playoff shares. American League rules, however, prohibited the pennant winners from barnstorming. Frazee reminded the press—and the public—that the players were profiting from a product that did not belong to them. "It's not the Red Sox team," he said. "They have no right to use the club's name or call these players the world's champions."[2]

The barnstorming "Red Sox" were not the only players benefitting from their notoriety. Babe Ruth also planned to profit from his growing celebrity. In the days after the Series, he acted as the official starter for a motorcycle race, refereed a boxing match, and pitched exhibition games in Connecticut. He contemplated making movies and appearing on the vaudeville stage, but the "work or fight" order lingered, and that meant that his best bet finding "essential" work was playing baseball in the industrial leagues. On September 25, 1918, he signed with Charles Schwab's Bethlehem Steel plant in Lebanon, Pennsylvania. "It looks as though it's hard work all winter for me," Ruth wrote Eddie Hurley of the *Boston Evening Record*. "All the boys have gone to work at some essential occupation and of course I'm big enough to do my bit. Before it's all over, I may be 'over there' yet."[3]

Ruth did not really believe he'd be fighting "over there" anytime soon, and he hardly worked at the Lebanon plant. He expected to play baseball and get paid for it. Years later, a Bethlehem worker complained that Babe and the other ballplayers avoided real work. They just played ball, as everyone suspected. "Babe Ruth used to show up at the plant an hour before practice. He'd be wearing fancy trousers, silk shirts and patent-leather shoes. He'd just walk around talking to people about baseball. There wasn't anything essential about what he was doing."[4]

Ruth played sporadically for the Lebanon team. There's little surviving evidence that proves exactly how many games he played, but he was back in Baltimore in early October. His playing time may have been limited after he singed his hand in a kitchen accident. But his extended disappearance from the team was more likely caused by a bout of Spanish influenza. By early October, Baltimore's city hospitals overflowed with flu victims and could no longer accept new patients. As in Boston, the city's health commissioner issued an order closing the theaters and prohibiting public gatherings. He also restricted the business hours of retail stores, though he allowed saloons to remain open—good news for the Ruth family business. In Pig Town, Ruth's old neighborhood, the grippe tore through the crowded, miserable hovels. The malignancy coursed throughout the city, spread by passengers on streetcars, rail yard workers, and the sailors whose ships docked at the piers.[5]

On October 16, the *New York Times* reported that the grippe had become a national crisis. "Spanish influenza now has reached epidemic proportions in practically every state in the country . . . Reports made public tonight by the public health service show that outside of Massachusetts, the epidemic is severe throughout New England." By that time, more than 3,500 Bostonians had died from the flu, including sportswriters Edward Martin and Harry Casey. Yet on October 20, Boston officials announced that the worst had passed and ended the closure order. Two days later, the city health commissioner declared that Boston's epidemic had finally ended, though officials implored people to remain cautious.[6]

After being confined to their homes for three weeks, Bostonians were desperate for fresh air, sunshine, and entertainment. Huge crowds flocked to the theaters and movie houses. Ticket sales boomed; many theaters had to turn away customers. Patrons swarmed cafés and saloons as well, celebrating the end of the closure order with suds and spirits.[7]

All told, Boston suffered nearly 4,800 fatalities from influenza and pneumonia by the end of the year. At a time when the nation had a population of about 105 to 110 million, the pandemic of 1918 and 1919 took the lives of more than 675,000 Americans—only a fraction of the estimated 50 million deaths worldwide. The virus killed with "extraordinary ferocity and speed," John Barry wrote in *The Great Influenza*. "Although the influenza pandemic stretched over two years, perhaps two-thirds of the deaths occurred . . . from mid-September to early December 1918."[8]

During those months, Babe Ruth and Harry Frazee both contracted the virus, as did about a quarter of all Americans. Fortunately, both recovered in a few weeks. Ruth spent much of the winter at his farm cottage in Sudbury, where he regained his strength. He built up his body that winter chopping pine trees, splitting wood, and shouldering logs. Always restless, Ruth pursued entertainment wherever he could find it—he enjoyed hunting, but fell when he tried playing hockey. He tried skiing, too, but grew weary after one incident in which he flew into the air, came crashing down, and ripped a hole in the seat of his pants.[9]

When Ruth got bored, he threw parties or invited children from an orphanage for a day of games. Ruth's wife, Helen, had hoped that a quiet life in the country, twenty miles away from Boston, might bring them closer together. She disliked the crowds and the spotlight that her husband drew whenever they went out in the city. Perhaps, she thought, Sudbury would be different. Perhaps, she would have him all to herself. "Someday people are going to find I've kidnapped my own husband and run away someplace where we can lead a simple life, away from grandstands and managers and photographers," she said.[10]

But Babe did not share Helen's fantasy. He loved the attention and the company of fawning women. He was always on the go, searching for his next adventure.

BY EARLY NOVEMBER, THE ALLIES knew that it was only a matter of time before Germany surrendered. On November 6, 1918, Supreme Allied Commander Marshal Foch received a peace proposal from Berlin. While Foch waited for the German delegation in his parked train car in the forest of Compiègne, a town fifty miles northeast of Paris, he ordered the Allied troops to hold fire so that the peace party could safely approach French lines. Somehow, a United Press correspondent named William Philip Simms mistakenly perceived the momentary truce in that single sector as the beginning of a general ceasefire. In a rush of excitement, he wired a garbled message back to New York: "URGENT ARMI-STICE ALLIES GERMANY SIGNED ELEVEN SMORNING

HOSTILITIES CEASED TWO SAFTERNOON SEDAN TAKEN SMORNONG BY AMERICANS."[11]

In New York, the bulletin rang like a fire alarm. The streets erupted with parades of jubilation. Newsboys waving special editions alerted the city: "Germany surrenders! Peace! War is over!" Suddenly, the workday stopped. "In the offices of Wall Street, in the great department stores uptown, in the loft buildings and sweat shops, men and women, sewing machine operators and bank presidents temporarily went insane," reported the *New York Tribune*. People tossed confetti out of office windows. Cascades of ticker tape swirled into the breeze. Similar celebrations took place in Boston, Chicago, and Washington.[12]

That same day newspaper editors published corrections informing readers that the peace announcement was premature. It was, the *New York Times* declared, "the most colossal news fake ever perpetrated upon the American people." The retractions deflated the hopes of the nation, though writers continued to predict that the Huns would soon wave the white flag. On November 9, the Kaiser resigned and fled the country, and German officials proclaimed a new republic. Then, at the eleventh hour of the eleventh day of the eleventh month, the "war to end all wars" ended. This time, the State Department confirmed the news. The early morning edition of the *Boston Globe* announced flatly: ARMISTICE SIGNED.[13]

During the nineteen months Americans fought the Great War, fifty-three thousand servicemen died in combat and another sixty-three thousand succumbed to disease, most of them victims of the global influenza pandemic. Death and destruction on the Western Front, the jarring explosions from mortar fire and constant shelling, traumatized American troops. They could hardly imagine a world without war. Many believed that the armistice was only a temporary reprieve. "After the long months of intense strain, of keying themselves up to the daily mortal danger, of thinking always in terms of war and the enemy, the abrupt release from it all was physical and psychological agony," recalled Colonel Thomas Gowenlock, an intelligence officer in the American 1st Division.

"Some suffered a total nervous collapse. Some . . . began to hope they would someday return to home and the embrace of loved ones. Some could think only of the crude little crosses that marked the graves of their comrades." The soldiers had been trained to focus all of their thoughts and energies into the war. What would their lives be like without it? "They did not know—and hardly cared. Their minds were numbed by the shock of peace. The past consumed their whole consciousness. The present did not exist and the future was inconceivable."[14]

On the home front, Americans celebrated like it was New Year's Eve, drinking champagne and dancing in the streets. In Boston, the pealing chimes at the Old North Church reverberated throughout the North End, signaling cessation of war. Before sunrise thousands upon thousands filled the city streets, extolling the Kaiser's abdication. By midafternoon massive crowds choked the thoroughfares, singing and cheering. The city closed every bar and saloon, but most people were too drunk with joy to care. People skipped work or forgot about it altogether. Tugboat whistles and foghorns echoed across the harbor. At Symphony Hall, the orchestra opened a celebratory program with a spirited rendition of "The Star-Spangled Banner." Then, when the new French conductor Henri Rabaud, Karl Muck's replacement, sang "La Marseillaise" himself, the crowd roared, affirming America's bond with one of its greatest allies.[15]

The city had never experienced such a day. "For Boston," Francis Russell wrote, "as for all the other thronged and delirious cities, that morning was the beginning of the new, the bright promise of a future that combined the ineradicable American belief in progress with the memory of a prewar golden past that never existed but was now to be recaptured."[16]

In Pittsfield, the mayor declared a holiday for the entire town. Every school, factory, office, bank, and store closed. Charles Whittlesey's father, Frank, marched near the front of a two-mile procession on North Street while twenty-five thousand people cheered. Men, women, and children congratulated one another while a military band played. The sound of drums and cannon shots pierced the crisp autumn air. Frank could not help but smile. His boy was coming home.[17]

THERE WAS NO ARMISTICE FOR Karl Muck. While the Boston Symphony Orchestra performed a victory concert, the *Globe* reported that "internment of dangerous enemy aliens" would continue. About a month later, the newspaper reported that approximately seventy-five alien enemies from the Boston district remained interned. Some German prisoners would not be set free for nearly two more years. Languishing behind the barbed wire fence at Fort Oglethorpe, Muck remained devastated by the agony of internment.[18]

Muck yearned for his old life—and for music. In the winter of 1918, Otto Willie, the camp's bandleader, persuaded him to direct a concert. "We convinced him," Erich Posselt wrote later, "that Ft. Oglethorpe was really Germany, and so he gave in." The image of Muck stepping onto the platform as the orchestra prepared to play Beethoven's *Eroica* symphony was seared into Posselt's memory. "The smelly, dirty mess-hall was jammed with two thousand listeners," he recalled, inmates wearing dirty overalls and black boots. "The orchestra numbered more than a hundred men. The first benches were reserved for the camp censors, some of the American officers, and an army doctor or two." In the silence before the first note, "an electric current" flowed through the room, as they anticipated "the most glorious musical event" in the camp.[19]

Muck raised his baton, and the music washed over the audience—mechanics, miners, seamen, and common laborers, men who had never attended a symphony orchestra concert. The men smiled and swayed, experiencing a sense of joy that they hardly ever felt at Ft. Oglethorpe. The music, Posselt wrote, "welded us into one, scorched us and purged us, and shook us to the very depths of our being."[20]

Muck mesmerized the audience with his command over the orchestra as the finale of Beethoven's "Heroic Symphony" reverberated across the camp yard. In that moment, on December 12, 1918, the maestro must have felt alive again. His last public concert had been more than eight months earlier, and now he once again commanded an orchestra. But the thrill was short lived. When the concert ended, he would still have to sleep in his cramped quarters.

For six more months he suffered, waiting for his release papers. Muck insisted that he should be allowed to live freely in the United States, but even after the war, the Justice Department treated him as a threat to the country's national security. He would never receive the unconditional discharge that he sought. The Justice Department "has notified us that they would not object to my husband's release, if he is willing to depart for Europe," Anita explained to their close friend Isabella Stewart Gardner. "But that's just the trouble. Anxious as he is to leave this country (for which he cannot be blamed!) he wants to go when he likes, not as a condition of his release."[21]

Anita grew increasingly worried about her husband's deteriorating health. He looked "poor, pale, and haggard." His heart condition had worsened to the point that the camp doctors warned him not to bend over to lace his own shoes. He spent most of his time resting, reading, and waiting—waiting for the day he could leave the camp. Sometimes he wondered if he would ever be able to conduct again. The stress of internment, he complained, had turned him into "an invalid, who is older than his years warrant."[22]

More than anything, Anita's love sustained him. Whatever he felt for Rosamond—passion, lust, infatuation—had faded. Anita, his "most devoted wife, the noblest friend, the bravest companion," never left his side. "I have always been a rather peculiar man," he admitted years later. "Anita was the only person who really knew and thoroughly understood me and to whom I could fully reveal my whole being."[23]

On a rainy day in late June 1919, a reporter from the *Boston Post* interviewed him. It was the first time a civilian other than Anita had spoken to him since his internment. Muck seemed almost unrecognizable to the writer. He appeared "meeker," a gaunt, tanned figure "hidden, almost beneath the folds of a raincoat." He looked nothing like the commanding maestro who led the Boston Symphony Orchestra with "a rod of iron." Stoop-shouldered with thinning hair, he shuffled into the stockade room wearing wrinkled white pants and a white collarless shirt. The reporter extended his hand toward Muck, but the prisoner ignored the gesture.[24]

A "square-jawed doughboy" sat nearby holding a shotgun, while the reporter peppered Muck with questions. "Where am I going?" Muck asked repeatedly, clearly perturbed at the reporter. "Where can I go? What can I do?" He had cut all ties to Germany, and he could never return to Boston. Muck still had friends in Boston who had supported him after his arrest. But even if the government allowed him to live in the United States, doing so now seemed pointless to him. "What could I do if I did stay here? Here in America there is no place for Germans," he said. Americans despised Germans and they would remain the enemy for years to come, he predicted. Speaking slowly, contemplating his answers between long drags on a cigarette, he explained how the US government had destroyed his life. He no longer had a job or a home. He refused to talk about the war or its outcome. "It is over, let it be."

All that remained was sadness. He mourned the loss of a life that he would never recover. It pained him to see his wife so distressed. "It has been doubly hard for her," he said. "But in an enemy country in war time it is best to be as inconspicuous as possible, and that is what Mrs. Muck has tried to do. She will go back to Germany with me, and what we shall do there we shall do together."

As the interview time expired, the reporter asked Muck one last question: why didn't he become an American citizen? Muck rose from his chair and looked out the window at the country that banished him, reflecting on a decision that may have changed the course of his life. "I intended to," he claimed. "You see, I came back to the United States in 1912, and in 1914 I decided to settle down in Boston, and in March of that year I bought a house at 50 Fenway, intending to take out my citizenship papers. Then came the war and, well, I intended to become a citizen and stay here."

The prison guard slung his rifle over his shoulder, and said, "Come on, Muck." It was time for him to return to his barracks. He extended his hand to the reporter and said, "Well, good-by."

That summer Muck finally agreed to the terms of forced depor-
tation. On August 10, he and Anita reunited in Chattanooga. It was
the first time in seventeen months that they embraced outside the
camp. About ten days later, the couple arrived in New York City,
accompanied by a government official. On August 21, an agent
from the Justice Department escorted them to a Scandinavian-
American luxury liner bound for Copenhagen.[25]

Before boarding the ship, he spoke to a reporter. Angry and
bitter, he denounced the American press for stoking anti-German
hysteria. "The country is being controlled by sentiment which
closely borders on mob-rule," he fumed. He reiterated that he had
never refused to play "The Star-Spangled Banner." Then he said
something that must have puzzled the agents in the Justice Department: "I am not a German, although they said I was. I considered
myself an American." Without a single regret he had become "a
man without a flag or country."[26]

When he boarded the *Frederick VIII*, a Secret Service agent
warned the ship captain that Muck was a dangerous man and that
he should be watched very carefully. Then the famous passenger
and his wife left the deck for their cabin. Unsure what lay ahead,
but certain he was leaving America behind for good, Karl Muck's
war ended as the ship steamed past the Statue of Liberty.

22

The Revolution

It made sense to Babe. The biggest stars deserved the most money. In 1918, Harry Frazee paid him $7,500, but that was no longer enough. He knew that his mere presence enhanced the value of the Red Sox. He could do it all: pitch, hit, and draw a crowd. In January 1919, he made it known that he wanted his salary doubled for the coming season. He had become, arguably, the most compelling figure in the game. "Is he not," a Boston fan asked, "the greatest attraction in the baseball world, as popular abroad as at home? Does anyone leave the ballpark, no matter what the score, if there is a chance of Babe busting up the game?"[1]

Ruth was as bold a negotiator as he was a ballplayer. His business manager, Johnny Igoe, a former Fenway Park peanut vendor turned local druggist, convinced him that he could demand more money. If Frazee was willing to give Ruth a bonus after he jumped for the shipyard league in the middle of the 1918 season, then he'd surely pay top dollar for him to wear a Red Sox uniform the following spring. Igoe and Ruth devised a strategy: Babe would threaten to quit baseball and become a boxer if Frazee didn't meet his price. After making his demands known, he staged a few boxing exhibitions and talked about arranging a match. "I always wanted to box," he claimed.[2]

Egotistical entertainers were nothing new to Frazee. He'd seen actors demand big money only to realize that without the spotlight their star would burn out. "They swear they are through with the show, they'll leave it flat," he said. "But it would take at least two squads of marines to keep them out of the theater and off the stage." The same was true of Ruth; he needed the exposure at Fenway. Unlike in the theater industry, however, baseball owners had complete control over the performers. What was known as the reserve clause in Ruth's contract gave Frazee complete ownership of his services. He could trade Ruth or sell him to another club. He did not have to negotiate with him or give him a raise; Frazee could force him to play under the exact terms of his previous contract, though he risked Ruth continuing his holdout if he did not offer better terms.[3]

Frazee appreciated Ruth's drawing power. He needed him, especially because the war had diminished attendance by 35 percent in 1918, and the baseball owners had already agreed to a reduced schedule of 140 games in 1919. Playing Ruth every day would allow Frazee to maximize profits. They negotiated throughout the winter; Ruth now said that if Frazee did not offer him $15,000 for the year, the only alternative he would consider was a three-year contract for $30,000. Frazee offered $8,500, but Ruth shrugged and the standoff continued into March. If Ruth did not sign a contract soon, Frazee countered, then he would trade him.[4]

When the Red Sox sailed for Florida without Babe on March 19, Frazee called Ruth into his New York office. After they talked face-to-face, Frazee finally caved: Ruth got his three-year contract for $30,000.

Ruth played spectacularly throughout the spring, launching baseballs into the sky with the same ease that "Sir Walter" Hagen displayed driving golf balls. On April 18, during the final stop of the Red Sox exhibition tour, Ruth put on a show in Baltimore against Jack Dunn's Orioles. Before the game began, he shook hands with old friends and neighbors. He worried that some of them did not believe that the pug-nosed kid from St. Mary's had become the greatest slugger in America.

Ruth gripped "his big war club" a little tighter that day, determined to show his hometown that he'd made it. By the end of the game, he had hit four home runs over the right-field fence—a triumphant demonstration of power that left Baltimore fans amazed. Who else could hit four home runs in a single game? How could a man learn to hit like *that*? Ruth smiled as a reporter interviewed him. No one could teach that kind of power, he said. "It's a gift."[5]

IN 1919, IT SEEMED THAT Ruth was the only player on the Red Sox who possessed any gift. Outside of his magnificent hitting, the season proved a total disaster for the team. The once dominant pitching staff suffered from injuries and incompetence. By the end of May, the Red Sox had fallen ten games out of first place. When the season ended, the defending champions had tumbled all the way to sixth, twenty and a half games behind the first-place Chicago White Sox. Ruth was the primary reason Boston fans showed up at Fenway, but not even he could distract them from the nation's upheaval.

In the aftermath of the Great War, the country experienced a wave of domestic turmoil—a combination of widespread inflation, rising unemployment, labor strikes, race riots, and terrorist bombings. The coming of Prohibition exacerbated the unrest, sparking a clash between temperance advocates and beer brewers. In New York almost no one worried more about Prohibition than the Yankees' co-owner, Jacob Ruppert. Born into the New York aristocracy, the son of a wealthy German-American brewer made a fortune running the family business. In 1915, Ruppert purchased the Yankees with Colonel Tillinghast L'Hommedieu Huston, a former US Army engineer who made a fortune from construction in Cuba after serving in the Spanish-American War. His Knickerbocker beer was synonymous with New York City, but the former president of the United States Brewers' Association feared that Prohibition would destroy his enterprise. Leading the charge of "wet" supporters, Ruppert, a four-term Democratic congressman from the 15th District, argued against the Volstead Act, claiming that beer was "a liquid food, healthful beverage, and in no way injurious to the system."[6]

Ruppert lost the argument and now had to prepare for a world in which his company's sole product was considered illegal. Without his brewery business, he needed a dependable source of income and reasoned that a winning baseball team could provide it. He worried, though, that if the New York Giants terminated his lease to use the Polo Grounds, he would not only be without a place to play but would have to come up with the cash to build a new ballpark. That would be a tall order. Despite Ruppert's ambitions, the Yankees were not yet a winning team; they had never captured a pennant and lacked a true star. He did notice, however, that Babe Ruth thrived at the Polo Grounds. The ballpark's short right-field porch made it an ideal venue for Ruth's pull-hitting, uppercut stroke. Perhaps, Ruppert hoped, Ruth could invigorate the team's fan base and offset his losses from Prohibition. When he asked his manager, Miller Huggins, what he needed to win the pennant, the skipper answered, "Get me Ruth."[7]

In the summer of 1919, even as the Red Sox continued to struggle, Ruth proved that he was, in the words of one Boston sportswriter, "far and away the greatest of all drawing cards in the game today." Although he continued pitching, he performed magnificently at the plate. At the end of July, he equaled the single-season American League record with sixteen homers, tying Seybold's mark. Reporters began tracking his barrage of home runs in exacting detail. Could he break Ned Williamson's obscure 1884 record of twenty-seven home runs? By August, Ruth appeared poised to claim the record. During one stretch he hit seven home runs in twelve days. Fan mail mushroomed in front of his locker.[8]

With the Red Sox long out of the pennant race, Frazee hyped the "Home Run King" as much as possible. On September 20, when Ruth trailed Williamson's record by just one, Boston celebrated "Babe Ruth Day," honoring the slugger with festivities and gifts in between a doubleheader against Chicago. More than thirty thousand fans packed Fenway, clamoring for him to hit a home run. In the first game, he struggled pitching and had to be removed from the mound in the sixth inning. In the bottom of the ninth, Ruth, then playing left field, came to the plate with the game tied. Claude "Lefty" Williams tossed a curveball that nearly fooled him, but with just a flick of the wrist, somehow the Babe managed to muscle it over the left-field wall onto Lansdowne Street. His dinger won the game, tied Williamson's record, and caused Lefty Williams to toss his glove into center field in a fit of anger. Afterward, the *Boston Globe* paid tribute to the city's "giant of a hero."[9]

A few days later, when the Red Sox visited the Yankees at the Polo Grounds, "the Boston mauler" broke the record, clubbing the longest ball ever hit there. The baseball soared over the roof of the stands and landed in Manhattan Field, a local park near the Harlem River. Jacob Ruppert took notice when Yankee fans showered Ruth with a standing ovation. Every time he came to the plate the crowd cheered. Ruppert must have sensed the possibilities. What would Ruth be worth to him and Huston if the New York fans could see Babe wear a Yankees uniform? How many home runs could he hit if he played half of his games at the Polo Grounds?[10]

Once again, after the season, Ruth contemplated his value. He had hit a record 29 home runs and led all hitters with 112 RBIs and 103 runs scored. Only twenty-four years old, he was a national sensation known from coast to coast. Before heading to Los Angeles where he played golf and exhibition games with other major leaguers, Ruth determined that he was severely underpaid. He wanted to shred his three-year contract. Seeking $20,000 a year— double his 1919 salary—Babe again threatened to become a boxer. "Frazee knows what I want and unless he meets my demands I will not play with the Boston club next year," he told a reporter.[11]

Trapped between unemployment and high inflation, hard-pressed Boston fans were unsympathetic to his financial woes. In 1919, the average worker made about 56 cents per hour during a 45-hour week. That amounted to about $25 each week or $1,332 each year—*if* the worker didn't miss any time on the job. One sportswriter thought that Ruth's ultimatum for a $20,000 contract appeared "ludicrous," if not offensive. "A sporting public has little use for contract breakers."[12]

Harry Frazee had bigger problems than Ruth's demands. On November 1, two days before Babe's public threat, Frazee missed a $125,000 payment on a promissory note to former Red Sox owner Joseph Lannin. If he did not get his money soon, Lannin warned, he would auction off Frazee's shares of Fenway Park. And if Frazee continued to default on his debts, his old nemesis Ban Johnson would move to oust him from the American League. Meanwhile, Frazee also wanted to buy the Harris Theater on West Forty-second Street in New York, but that plan was put on hold as his finances became precarious. Diminished attendance at baseball games and theater productions had reduced revenues at Fenway Park and the Cort Theatre in Chicago. Just to cover his personal expenses, Frazee borrowed money from the Red Sox. Though selling Ruth clearly wasn't ideal, it *would* solve some of his financial problems while also handing his friend Ruppert the star player he desired.[13]

From Boston to New York, rumors swirled that Frazee planned to unload Ruth. In late December, the *Boston Post*'s Paul Shannon hinted that the ballplayer might be on the auction block. Although Babe was immensely talented, Shannon believed that the tension over his contract may have pushed Frazee over the edge. The *Boston Globe*'s Arthur Duffey argued that no player was worth $20,000 a year. Under the circumstances, Frazee thought it impractical to pay Ruth that much—a quarter of the team's payroll. How could he justify it while the rest of the players made on average about $3,000?[14]

Before Frazee finalized a deal with Ruppert, he met with Ed Barrow in the café at the Hotel Knickerbocker. Years later, Barrow recalled Frazee telling him, "Lannin is after me to make good on my notes. And my shows aren't going so good. Ruppert and Huston will give me $100,000 for Ruth and they've also agreed to loan me $350,000." Frazee prepared to sign the agreement. When newspaper writers first announced the deal on January 6, 1920—ten days before Prohibition went into effect—they did not mention the loan Frazee received from the Yankees' owners. The final terms of the sale included Ruppert and Huston paying Frazee $100,000 in installments—$25,000 cash, plus three promissory notes for $25,000 at 6 percent interest—plus a $300,000 loan, which was secured using Fenway Park as collateral. Essentially, Ruppert had acquired both Ruth and a mortgage on Fenway Park, all for the astronomical price of $400,000 plus interest on the notes. Hungry for cash, Frazee immediately borrowed against his three $25,000 notes.[15]

When reporters asked Frazee why he sold Ruth, he made no mention of his financial hardships or any loan from Ruppert. He insisted that the deal was not about money. Babe's ego made him impossible to manage, he lamented. "While Ruth, without question, is the greatest hitter the game has ever seen, he is likewise one of the most selfish and inconsiderate men that ever wore a uniform . . . Had he been willing to take orders and work for the good of the club like the other men on the team, I never would have dared let him go." Frazee reminded the public that twice Ruth had abandoned the team—and he often defied his manager, Barrow. In other words, Babe made a terrible soldier. He did not follow orders.[16]

Frazee's decision did not surprise Ruth. He figured there was a good chance that the owner would rather sell him than pay him more money. He resented that Frazee profited from his talents, selling him off like a piece of chattel. The Yankees owners satisfied his demands for a raise and worked out a deal where he made more than $40,000 over the next two seasons.[17]

Yet his departure stunned Boston fans. Critics could not understand why Frazee sold the best player in the game. One fan lamented to a reporter, "I figure the Red Sox is ruined." It proved a prophetic statement. The Ruth deal precipitated a fire sale by Frazee that transformed both organizations for years to come. In 1920, the Red Sox finished twenty-five and a half games out of first place. After that season, Ed Barrow left Boston and became general manager of the Yankees. Over the next decade, the Red Sox finished last in the American League seven times. During

Ruth's fifteen seasons playing for the Yankees, the Bronx Bombers dominated baseball, winning seven American League pennants and four World Series. When they won their first World Series in 1923, eight of the team's starting position players and four-fifths of the starting pitching rotation had come from the Red Sox. Studying Frazee's dubious transactions, Ban Johnson called him "the champion wrecker of the baseball age."[18]

No single athlete embodied the Roaring Twenties more than Babe Ruth. In the age of ballyhoo, a time when newsreel films, tabloid newspapers, radio broadcasts, magazines, and national advertising campaigns shaped a new celebrity culture, prominent athletes became more famous than ever before. In the aftermath of the Great War, many Americans sought "a return to normalcy," an escape from politics and foreign affairs. Sports provided the perfect outlet. After the war, baseball remained the national pastime and Ruth became a national hero.[19]

Everything about Ruth, sportswriter Paul Gallico observed, seemed massive—"his frame, his enormous head surmounted by blue-black curly hair, his great blob of a nose spattered generously across his face." In the coming years, writers covered every detail of his exploits, reporting on his daily diet and the growing measurements of a body that became increasingly portly, stretching the middle of his pinstripe jersey. Unrestrained, he lived his life spending like a sailor on shore leave. In every way, Ruth personified the decade's excess, the instant gratification, the buy-now-pay-later, *carpe diem* zeitgeist.[20]

Above all, what drew Americans to Ruth was his unprecedented power. Baseball historian Harold Seymour explained, "He attracted people who might be untutored in the subtleties and refinements of inside baseball but who could understand and respond to the clear, uncomplicated drama and beauty of one of his towering drives, which had the directness and impact of one of Jack Dempsey's knockout punches."[21]

In the 1920s, Ruth became a one-man revolution, single-handedly pounding the game into an entirely different shape. In the first year of that decade alone, he obliterated his own single-season home run record, smashing fifty-four dingers. That season *no team* hit more home runs than Ruth. The following year, he hammered fifty-nine home runs. In 1927, he broke his own record again with sixty homers, which represented nearly 14 percent of all home runs hit in the entire American League.[22]

Baseball historians have debated the causes in the explosion in home runs and scoring during the 1920s. They have posited different theories: the introduction of a livelier "rabbit ball"; the elimination of "trick" pitches, particularly the spitball; the number of brand new baseballs used in each game; and the increasing tendency of batters swinging for the fences. But the truth is that the "home run fever" was mostly a result of Ruth's astonishing hitting success, inspiring other players to emulate his swing. "We are irresistibly impelled to see in Babe Ruth the true cause for the amazing advance in home runs," F. C. Lane wrote in *Baseball Magazine* in 1921. By the early twenties, Lane noticed that strategy had changed. Batters were no longer chopping at the ball. Instead, each player was "swinging from the handle of the bat with every ounce of strength that nature placed in his wrists and shoulders."[23]

Suddenly and unexpectedly, Ruth had revolutionized baseball.

23

Homecoming

CHARLES WHITTLESEY HAD NEVER PLANNED FOR THE LIFE HE fell into when he reached America. On the Western Front, he had become an overnight hero, celebrated as much for a sentence he never uttered as for his tenacity and bravery. Not long after his return to New York the ad men and propagandists went to work, chiseling his image into stone. During the Fifth Liberty Loan campaign, for instance, the Overland-Harrisburg Company incorporated Whittlesey's line into their drive, using the slogan "Tell Them to Go to Hell!"[1]

Yet what made Whittlesey so appealing was his total lack of interest in popular acclaim. As reporters often implied in their descriptions of him, nothing was heroic in how he looked, spoke, or behaved. Stooped shoulders, wire-rimmed glasses, soft-spoken— he was no Lancelot. He did, however, display a certain magical quality—a genuine noblesse oblige that was rare. He did his duty as he saw it, seeking no praise and without aggrandizement. He *was* a modern George Washington, a twentieth-century Cincinnatus who answered his nation's call to arms and now only wanted to return to his farm (or Wall Street firm). It was that fundamental honesty that his men and the public found so reassuring and attractive. As one of the survivors explained the doggedness of the Lost Battalion: "*We* held out because *he* did. We were all right if we could see him once a day." It was that irreducible essence that writers wanted to celebrate, advertisers sought to package, and Americans at home desired to honor.[2]

A few days after he returned to the United States, he elaborated on his war experiences before a hometown audience. Speaking in a quiet, undramatic voice to 350 members and invited guests of the Pittsfield Park Club, Whittlesey detailed his activities from the time he sailed for England until his return. The audience packed the parlor of the club, spilling over into the antechamber. He presented an uncommon address. It was as if Travis had survived the Alamo or Custer the Little Bighorn and then refused to discuss the engagements that had won them immortality. To truly convey a sense of "the fighting end of the war," he claimed, required "a man of imagination and technical grasp of the situation," neither of which he possessed. Instead, he detailed the life of an average American division.[3]

He spoke of the culinary defects of the British and the practical sense of French soldiers, of the ghastly weather in England and the superiority of German trenches. His talk was long on everyday details, short on the gore of battle, and lacking almost entirely anything about the Lost Battalion. Other than saying that "it was very hard going toward the last," he never mentioned the one topic his listeners had come to hear. Nor did he address the peace, an event that a week before had caused paroxysms of celebration in the Massachusetts town.[4]

Surprisingly, however, Whittlesey spoke passionately about America's enemy, the Germans who had attacked his fragile sanctuary in the Pocket, ripping his men apart with artillery, cutting them to pieces with machine guns, and burning them alive with flame-throwers. He respected them as "scrappers," he said. "As far as I know they always fought fair with us. You will remember that there were no atrocities reported from the east end of the line ...They were all in the west."[5]

SPEAKING BEFORE HIS FORMER NEIGHBORS and childhood friends, perhaps Whittlesey made a decision. If he were destined to be the evening's entertainment, telling his story like a veteran of the Chautauqua circuit, then the audience was going to hear his politics. Though he spoke as mildly as a banking lawyer, there was nothing mealy about his opinions and agenda. He supported President Wilson's notion of "a peace without victory," the belief that harsh peace terms created a hostile environment that would inevitably lead to future wars. On a more personal level, he sought to use his celebrity—something he cared nothing about—to publicize the anonymous privates and noncommissioned officers who fought and died for their country.

Two days after speaking in Pittsfield, he was back in New York on Madison Avenue for a "War Night" engagement at the Williams Club. Although half of the club's nine hundred members were still in the service, nearly three hundred attended the talk. After a bout of singing that included "La Marseillaise" and "The Star-Spangled Banner," Whittlesey began to speak in a quiet, almost reverent tone, praising the legions of Williams graduates who fought in the war, such as Captain Belvidere Brooks and Lieutenant Meredith Wood, and the French soldiers who taught Americans how to fight. "Not a word of the Forest of Argonne, of his 'Lost Battalion,' of his 'Go To Hell!' reply to the German demand that the trapped Americans surrender did Lieut. Col. Charles W. Whittlesey of the 308th Infantry say," commented a *New York Sun* reporter.[6]

He spoke instead about those enlisted and conscripted men from New York and across the country—"the soul of honor and courage"—who carried the burden of the war. "You don't hear enough of the enlisted men in France," he said. "They were just ordinary American boys when they went over, but now they're changed, and officers have adopted a different attitude toward them. I can't describe the fondness that we acquired for them as we saw them day after day doing their work without complaint. It makes you proud of America to think of these common soldiers of ours. And remember that those who have been picked out for special praise are the symbols of the men behind them. No man ever does anything alone."

Eventually, toward the conclusion of a long evening, one audience member shouted the question that was on everybody's mind: "But did you tell them to go to hell?"

Whittlesey modestly nodded.

"But did they?" several others inquired.

"A hundred voices" drowned Whittlesey's measured reply: "They sure did."

It was that bravado his audience craved, the memorable line that summoned a soldier's highest sacrifice—"Remember the Alamo!," "They shall not pass!," "Lafayette, we are here!" "Go to Hell!" was it, and no one listening to Whittlesey truly cared if he really said it any more than they cared if General Nivelle or General Pétain uttered, "*Ils ne passeront pas!*" They only wanted him to acknowledge that in the heat of battle, with the whiff of powder in the air and the sound of death all about him, he had dramatically rejected the request to surrender. The words even more than the stand had captivated Americans. Yet even the mildest suggestion that he had shouted or whispered it tortured him. He was a man who trafficked in truth, and the truth was that the lie sullied the genuine heroics of the Charlevaux Valley. He never resolved the dilemma between his public and private lives.[7]

In the weeks after returning to America, he labored to diminish his celebrity by sharing it. On December 6, the same day the army honorably discharged him, President Wilson designated Whittlesey as a Medal of Honor recipient. Not only would he receive the nation's highest military decoration, he was among the first three recipients in the war against Germany.

In a ceremony held the day before Christmas on the snow-covered Boston Common, General Clarence R. Edwards, former commander of New England's famed Yankee Division, pinned the Medal of Honor on Whittlesey's chest. Twenty thousand people, including his mother, father, and brother Elisha who had come down from the Berkshires, stood in the cold to see the hero of the Argonne, still popularly called "Go to Hell" Whittlesey. The ceremony was simple. After a Naval Aviation School band played "The Star-Spangled Banner," General Edwards told Whittlesey, "I was in France at the time your act thrilled the entire American Expeditionary Force, and it gives me great pleasure to present this medal." As the ceremony ended, Whittlesey's mother leaned over and gave her son a peck on the cheek. That kiss, far more than any other aspect of the event, put a smile on his lips. He "was essentially his mother's son more than the hero of any battle," wrote a Boston reporter.[8]

What did the medal mean to Whittlesey? It was meaningless to him personally, but it did remind him of his continuing duty to his men. The medal, along with others he would receive—French Legion of Honor, French Croix de Guerre, Italian Croce di Guerra, and Montenegrin Ordre du Prince Danilo I—held just enough significance to be placed and stored in a box. They made his mother, Anna, proud, and that was enough for him. Nevertheless, the awards compelled him to do something that he did not want to do. In this case, to take a public stand on issues vital to America, and become a spokesman for Wilsonian internationalism. The future peace of the world, he felt, depended on the decisions that politicians gathering outside of Paris would make in 1919.

The reintegration of Germany into the world community, Whittlesey knew, would be critical to maintaining peace. Even before the Boston ceremony, he had cautioned Americans against accepting his nation's wartime anti-German propaganda. German soldiers were not mindless Huns ransacking villages, raping women, and killing babies—in short, the villains portrayed in Comittee on Public Information publications and such Germanophobic films as *The Kaiser, the Beast of Berlin*. In mid-December, he appeared at the Sixty-ninth Regimental Armory for the opening of the Union Peace Jubilee. Taking a seat beside the main speaker, President Wilson's son-in-law and secretary of the treasury William Gibbs McAdoo, the tall, mufti-dressed Whittlesey attracted scant attention from the more than six thousand attendees.[9]

Whittlesey Medal Ceremony: In 1918, on the day before
Christmas, in a ceremony on Boston Common, General Clarence
R. Edwards, former commander of the Yankee Division, pinned
the Medal of Honor on Whittlesey's chest. Twenty thousand
people stood in the cold and snow to see the hero of the Lost
Battalion. *(Courtesy of the Williams College Archives.)*

At least, that is, until the event organizer introduced him as
"Lieut.-Col. Charles W. Whittlesey, U.S.A.," commander of the
"Lost Battalion." With a "gasp of astonishment," six thousand pairs
of eyes fixed on the bookish-looking man because "there were few
in the hall who did not know the history of that salient band of
Americans." As he arose, noted a *New York Sun* scribe, "a mighty
cheer" shook the armory, billowing and swelling, lasting a full three

minutes. He just stood there, embarrassed, shifting his weight from one foot to the other, waiting to have his brief say.

When the cheering stopped, he began a restrained address, partly a tale of heroics but also a serious request for a return to national sanity. After a few stories about the gallantry of his men that the audience received with even more applause, he turned to a pressing political issue. "The American soldiers are not going to come back hating the Germans," he said. "No man who has been out in the front line trenches facing the enemy is going to return with malice in his heart. The paramount trait of the American soldier is kindliness. If he met the Kaiser on the road he would be willing to share his cigarettes with him as with anyone."

Of course, he added, Britain and France had suffered far more than Americans had in the war, and their terrible losses could not be ignored. "Mind you I do not want to let the Germans off too easily. I merely want to see justice done. Germany after the war, it must be remembered, is going to be part of the world community."

Silence met his plea. With the Great War just a few days more than a month concluded, many Americans found it difficult to accept Whittlesey as the Wilsonian prophet of "peace without victory" and to embrace Germany. Others used his words to show the hypocrisy of the president's repressive wartime legislation aimed at ending all radical dissent. What "are we going to do about Lieut. Col. Whittlesey?" poet and socialist Louis Untermeyer asked sarcastically in *The New Republic*. "Should he be lynched? Should we deprive him of the power of free speech and free assembly? Should we deny him the use of the mails? Or should we merely sentence him to one year in Atlanta for the dissemination of seditious remarks?"

For the next several months, Whittlesey continued to speak out in favor of Wilsonian ideals. "Peace without victory," the League of Nations, liberal internationalism—these topics, not his battlefield decisions, occupied his mind. The war, he told a forum at the Church of the Ascension in New York, had broadened the thinking of the servicemen who had gone to France. Unlike Americans at home, conditioned by the Creel Committee to consider anything German to be detestable, the soldiers had undergone an enlightening experience. They had become more liberal and more international, believing that "if the German people were destroyed the world's morale would suffer."[10]

Unfortunately, Whittlesey's political timing misfired. The causes he championed were unpopular. At the Versailles Peace Conference, British prime minister David Lloyd George and especially French prime minister Georges Clemenceau schemed to cripple and bankrupt Germany, and in the United States President Wilson clumsily dithered away whatever support he could muster in Congress. Whittlesey had returned to America two weeks after the Democratic Party suffered a crushing defeat in the 1918 midterm elections. As a result, the Republicans captured both houses of Congress, and combined with Wilson's intransigence eventually doomed America's entry into the League of Nations.

As he had in the Pocket, Whittlesey clung desperately to hope, even after Wilson collapsed from a stroke and the Senate rejected the Treaty of Versailles. In the 1920 presidential election—proclaimed by Wilson as "a great and solemn referendum" on the treaty—Whittlesey gave a series of whistle-stop speeches supporting the Democratic ticket of James Cox and Franklin D. Roosevelt, and America's entry into the League of Nations. He argued that opposition to the League "is simply the manifestation of a reactionary spirit with which every great moment in history has to contend." He promised to cast his vote for Cox, the League, and the dream of world peace. "I think the sooner we get into it the better it will be for the world," he said.[11]

Cox's defeat was troubling, but not nearly as much as his own family worries. Intensely concerned about his family, he now had to witness the slow, painful decline of his brother Elisha. In 1920, Whittlesey had ended his legal partnership—though not his deep friendship—with John Bayard Pruyn and joined the Wall Street firm of White & Case, a house that had worked closely with J. P. Morgan during the years leading up to America's entry into the war. The position allowed him to specialize in banking law and provided more time for activities outside the office. About the same time,

Elisha completed an MBA at Harvard and obtained a job in New York as a statistician for Case, Pomeroy & Company. Often ill, suffering from a long-standing heart condition and the lingering impact of exposure to poisonous gases during the war, his health worsened steadily, and Charles provided what care he could.[12]

Increasingly, as during the 1918 flu pandemic, it was a case of the sick caring for the sicker. Though stronger than Elisha, Charles also suffered from a persistent, hacking cough that drained his energy and left him breathless. In the Argonne, he had written it off as a "cold," a condition that on the front covered a multitude of ailments ranging from exhaustion to tuberculosis. But common colds get better; the effects of poison gas often don't. In the Vesle, he had trampled across ground saturated with gas, eating meals on it during the day and bedding down on it at night. By 1921, his racking cough was so troubling that it disturbed his sleep and woke other residents in his boarding house. Sadly, it was an all too familiar sound, one he had heard often in veteran hospitals and sick wards where gassed soldiers had gone to die.

HE WAS ONE OF THEM. He had marched them into the Pocket, watched artillery shells tear them apart, and heard them cough their lungs out in the hours before dawn. At night, he could see and hear it all in feverish sweaty dreams that woke him as often as the cough. By November 11, 1921—just short of three years since he had returned to America, he found that he could do no more for the soldiers who had shipped to France. He had used his celebrity in support of joining the League of Nations, hoping that the greatest of wars would be the last. He had served in more than name on veterans' aid groups, especially the Roll Call campaign of the American Red Cross, raising money, visiting hospitals, and chairing committees.[13]

Informally, he had also done what he could. He was a soft touch for a veteran's hard luck story. It didn't matter if they had served under him or someone else. And there were plenty of hard luck stories among the members of the 77th Division tramping the streets of New York during the economic slump in the years immediately after the war. He always found time to talk to the mothers or wives of fallen members of the Lost Battalion. They all wanted some variation of the same thing: How did he die? What were his last words? Did he speak of me? Whittlesey was at a loss. What could he say? *Your son (or husband) took a gut shot that became infected and he died after three days of agony crying out in pain and thirst with the smell of gangrene in the air.* Of course not. He lied. The slow and obscene deaths became quick and clean. Charles Whittlesey remained the good soldier—always protecting the memory of the army, the campaign, and the men, even when he had to bend the truth beyond all recognition.

He had experienced too much of death. His sister Annie and his brother Russell. Captain Belvidere Brooks, Williams grad and commander of D Company in the 308th Infantry. Captain Eddie Grant, who went to Harvard Law with Whittlesey and served in the 307th Infantry. Attempting to rescue his friend Whittlesey, Eddie was killed instantly by an artillery shell. All those men of the 308th and 307th surrounded by Germans, subjected to withering fire. So many funerals. Some weeks he attended two or three. It had worn him out. But at least one more remained. A service for a man no one knew.

Epilogue

"A Misfit by Nature and by Training"

THE FOUR SHIPPING CASES ARRIVED AT THE DIMLY LIT HOTEL DE Ville in Châlons-sur-Marne from the French cemeteries of Belleau Wood, Bony, Thiaucourt, and Romagne-sous-Montfaucon. Outside a band played a hymn. Inside the cases were flag-covered caskets and remains of four unidentified American servicemen who had died in the war. Military officials had already burned the paperwork detailing the exhumations. To ensure even further anonymity, a detachment of soldiers and embalmers played two macabre shell games, switching the bodies from casket to casket until even they did not know which body had arrived in which case.[1]

Only one casket would make the trip back to the United States for burial in Arlington Cemetery in the recently created Tomb of the Unknown Soldier. War hero Sergeant Edward F. Younger, survivor of the Château-Thierry, St. Mihiel, Somme, and Meuse-Argonne campaigns, a wounded soldier himself, stood near the caskets, feeling the solemnity of the moment. Holding a clutch of white roses, he had the duty to make the final selection.[2]

He walked past the caskets, he recalled. Once. Twice. Three times. And then—"It was as though something had pulled me," he later recalled. He couldn't take another step. "It seemed as if

God raised my hand and guided me . . ." He was overwhelmed by a premonition, as if a voice was calling out, "This is a pal of yours."

Younger placed the white roses on that coffin. Turning, he saluted the fallen and walked back into the sunlight. He had finished his somber duty, but the memory stayed with him for the rest of his life. He told people, "I still remember the awed feeling I had, standing there alone."

From the sunlight of Châlons-sur-Marne a new sealed ebony and silver casket holding the remains was trained to Le Havre, loaded onto the ship USS *Olympia*, and carried to the gray gloom of the Washington Naval Yard. The *Olympia* had won fame more than two decades earlier as Commodore George Dewey's flagship in the Battle of Manila Bay, a victory that thrilled Americans and signaled the country's presence in the western Pacific, but now the old ship was returning on a sadder mission. On November 9, 1921, as the cruiser entered the Potomac, cannons boomed a salute, and as it slowly moved up the river, largely hidden by a thick fog and rain, "fort by fort, post by post, the guns took up the tale of honors for the dead as she moved past."[3]

A regiment of cavalry waited on the cobbled patch of the Navy Yard to transport the casket to the Capitol Rotunda, where it would lie in state. That in itself was a singular honor, one that the unknown, fallen soldier shared with martyred presidents Lincoln, Garfield, and McKinley. "Far above," wrote a *New York Times* reporter, "towering from the great bulk of the dome, the brooding figure of Freedom watched, . . . as though it said 'Well done' to the servant, faithful unto death, asleep in the dim chamber below."

On the morning of November 11, exactly three years since the armistice ending the World War, pedestrians and automobiles swelled the streets of the capital—all heading toward Arlington National Cemetery. The traffic became so snarled that President Warren Harding's driver had to cut across a field to reach Arlington's amphitheater in time for the ceremonies.[4]

When the president finally arrived, he joined the other civilian and military dignitaries gathered for the solemn occasion. Former president Woodrow Wilson, still suffering the effects of his 1919 stroke, was not in the amphitheater, but he had traveled in his old-fashioned topless Victoria as far as the White House, cheered all along Pennsylvania Avenue. In addition to Harding, former president and current chief justice of the United States William Howard Taft, "in the vigor of health," was there, joined by Premier Aristide Briand and Marshal Foch of France and Prime Minister David Lloyd George of Great Britain. Other lesser officials filled in the seats around them. A generalissimo from Italy, a prince of Japan, six American Indian chiefs in full war dress and war paint led by Chief Plenty Coups, and a host of other illustrious officials joined one thousand Gold Star mothers and the more than one hundred thousand people gathered in the cemetery.

Hundreds of servicemen from the war looked on as well. In one section close to the stage were the crippled and the blind from Walter Reed and other area hospitals. They were under the care of army nurses dressed in soft gray gowns and long gray veils. Not far from this section of battle-scarred soldiers was another for the Medal of Honor recipients, most of them dressed in khaki uniforms. They served as the honorary pallbearers, visible symbols of the heroism of the Unknown Soldier. Their ranks would be increased by one when President Harding pinned the highest medal for valor to the flag-covered coffin.

From his place of honor Charles Whittlesey observed the proceedings. He watched the dignitaries take their seats, listened as the Marine Band played Chopin's Funeral March and "The Star-Spangled Banner," and gazed at the legless, armless, and blind men in the wounded veteran section. He stood silently at noon for two minutes with everyone else while a terrible hush embraced the cemetery.[5]

What did he think about Harding's oration? Whittlesey had stumped for Wilson's vision of peace without victory, for a world safe for democracy and free from the horrors he had endured. Now, all of that was lost. America had a new president, one who spoke in vague, mangled abstractions unencumbered by even a hint of a larger policy. Looking "strong and vigorous," the president doffed his overcoat, stood next to the coffin, and began speaking from prepared notes. He spoke nebulously about his desire for peace, declaring that although he was no pacifist, he believed that "the highest function of government is to give its citizens security and peace." Without detailing any specifics, he intoned, "There must be, there shall be, a commanding voice of a conscious civilization against armed warfare." Closing, he said that he sensed "that this Armistice Day shall mark the beginning of a new and lasting era of peace on earth, good-will among men." With that, he asked the gathering to join him in the Lord's Prayer. "While he said the words," reported the *New York Times*, "his right hand remained uplifted—a touch that emphasized the solemnity and force of the moment."[6]

For many, it was a moving ceremony, and Whittlesey was no different. He told George McMurtry, who as a Medal of Honor recipient had come to the event with him, that he should not have attended. "I kept wondering if the Unknown Soldier is one of my men," he said. Marguerite Babcock, his former business partner John Pruyn's sister-in-law and one of Whittlesey's friends, commented a few weeks after the event, "We are all convinced that it was the burial of the Unknown Soldier that was the climax of his mental suffering because of the war. He was the sort of man who would say: 'Look at that poor fellow, and think of all the poor boys who were killed. What right have I to be alive?'"[7]

Unfortunately, Whittlesey could not evade reminders of the war. He was chairman of the New York County Chapter of the Red Cross Roll Call, spearheading the organization's efforts to enroll five hundred thousand members between Armistice Day and Thanksgiving. This position, combined with his wartime celebrity, obliged him to attend a variety of war-related functions. On the evening of Sunday November 20, for instance, he went to the American Legion of New York's farewell reception for Marshal Ferdinand Foch at the Hippodrome. Once again, he sat on the stage with a group of maimed soldiers, only this time it was not accompanied by guarantees of future world harmony. Foch talked about the blood ties between the United States and France, and America's obligation to protect France's territorial integrity.[8]

Whittlesey craved to escape the war, but memories trapped him at every turn. At night, he dreamed of his time in the Pocket and awoke coughing. During the days, he talked with his men and their families, worked on the Red Cross Roll Call and other veterans projects, and provided the face of heroism at any number of conclaves. There seemed no end to the demands on his time. "Recently Colonel Whittlesey had been besieged by wounded soldiers and widows of soldiers seeking aid," said Joseph M. Hartfield, who worked alongside him at White & Case. "He was very sentimental and these distressing appeals made him most anxious and worried." But there was no let up. After all, he was "Go to Hell" Whittlesey, acclaimed in newspapers, magazines, books, and cinema. He must have seen no way to bail out gracefully—unless, of course, he simply disappeared.[9]

Thanksgiving would come the following week, but before he went to Pruyn's home for the holiday, he had a few chores to finish. One was personal. On Monday, he dropped by the American Express office on Broadway, not far from his law firm, and purchased a ticket for passage to Havana on the United Fruit Company liner SS *Toloa*. The others were mostly work related. Whittlesey, a conscientious lawyer—Robert Little, an associate at White & Case, called him "one of our most promising assistants" and said he had "a brilliant future" in the firm—handled significant, complex banking cases. Throughout the week, including the evening on Wednesday, he wrapped up his work, drafting detailed memoranda on his twelve cases, and placing the documents in the upper left-hand drawer of his desk.[10]

Earlier that Wednesday, he drew up and signed a new will. Associates Fitzhugh McGrew and Jesse Wald witnessed it. No one in the office gave it a second thought. "Nobody considered it at all out of the ordinary," Little said, "for lawyers are always drawing up their own wills and asking somebody in the office to witness them." Furthermore, it was such a brief document, leaving most of what he had to his mother and naming Pruyn as the executor. That finished, he locked it away in his safety deposit box at the Mercantile Trust Company.[11]

There was really only one curious aspect of his behavior. For months, he had been plagued by acute melancholia caused by "his brooding over the suffering of disabled soldiers." He was "engulfed in a sea of woe," thought Little. As part of his work as chairman of the Red Cross Roll Call, "he would go to two or three funerals every week, visit the wounded in the hospitals, and try to comfort the relatives of the dead." Yet when Pruyn saw him Wednesday night, he appeared in "unusually cheerful spirits."[12]

His spirits remained high the next day with the Pruyns. Not only was it Thanksgiving, but it was also the first birthday of the baby of Bayard and his wife, Edith. Whittlesey brought the child—his goddaughter—pins as a gift, and spent time playing with her. He talked about a weekend trip to Pittsfield to see his family. Neither Elisha nor his mother were in good health, but he did not dwell on their conditions. Marguerite Babcock was struck by his "very gay spirits." "He was usually very quiet," she said. "He never talked about the war, and we never dared to ask him." But this time he was different. "His cheerfulness was in great contrast to his usual solemnity."[13]

He had a date on Friday with a woman, an old, close friend. It was nothing romantic, more a friendly get-together, for as all his friends knew, he was a "confirmed bachelor." "In the ten years or more that I knew him," Little claimed, "I never heard him mention the name of a woman." When he was not in his boarding house rooms or law office, friends normally could find him reading, studying, or talking at the Williams Club or Harvard Club.[14]

His only other notable action on Friday involved his house-keeper, Mrs. Sullivan. He called her that evening asking for an early 8:00 a.m. breakfast. "I'm going away to be alone for a few days," he said. "I am tired." After eating the next morning, he gave Mrs. Sullivan a check for his December rent. "You had better cash this right away," he suggested. Then, for the last time, he walked out of his East Forty-fourth Street digs.[15]

A few friends thought he was going to Pittsfield to spend time with his family. Others believed he was staying in town to at-tend the Army-Navy football game at the Polo Grounds. Instead, shortly before noon, he boarded the SS *Toloa*, which lifted anchor a brief time later.

A celebrity aboard a cruise has no chance of anonymity, and Colonel Whittlesey of the Lost Battalion was soon recognized, introduced to Captain Farquahar Grant, and invited to dine that night at the captain's table. Grant thought his passenger was entirely normal, not "morose" at all, and chiefly interested in the afternoon's big game, which Army lost, 7–0.[16]

Not long after 9:00 p.m., Whittlesey joined Mr. A. Maloret, a veteran from the Puerto Rico campaign, for a single drink in the smoking room. For more than an hour, they talked pleasantly, mostly about war experiences, normally a taboo for Whittlesey. Maloret saw no signs of agitation, no indication of "a man with a heavy load on his mind." Then at 11:15 Whittlesey abruptly rose from the table, like a man late for an appointment. He said he had to "retire."[17]

The sea was not rough, but the night was drenched in a heavy fog. Although a few passengers strolled along the decks, Whittlesey must have felt invisible, shrouded by the darkness.

What must he have felt walking on the deck of the ship? Did he think about his responsibilities? Did he reflect on the nine envelopes and a note for the captain that he had addressed and placed on his bedspread?

Did he look at the water? The moon shimmering on the dark sea like a silent yellow light? Did he think about the war? The cold dead soldier he woke up next to cheek-to-cheek in the Pocket? All the young men under his command now dead? Some scorched by flamethrowers. Or bayonetted through the stomach. Or shot in the face. Or torn apart by artillery shells fired by their own compatriots.

Did he think of his friends? He had many, though even some of the closest would later say that they didn't know him well. Not really well. After the war, he just couldn't explain himself. What troubled him seemed too personal, too elusive.

He had dashed off a hurried letter to Bayard Pruyn. "Just a note to say good by," he wrote. "I'm a misfit by nature and by training, and there's an end to it."[18]

Then he apologized for dumping the burden of executor duties on his friend. In an act of penitence, he quickly outlined his assets, insurance policies, safety deposit boxes, and such mundane matters. As he jotted all the instructions, his handwriting became chicken scratch, bordering on illegible, improving only when he noted, "Medals etc. in Safe Deposit box in Mercantile Safe Deposit Co. No. 69-175. Keys are in envelope with my will in White & Case safe."

That was about it. Nothing more to add. "I won't try to say anything personal, Bayard, because you and I understand each other."

Remembering his always courtly manners, he added one more line: "Give my love to Edith."

That was the end of it. He climbed over the rail of the SS *Toloa*, and then did something that he wanted to do. As surely as his men who had died or suffered wounds in the Pocket, Charles White Whittlesey was a casualty of the war to end all wars.

Acknowledgments

In all of our collaborations we have relied upon a dedicated group of people who have made writing our third book together as rewarding as the first. Throughout our journey, we have benefitted from a great team at Fletcher & Company, especially our literary agent, Sylvie Carr, whose enthusiasm and insight helped us transform *War Fever* from an idea into a book. As always, our publisher, Lara Heimert, remains an incredible advocate. Her guidance and generous support has made publishing with Basic Books an absolute pleasure. Our editor Connor Guy provided an invaluable critique of the manuscript that helped us improve every chapter. And as always, our good friend Aram Goudsouzian read the manuscript closely and helped us sharpen our arguments and strengthen the narrative.

A number of people and institutions made our research for this book possible. In particular we wish to thank the staff at the National Archives and Records Administration who helped us locate documents related to Charles Whittlesey, Karl Muck, and the Boston Red Sox. We are especially grateful for the staffs at the Library of Congress; the Boston Public Library; the Baseball Hall of Fame's A. Bartlett Giamatti Research Center; the Boston

Acknowledgments

Symphony Orchestra Archives; the Harvard University Archives; and the Williams College Archives.

A sincere thank-you to two Lost Battalion scholars: Alan D. Gaff read our chapters on the event, and Robert J. Laplander shared his extensive understanding of that week in October 1918 with Randy Roberts on the ground in the Meuse-Argonne as they followed in the footsteps of Charles Whittlesey. Military historian Robert Kirchubel read and improved the Whittlesey chapters, and Randal G. Gaulke shared his knowledge of the Meuse-Argonne Offensive on the battlefield.

Our home universities made it possible for us to write this book. Purdue University has long facilitated Randy Roberts's career. In recent years, President Mitch Daniels, College of Liberal Arts dean David Reingold, and Department of History head Doug Hurt have created an ideal environment to teach and write. At Georgia Tech, the Julius C. "Bud" Shaw Professorship and the Ivan Allen College Small Grant Award for Research provided research support to Johnny Smith. He wishes to thank Ivan Allen College of Liberal Arts dean Jackie Royster for making it all possible at Georgia Tech.

Lastly, but most important, we wish to thank our wives, Marjie Roberts and Rebecca Smith. For all the times we were away from home or distracted at the dinner table, we offer our most sincere gratitude and love.

Notes

PREFACE

1. Brian Bell, liner notes for *The First Recordings of the Boston Symphony Orchestra* (Boston Symphony Orchestra, 1995).

2. The architect of the US propaganda campaign during the Great War was George Creel, the director of the Committee on Public Information. See Creel, *How We Advertised America: The First Telling of the Amazing Story of the Committee on Public Information That Carried the Gospel of Americanism to Every Corner of the Globe* (New York: Harper and Brothers Publishers, 1920).

3. *BP*, November 14, 1919.

4. *BP*, April 3, 1917; *BG*, April 21, 1917, June 8, 1917; Steve A. Riess, *Touching Base: Professional Baseball and American Culture in the Progressive Era* (Urbana and Chicago: University of Illinois Press, 1999), 29.

5. *BG*, April 7, 1917.

6. *BG*, July 21, 1918.

1. SOMETHING THAT I *DON'T* WANT TO!

1. Max Eastman, *Enjoyment of Living* (New York: Harper and Brothers, 1948), 216; Richard Slotkin, *Lost Battalions: The Great War and the Crisis of American Nationality* (New York: Henry Holt and Company, 2005), 80; Robert J. Laplander, *Finding the Lost Battalion: Beyond the Rumors, Myths and Legends of America's Famous WW 1 Epic*, 3rd ed. (Waterford, WI: Lulu Press, 2017), 43.

2. Christoph Irmscher, *Max Eastman: A Life* (New Haven: Yale University Press, 2017), 30; Charles White Whittlesey College Transcript, Williams College.

3. Theodore Roosevelt, "The Strenuous Life," speech presented to the Hamilton Club, Chicago, April 10, 1899.

4. Laplander, *Finding the Lost Battalion*, 42.

5. Eastman, *Enjoyment of Living*, 228–229.

6. Eastman, *Enjoyment of Living*, 215–216.

7. *The Gulielmensian* (1906), Williams College, 47, 52.

8. Max Forrester Eastman, "Systematic Suppression of Freshmen," *Williams Literary Monthly* (November 1904): 50, 53, 55.

9. Charles White Whittlesey, "Liberal Culture," *Williams Literary Monthly* (December 1904): 197–198, 200.

10. Charles White Whittlesey, "The Lotos," *Williams Literary Monthly* (May 1903); "The Telegram," *Williams Literary Monthly* (November 1903); "The Ides of November," *Williams Literary Monthly* (January 1903); "A Fair Exchange," *Williams Literary Monthly* (October 1902): 12; "A Lonely Post," *Williams Literary Monthly* (November 1902): 67, 72.

11. Charles White Whittlesey, "The Twins Mine," *Williams Literary Monthly* (February 1903): 239.

12. Whittlesey, "The Twins Mine," 242.

13. Eastman, *Enjoyment of Living*, 216.

14. *The Williams Record*, November 7, 1904, November 10, 1904, June 22, 1905.

15. *The Williams Record*, June 22, 1905.

16. *The Williams Record*, June 22, 1905.

17. Slotkin, *Lost Battalions*, 81–82; *NYT*, November 30, 1921.

18. Charles White Whittlesey, "Brook Farm," *Williams Literary Monthly* (February 1904): 177–186.

19. Charles Whittlesey to Max Eastman, August 23, [1913], Max Eastman Papers, Series II, Box 1, Lilly Library, Indiana University.

20. Slotkin, *Lost Battalions*, 81.

21. Laplander, *Finding the Lost Battalion*, 47.

22. Robert Zieger, *America's Great War: World War I and the American Experience*, rev. ed. (Lanham, MD: Rowman and Littlefield, 2000), 22; Slotkin, *Lost Battalions*, 82.

23. John Garry Clifford, *The Citizen Soldiers: The Plattsburg Training Camp Movement, 1913–1920* (Lexington: University Press of Kentucky, 2015), 54–55.

24. For the history of the Plattsburg Camp, see Francis Russell, "When Gentlemen Prepared for War," *American Heritage* (April 1964): 24–27, 89–93; Clifford, *The Citizen Soldiers*, 56–91.

25. Clifford, *The Citizen Soldiers*, 63.

26. Clifford, *The Citizen Soldiers*, 58.

27. Corydon Ireland, "'The Choicest of Their Kind,'" *Harvard Gazette*, July 25, 2014, http://news.harvard.edu/gazette/story/2014/07/the-choicest-of-their-kind/.

28. Charles W. Whittlesey, Military Service Records, War Records Office, Harvard University Archives, Box 121.

29. Laplander, *Finding the Lost Battalion*, 48–49; Charles W. Whittlesey, Honorable Discharge, August 14, 1917, CWP; Appointment to Captain, August 8, 1917, CWP.

2. MUCK RAKING

1. French Strother, "'The Providence Journal Will Say This Morning,'" *The World's Work*, December 1917, 149–153; *BG*, November 18, 1917; "WWI 100 Years: Journal Editor Rathom Lied About Personal, Paper's Role in Exposing German Spies," *PJ*, July 20, 2014, www.providencejournal.com/article/20140720/SPECIAL-REPORTS/307209929.

2. "Conscience of New England," *Time*, July 6, 1953, 70; "'More Thrilling Than Fiction,'" *The Nation*, November 10, 1920, 522.

3. Erik Kirschbaum, *Burning Beethoven: The Eradication of German Culture in the United States During World War I* (New York: Berlinica Publishing, LLC, 2015), 58–76; Mark Ellis, "German-Americans in World War I," in Ragnhild Fiebig-von Hase and Ursula Lehmkuhl, eds., *Enemy Images in American History* (Providence and Oxford: Berghahn Books, 1997), 189–190.

4. *PJ*, October 1, 1917.

5. Out of the one hundred musicians in the BSO during the 1917–1918 season, forty-four were from Germany and twelve from Austria. Only fourteen were native-born Americans. See 1917–1918 BSO Roster, BSO Archives. Jessica C. E. Gienow-Hecht, *Sound Diplomacy: Music and Emotions in Transatlantic Relations, 1850–1920* (Chicago: University of Chicago Press, 2009), 181–182; Kirschbaum, *Burning Beethoven*, 130–131.

6. *PJ*, October 30, 1917.

7. *PJ*, October 31, 1917.

8. Muck quoted in Thomas Boynton to Attorney General Thomas Gregory, April 10, 1918, NA Record Group 60, Box 30, Folder 9-5-542.

9. Janet Baker-Carr, *Evening at Symphony: A Portrait of the Boston Symphony Orchestra* (Boston: Houghton-Mifflin, 1977), 50; Joseph Horowitz, *Classical Music in*

America: A History of Its Rise and Fall (New York: W. W. Norton and Company, 2005), 26–27.

10. Baker-Carr, *Evening at Symphony*, 41; Lawrence W. Levine, *Highbrow/Lowbrow: The Emergence of Cultural Hierarchy in America* (Cambridge, MA: Harvard University Press, 1988), 83–168.

11. Baker-Carr, *Evening at Symphony*, 1–2; Joseph Horowitz, *Moral Fire: Musical Portraits From America's Fin de Siècle* (Berkeley and Los Angeles: University of California Press, 2012), 26, 57; Levine, *Highbrow/Lowbrow*, 124.

12. *BG*, March 10, 1940; Horowitz, *Classical Music in America*, 78.

13. *NYT*, November 18, 1906.

14. Gienow-Hecht, *Sound Diplomacy*, 190; *NYT*, March 26, 1918.

15. Harold C. Schonberg, *The Great Conductors* (New York: Simon and Schuster, 1967), 218–220.

16. Gienow-Hecht, *Sound Diplomacy*, 178; "Carl Muck," February, 14, 1918, Report, NA Record Group 165, Box 2101, Folder 9140-4175/18; Gayle Turk, "The Case of Dr. Karl Muck," Harvard University B.A. Thesis, 1994, 23–24.

17. Bliss Perry, *Life and Letters of Henry Lee Higginson* (Boston: Atlantic Monthly Press, 1921), 470–471.

18. Perry, *Life and Letters of Henry Lee Higginson*, 471–473, 481; Horowitz, *Moral Fire*, 63.

19. Perry, *Life and Letters of Henry Lee Higginson*, 474–476; Muck quoted in Boynton to Gregory, April 10, 1918.

20. Perry, *Life and Letters of Henry Lee Higginson*, 477–478.

21. Norman L. Gifford, "Dr. Karl Muck," Report, March 26, 1918, BSO Archives; George Kelleher, "Dr. Karl Muck," Report, February 18, 1918, NA Record Group 165, Box 2101, Folder 9140-4175/18.

22. Gienow-Hecht, *Sound Diplomacy*, 192; Boynton to Gregory, April 10, 1918; *BP*, November 16, 1919.

23. Barbara W. Tuchman, *The Zimmermann Telegram* (New York: Random House, 1985), 135–137.

24. Tuchman, *The Zimmermann Telegram*, 65–66; Howard Blum, *Dark Invasion: Germany's Secret War and the Hunt for the First Terrorist Cell in America* (New York: Harper Perennial, 2015), 32; Chad Millman, *The Detonators: The Secret Plot to Destroy America and an Epic Hunt for Justice* (Boston: Little, Brown, and Company, 2006), 9–10, 54–55.

25. *NYTR*, February 14, 1917; Boynton to Gregory, April 10, 1918; Christopher Capozzola, *Uncle Sam Wants You: World War I and the Making of the Modern American Citizen* (New York: Oxford University Press, 2010), 186.

26. Tuchman, *The Zimmermann Telegram*, 125–160; Meirion Harries and Susie Harries, *The Last Days of Innocence: America at War, 1917–1918* (New York: Random House, 1997), 68.

27. *Official Bulletin*, published by the Committee on Public Information, October 10, 1917, 1; Blum, *Dark Invasion*, 69–70.

28. Turk, "The Case of Dr. Karl Muck," 49–50; Capozzola, *Uncle Sam Wants You*, 177.

29. Blum, *Dark Invasion*, 419.

30. Capozzola, *Uncle Sam Wants You*, 151–152; Harries and Harries, *The Last Days of Innocence*, 167.

31. David M. Kennedy, *Over Here: The First World War and American Society* (New York: Oxford University Press, 2004), 67–68; John Higham, *Strangers in the Land: Patterns of American Nativism, 1860–1925*, rev. ed. (New Brunswick, NJ: Rutgers

University Press, 2002), 195–196; Glenn Watkins, *Proof Through the Night: Music and the Great War* (Berkeley and Los Angeles: University of California Press, 2003), 282.

32. Higham, *Strangers in the Land*, 198, 208; Kennedy, *Over Here*, 54; Kirschbaum, *Burning Beethoven*, 130; Gienow-Hecht, *Sound Diplomacy*, 183–184.

33. Perry, *Life and Letters of Henry Lee Higginson*, 480–484.

34. Perry, *Life and Letters of Henry Lee Higginson*, 486; Watkins, *Proof Through the Night*, 288–290; Barbara Tischler, "One Hundred Percent Americanism and Music in Boston During World War I," *American Music* 4 (Summer 1986): 169; Gienow-Hecht, *Sound Diplomacy*, 185; *BG*, November 1, 1917.

35. *PJ*, October 31, 1917.

36. *PJ*, November 1, 1917, November 3, 1917; *NYT*, November 1, 1917; Turk, "The Case of Dr. Karl Muck," 30.

37. "The Boston Symphony and Patriotism," *Literary Digest*, November 17, 1917, 28; Turk, "The Case of Dr. Karl Muck," 18; *BG*, November 22, 1917.

38. Perry, *Lives and Letters of Henry Lee Higginson*, 487.

39. Perry, *Lives and Letters of Henry Lee Higginson*, 487.

40. Norman L. Gifford, "Dr. Carl Muck," Report, February 15, 1918, NA, RG 165, Box 2101, Folder 9140-4175/18.

41. *PJ*, November 3, 1917; *BG*, November 3, 1917; James Badal, "The Strange Case of Dr. Karl Muck," *High Fidelity*, October 1970, 57.

42. Matthew Mugmon, "Patriotism, Art, and 'The Star-Spangled Banner' in World War I: A New Look at the Karl Muck Episode," *Journal of Musicological Research* 33 (2014): 22.

43. Badal, "The Strange Case of Dr. Karl Muck," 57; Mugmon, "Patriotism, Art, and 'The Star-Spangled Banner' in World War I," 13.

44. *BS*, November 7, 1917.

45. *WP*, December 2, 1917; Edmund Bowles, "Karl Muck and His Compatriots: German Conductors in America During World War I (And How They Coped)," *American Music* 25 (Winter 2007): 411–412.

46. John B. Hanrahan, "Dr. Karl Muck (alleged German activities)," September 18, 1917, Report, NA Record Group 165, Box 2100, Folder 9140-4161 to 9140-4175/17; Charles H. McCormick, *Hopeless Cases: The Hunt for the Red Scare Terrorist Bombers* (Lanham, MD: University Press of America, 2005), 18–21. For the Hanrahan quote, emphasis ours.

47. J. Scully, "Dr. Karl Muck," November 9, 1917, Report, NA Record Group 165, Box 2100, Folder 9140-4161 to 9140-4175/17.

3. OUT OF THE CAGE

1. *BS*, November 9, 1917; *BDA*, November 9, 1917; Kal Wagenheim, *Babe Ruth: His Life and Legend* (New York: Praeger, 1974), 37.

2. For Ruth's early childhood through his years at St. Mary's Industrial School for Orphans, Delinquent, Incorrigible, and Wayward Boys and the Baltimore Orioles, see Robert Creamer, *Babe: The Legend Comes to Life* (New York: Simon and Schuster, 1992), 24–83; Marshall Smelser, *The Life That Ruth Built: A Biography* (New York: New York Times Book Co./Quadrangle, 1975), 3–49; Wagenheim, *Babe Ruth*, 9–23; Leigh Montville, *The Big Bam: The Life and Times of Babe Ruth* (New York: Doubleday, 2006), 7–41; Bill Bryson, *One Summer: America, 1927* (New York: Doubleday, 2013), 107–111.

3. John J. Ward, "The Coming Southpaw," *BM*, July 1916, 44.

4. Babe Ruth, *Babe Ruth's Own Book of Baseball* (New York: G.P. Putnam's Sons, 1928), 3–4.

5. Smelser, *The Life That Ruth Built*, 4; Fred Lieb, *Baseball As I Have Known It* (New York: G.P. Putnam's Sons, 1977), 153–154.

6. According to biographer Jane Leavy, records in the Maryland State Archives belie Mamie's memory of how many children her mother Katie bore. Records only confirm the births of six children and four deaths. See Leavy, *The Big Fella: Babe Ruth and the World He Created* (New York: Harper, 2018), 41–42.

7. Babe Ruth with Bob Considine, *The Babe Ruth Story* (New York: E. P. Dutton, 1948), 12; Creamer, *Babe*, 29.

8. Allen Wood, *1918: Babe Ruth and the World Champion Boston Red Sox* (San Jose, CA: Writers Club Press, 2000), 47–50.

9. Creamer, *Babe*, 32.

10. Ruth, *Babe Ruth's Own Book of Baseball*, 4–5.

11. Creamer, *Babe*, 38; Montville, *The Big Bam*, 21.

12. Montville, *The Big Bam*, 25.

13. Creamer, *Babe*, 37.

14. Montville, *The Big Bam*, 26.

15. Creamer, *Babe*, 45.

16. Creamer, *Babe*, 45.

17. Creamer, *Babe*, 52.

18. Creamer, *Babe*, 61.

19. Creamer, *Babe*, 63.

20. Wood, *1918*, 83; Montville, *The Big Bam*, 54.

21. Stout, *The Selling of the Babe*, 12–13; Thomas Whalen, *When the Red Sox Ruled: Baseball's First Dynasty, 1912–1918* (Chicago: Ivan R. Dee, 2011), 69.

22. Creamer, *Babe*, 21.

23. Bryson, *One Summer*, 110–111; Lawrence Ritter, *The Glory of Their Times: The Story of the Early Days of Baseball Told by the Men Who Played It* (New York: Harper Perennial Classics, 2010), 205–206.

24. Wood, *1918*, 79–81; Montville, *The Big Bam*, 53–54.

25. Montville, *The Big Bam*, 44; Bryson, *One Summer*, 111; Creamer, *Babe*, 321–322.

26. Wood, *1918*, 79.

27. Creamer, *Babe*, 186.

28. Leavy, *The Big Fella*, 49–55, 206.

29. Ritter, *The Glory of Their Times*, 145.

30. Montville, *The Big Bam*, 50.

31. Ward, "The Coming Southpaw," 45.

32. For Ruth's signing, see *BH*, January 12, 1918; *BP*, January 12, 1918; *BG*, January 10, 1918, January 12, 1918.

33. For John L. Sullivan, see Michael T. Isenberg, *John L. Sullivan and His America* (Urbana: University of Illinois Press, 1988).

34. There's some dispute about the salary terms of Ruth's 1918 contract. His biographers Creamer and Smelser claim that Ruth signed for $7,000. However, a recent auction sale of the original contract shows that Ruth signed for $5,000. Ruth later earned $2,000 more because of two separate bonuses Frazee paid him. For more on the bonuses, see Chapter 13. Creamer, *Babe*, 148; Smelser, *The Life That Ruth Built*; 95; *BP*, January 12,

1918; for a copy of the auctioned contract, see https://goldinauctions.com/1918_Babe _Ruth_Boston_Red_Sox_Contract___Ruth_s_Ow-LOT10392.aspx.

35. *BG*, January 20, 1918.

36. Ward, "The Coming Southpaw," 46.

4. THE WAR GAME

1. Wood, *1918*, 7; *BG*, January 20, 1918.

2. *BG*, December 7, 1917.

3. Unless otherwise cited, the sketch of Frazee is drawn from F. C. Lane, "The Fire Brand of the American League," *BM*, March 1919, 268–272; Glenn Stout and Richard Johnson, *Red Sox Century: 100 Years of Red Sox Baseball* (Boston: Houghton Mifflin, 2000), 116–118; Glenn Stout, *The Selling of the Babe: The Deal That Changed Baseball and Created a Legend* (New York: Thomas Dunne Books, 2016), 22–75; Michael T. Lynch, *Harry Frazee, Ban Johnson, and the Feud* (Jefferson, NC: McFarland and Co., 2008), 41–44.

4. Geoffrey C. Ward, *Unforgiveable Blackness: The Rise and Fall of Jack Johnson* (New York: Knopf, 2004), 172–173.

5. Wood, *1918*, 88.

6. *BG*, November 2, 1916; Daniel R. Levitt, Mark L. Armour, and Matthew Levitt, "History versus Harry Frazee," *Baseball Research Journal* 37 (2008): 27; quote from Stout and Johnson, *Red Sox Century*, 117.

7. Eugene C. Murdock, *Ban Johnson: The Czar of Baseball* (Westport, CT: Greenwood Press, 1982), 67, 74.

8. Murdock, *Ban Johnson*, 67; Eliot Asinof, *Eight Men Out: The Black Sox and the 1919 World Series* (New York: Holt Paperbacks, 2000), 75; Harold Seymour and Dorothy Seymour, *Baseball: The Golden Age* (New York: Oxford University Press, 1989), 11.

9. *NYT*, March 28, 1917.

10. Robert Elias, *The Empire Strikes Out: How Baseball Sold U.S. Foreign Policy and Promoted the American Way Abroad* (New York: The New Press, 2010), 78.

11. H. Addington Bruce, "Baseball and the National Life," *The Outlook*, May 17, 1913, 107.

12. Morris R. Cohen, "Baseball as a National Religion," *The Dial*, July 26, 1919, 57–58.

13. Rev. Wm. A. Sunday, "A Defense of the Grand Old Game," *BM*, July 1917, 361; Sean Deveney, *The Original Curse: Did the Cubs Throw the 1918 World Series to Babe Ruth's Red Sox and Incite the Black Sox Scandal?* (New York: McGraw-Hill, 2009), 67; Robert F. Martin, *Hero of the Heartland: Billy Sunday and the Transformation of American Society, 1862–1935* (Bloomington: Indiana University Press, 2002), 90–91.

14. Sunday, "A Defense of the Grand Old Game," 361; Elias, *The Empire Strikes Out*, 87.

15. Seymour and Seymour, *Baseball: The Golden Age*, 245; "Baseball Players and National Defense," *The Outlook*, February 28, 1917, 342–343.

16. Seymour and Seymour, *Baseball: The Golden Age*, 246; Elias, *The Empire Strikes Out*, 79–80.

17. *BG*, May 2, 1917; Murdock, *Ban Johnson*, 122–123; Creamer, *Babe*, 138; Capozzola, *Uncle Sam Wants You*, 28; Seymour and Seymour, *Baseball: The Golden Age*, 247; *NYT*, July 28, 1917.

18. Jim Leeke, *From the Dugouts to the Trenches: Baseball During the Great War* (Lincoln: University of Nebraska Press, 2017), 62–63; Charles Fountain, *The Betrayal: The 1919 World Series and the Birth of Modern Baseball* (New York: Oxford University Press, 2015), 45.

19. Leeke, *From the Dugouts to the Trenches*, 63–64.

20. Annual Meeting of the American League, December 12, 1917, American League Meetings and Minutes, BHOF, Box 1, Folder 5; Joint Meeting of National and American Leagues, December 14, 1917, BHOF, Box 1, Folder 5; Seymour and Seymour, *Baseball: The Golden Age*, 247–248; Deveney, *The Original Curse*, 18; Fountain, *The Betrayal*, 46.

21. Leeke, *From the Dugouts to the Trenches*, 67.

22. Wood, *1918*, 89–90; Stout, *The Selling of the Babe*, 27–28; Creamer, *Babe*, 146–147.

23. *TSN*, March 14, 1918; Bill Nowlin, ed., *When Boston Still Had the Babe: The 1918 World Champion Red Sox* (Burlington, MA: Rounder Books, 2008), 10; Creamer, *Babe*, 147; *TSN*, January 31, 1918.

24. Stout and Johnson, *Red Sox Century*, 122; "Captain, Commandant" to Harry H. Frazee, December 29, 1917, NA Record Group 181, Records of Naval Districts and Shore Establishments, Correspondence Concerning Red Sox Players at the Boston Navy Yard; H. H. Frazee to Hon. Franklin D. Roosevelt, January 23, 1918, NA, Record Group 181, 12/1917–2/1918; Frazee to Commandant W. R. Rush, January 11, 1918, NA, Record Group 181; Franklin D. Roosevelt to Captain Rush, January 24, 1918, NA, Record Group 181.

25. *TSN*, February 14, 1918.

26. District Enrolling Officer to Commandant, Boston Navy Yard, January 17, 1918, NA, Record Group 181; Boston Navy Yard Commandant, Press Statement, February 9, 1918, NA, Record Group 181.

5. BANG THAT OLD APPLE

1. *BG*, March 8, 1918, March 9, 1918; *BHJ*, March 10, 1918; *BP*, March 10, 1918; Stout, *The Selling of the Babe*, 11.

2. *BP*, March 10, 1918, March 11, 1918.

3. *BG*, March 10, 1918.

4. *BG*, March 10, 1918.

5. *BG*, October 4, 1918, October 5, 1918, October 6, 1918.

6. Arthur Mann, "Edward Grant Barrow" manuscript, Arthur Mann Papers, Box 6, Library of Congress; Stout, *The Selling of the Babe*, 19–20.

7. Nowlin, ed., *When Boston Still Had the Babe*, 156–158.

8. Whalen, *When the Red Sox Ruled*, 152.

9. *BHJ*, March 12, 1918; *BA*, March 12, 1918; *BP*, March 12, 1918; *BG*, March 12, 1918.

10. *BG*, March 17, 1918.

11. *BHJ*, March 14, 1918.

12. *BHJ*, March 14, 1918.

13. At the time, reporters referred to the Brooklyn club as the "Dodgers" and "Robbins." To avoid confusion, we use "Dodgers." See *BG*, March 18, 1918.

14. *BG*, March 18, 1918; *BHJ*, March 18, 1918.

15. *BG*, March 18, 1918.

16. *BA*, March 20, 1918.
17. *BG*, July 14, 1918.
18. *BG*, March 24, 1918.
19. *BA*, March 24, 1918; *BG*, March 24, 1918.
20. *BG*, March 25, 1918; *BP*, March 25, 1918; *BA*, March 25, 1918.
21. *BHJ*, March 25, 1918.
22. *BG*, March 22, 1918; *BA*, March 20, 1918.

6. THE KEYS

1. Harries and Harries, *The Last Days of Innocence*, 303–304.
2. Randy Roberts, *Papa Jack: Jack Johnson and the Era of White Hopes* (New York: Free Press, 1985), 148–151, 161–164.
3. *WP*, December 2, 1917; Turk, "The Case of Dr. Karl Muck," 31.
4. George Kelleher, "Carl Muck (War Matters)," Report, January 16, 1918, NA Record Group 165, Box 2101, Folder 9140-4175/18; Von Ende School advertisement, *The Musician*, October 1915, 676; "Annual Concert of the Von Ende School," *Musical America*, June 12, 1915, 8.
5. George Kelleher, "Carl Muck (War Matters)," Report, January 18, 1918, NA, RG 165, Box 2101, Folder 9140-4175/18.
6. *BG*, February 15, 1931; John William Leonard, *Woman's Who's Who of America* (NY: The American Commonwealth Company, 1914), 913; Rosamond Young to A. Mitchell Palmer, March 3, 1922, NA Record Group 60, Box 30, Folder 9-5-542.
7. Francis G. Caffey to the Attorney General, February 8, 1918, NA Record Group 60, Box 30, Folder 9-5-542; Turk, "The Case of Dr. Karl Muck," 32.
8. *BP*, November 12, 1919.
9. Henry L. Higginson to Karl Muck, March 6, 1918, NA Record Group 165, Box 2101, Folder 9140-4175/18; Henry L. Higginson to the Attorney General of the United States, March 13, 1918, NA Record Group 60, Box 30, Folder 9-5-542.
10. *BG*, January 20, 1918, February 5, 1918; Turk, "The Case of Dr. Karl Muck," 35.
11. Lucy Claire Church, "Music, Morality, and the Great War: How World War I Molded American Musical Ethics," (PhD diss., Florida State University, 2015), 125–139; quote from *The Chronicle* found in *The Musical Leader*, August 15, 1918, 160.
12. *NYTR*, March 12, 1918; Irving Lowens, "L'Affaire Muck: A Study in War Hysteria (1917–18)," *Musicology* I (1947): 269–270.
13. Lowens, "L'Affaire Muck," 271.
14. *BG*, March 15, 1918; Lowens, "L'Affaire Muck," 271–272.
15. *BP*, November 12, 1919.
16. *BP*, November 11, 1919.
17. *BP*, November 12, 1919.
18. Norman L. Gifford, "Dr. Karl Muck," Report, March 20, 1918, NA Record Group 165, Box 2101, Folder 9140-4175/18.
19. Feri Weiss, "Dr. Karl Muck," March 20, 1918, Report, NA Record Group 165, Box 2101, Folder 9140-4175/18; *Pittsburgh Press*, November 9, 1919; McCormick, *Hopeless Cases*, 18–19.
20. *WT*, December 20, 1919.
21. *WT*, December 22, 1919.
22. Young to Palmer; *WT*, December 20, 1919.

23. Young to Palmer; *WT*, December 20, 1919.

24. Young to Palmer; Feri Weiss, "Dr. Karl Muck," Report, March 20, 1918, NA Record Group 165, Box 2101, Folder 9140-4175/18.

25. Young to Palmer.

26. Young to Palmer.

27. Young to Palmer.

28. Young to Palmer.

29. Norman Gifford, "Carl Muck," Report, March 21, 1918, NA Record Group 165, Box 2101, Folder 9140-4175/18; Thomas Boynton to Attorney General Thomas Gregory, April 1, 1918, NA Record Group 60, Box 30, Folder 9-5-542; *WT*, December 24, 1919.

30. Norman Gifford, "Dr. Karl Muck," Report, March 25, 1918, NA Record Group 165, Box 2101, Folder 9140-4175/18; Attorney General Thomas Gregory to U.S. Marshal, Boston, March 26, 1918, NA Record Group 165, Box 2101, Folder 9140-4175/18.

31. Feri Weiss, "Dr. Karl Muck," Report, March 25, 1918, NA Record Group 165, Box 2101, Folder 9140-4175/18.

32. Weiss, "Dr. Karl Muck," Report, March 25, 1918; Karl Muck to Carl Huebscher, Counselor of the Legation of Switzerland, July 19, 1919, NA Record Group 407, Box 23, Folder "Muck, Karl."

33. *BT*, March 26, 1918.

7. FAMILY TRADITIONS

1. *PE*, October 26, 1917.

2. *Harvard Class of 1918, Twenty-fifth Anniversary Report* (1943), 905–906.

3. *Harvard Class of 1918, Twenty-fifth Anniversary Report* (1943), 905–906; *Harvard Class Album, 1918*; Elisha Whittlesey Harvard Record Card, Harvard University Archives, UAIII 15.75.12 1910–1919, Box 22.

4. Michael S. Neiberg, *The Path to War: How the First World War Created Modern America* (New York: Oxford University Press, 2016), 109; "Harvard and the War," *The Harvard Advocate*, October 19, 1917, 1–2.

5. H. A. Yeomans to Dear Sir, May 5, 1917; Elisha Whittlesey to H. A. Yeomans, May 11, 1917, War Records Office, Personal Service Records, Harvard University Archives, UAV 874269.

6. *Harvard Alumni Bulletin*, vol. 24 (1922); *PE*, October 26, 1917.

7. *PE*, October 26, 1917.

8. *PE*, October 26, 1917; Elisha Whittlesey Harvard Record Card, Harvard University Archives, UAIII 15.75.12 1910–1919, Box 22.

9. *PE*, October 26, 1917.

10. *PE*, October 26, 1917.

11. *PE*, October 26, 1917.

12. Laplander, *Finding the Lost Battalion*, 41, 45.

13. For details on Camp Upton, see Alan D. Gaff, *Blood in the Argonne: The "Lost Battalion" of World War I* (Norman: University of Oklahoma Press, 2005), 9–53; L. Wardlaw Miles, *History of the 308th Infantry 1917–1919* (New York: G.P. Putnam's Sons, 1927), 1–23; Richard S. Faulkner, *Pershing's Crusaders: The American Soldier in World War I* (Lawrence: Kansas University Press, 2017), 161–163.

14. Slotkin, *Lost Battalions*, 74–75.

15. Slotkin, *Lost Battalions*, 78–79.

16. Gaff, *Blood in the Argonne*, 17–18, 34–35; W. K. Rainsford, *From Upton to the Meuse* (New York: D. Appleton and Company, 1920), 4.

17. Gaff, *Blood in the Argonne*, 17–18.

18. Julius Ochs Adler, *History of the Seventy Seventh Division August 25th, 1917–November 11th, 1918* (New York: Wynkoop Hollenbeck Crawford Company, 1919), 8.

19. For Whittlesey and his men, see *NYT*, September 25, 1938; Laplander, *Finding the Lost Battalion*, 50; Gaff, *Blood in the Argonne*, 36.

20. Laplander, *Finding the Lost Battalion*, 51; Miles, *History of the 308th Infantry 1917–1919*, 19, 115.

21. For the parade, see *NYT*, February 22, 1918, February 23, 1918, Gaff, *Blood in the Argonne*, 39–40; Adler, *History of the Seventy Seventh Division*, 17.

8. THE MAD BRUTE

1. *BP*, March 27, 1918; *BG*, March 27, 1918; *BA*, March 27, 1918.

2. *BA*, March 26, 1918; *BG*, March 27, 1918; *BHJ*, March 26, 1918.

3. *BP*, March 27, 1918; *NYT*, March 27, 1918.

4. *NYT*, March 27, 1918; Nathaniel C. Nash Jr., "Dr. Karl Muck, Alleged German Spy," Report, June 19, 1918, NA Record Group 165, Box 2101, Folder 9140-4175/18.

5. *NYT*, March 26, 1918; *BP*, March 27, 1918; *BG*, March 27, 1918.

6. Norman L. Gifford, "Dr. Carl Muck," Report, March 26, 1918, NA Record Group 165, Box 2101, Folder 9140-4175/18; "Dr. Karl Muck," Report, April 2, 1918, NA Record Group 165, Box 2101, Folder 9140-4175/18.

7. *BA*, March 27, 1918; Karl Muck to Carl Huebscher, Counselor of the Legation of Switzerland, July 19, 1919, NA Record Group 407, Box 23, Folder "Muck, Karl."

8. *BP*, March 28, 1918; *BA*, March 29, 1918, March 30, 1918; *BG*, March 27, 1918; Perry, *Life and Letters of Henry Lee Higginson*, 502–503.

9. *NYTR*, April 2, 1918; *BA*, April 2, 1918; Unless otherwise cited, quotes from the interrogation come from Thomas Boynton's interview with Karl Muck, April 1, 1918, Boston Symphony Orchestra Archives.

10. *BP*, November 12, 1919.

11. *BP*, November 12, 1919.

12. Norman Gifford, "Dr. Karl Muck," March 29, 1918, Report, NA Record Group 165, Box 2101, Folder 9140-4175/18.

13. *NYT*, February 27, 1918; "'More Thrilling Than Fiction,'" *The Nation*, November 10, 1920, 522.

14. Thomas Boynton to Thomas Gregory, April 1, 1918, NA Record Group 60, Box 30, Folder 9-5-542.

15. Boynton to Gregory; *BP*, November 9, 1919.

16. David J. Langum, *Crossing Over the Line: Legislating Morality and the Mann Act* (Chicago: University of Chicago Press, 1994), 3–7.

17. *BA*, May 28, 1918; *BG*, June 20, 1918, September 19, 1918.

18. Henry Rood to John Lord O'Brian, May 30, 1918; O'Brian to Rood, June 10, 1918, NA Record Group 60, Box 30, Folder 9-5-542; Nathaniel C. Nash Jr., "Dr. Karl Muck, Alleged German Spy," Report, June 3, 1918, NA Record Group 165, Box 2101, Folder 9140-4175/18; *WT*, December 27, 1919.

19. Roberts, *Papa Jack*, 144; Langum, *Crossing Over the Line*, 4–9.

20. Langum, *Crossing Over the Line*, 10.

21. Rosamond Young to A. Mitchell Palmer, March 3, 1922, NA Record Group 60, Box 30, Folder 9-5-542; Boynton to Gregory; *BP*, November 11, 1919.

22. The description of the Prager lynching is drawn from the following: *St. Louis Globe-Democrat*, April 5, 1918; *St. Louis Post-Dispatch*, April 6, 1918; Frederick Luebke, *Bonds of Loyalty: German-Americans and World War I* (DeKalb: Northern Illinois University, 1974), 3–13; Kirschbaum, *Burning Beethoven*, 15–19.

23. "Lynching: An American Kulture?" *The New Republic*, April 13, 1918, 311; Capozzola, *Uncle Sam Wants You*, 117.

24. Kennedy, *Over Here*, 68; *BG*, April 6, 1918; "The First War Lynching," *Literary Digest*, April 20, 1918, 16–17.

25. *BA*, March 26, 1918.

26. Turk, "The Case of Dr. Karl Muck," 61.

27. Turk, "The Case of Dr. Karl Muck," 61.

28. John Lord O'Brian to Thomas Boynton, April 6, 1918, NA Record Group 60, Box 30, Folder 9-5-542; *BA*, April 6, 1918.

9. THE SEASON OF DOUBT

1. *BG*, April 12, 1918; *BA*, April 12, 1918; *BP*, April 13, 1918.

2. *BG*, April 14, 1918; *BHJ*, April 14, 1918.

3. *BHJ*, April 14, 1918; *BG*, April 15, 1918.

4. Leeke, *From the Dugouts to the Trenches*, 82; Wood, *1918*, 7.

5. *BHJ*, April 16, 1918; Glenn Stout, *Fenway 1912: The Birth of a Ballpark, a Championship Season, and Fenway's Remarkable First Year* (New York: Mariner Books, 2012), 73–74.

6. Patrick R. Redmond, *The Irish and the Making of American Sport, 1835–1920* (Jefferson, NC: McFarland and Co., 2014), 148–152, 124–125; Francis Russell, "Honey Fitz," *American Heritage*, August 1968; Thomas H. O'Connor, *The Boston Irish: A Political History* (Boston: Back Bay Books, 1997), 142–144, 168; William V. Shannon, "Boston's Irish Mayors: An Ethnic Perspective," in *Boston, 1700–1980: The Evolution of Urban Politics*, eds. Ronald P. Formisano and Constance K. Burns (Westport, CT: Greenwood Press, 1984), 204–205.

7. Wood, *1918*, 12–14; Stout, *The Selling of the Babe*, 39; *BP*, April 16, 1918; *BG*, April 16, 1918, April 13, 1916.

8. *BHJ*, April 16, 1918; *BP*, April 16, 1918; *BG*, April 16, 1918.

9. Marc Ferris, *Star-Spangled Banner: The Unlikely Story of America's National Anthem* (Baltimore: Johns Hopkins University Press, 2014), 77.

10. Thomas H. O'Connor, *Bibles, Brahmins, and Bosses: A Short History of Boston*, rev. ed. (Boston: Boston Public Library, 1991), 84; Francis Russell, *A City in Terror: Calvin Coolidge and the 1919 Boston Police Strike* (Boston: Beacon Press, 2005), 68–70; James J. Connolly, *Triumph of Ethnic Progressivism: Urban Political Culture in Boston, 1900–1925* (Cambridge: Harvard University Press, 1998), 159–160.

11. *BHJ*, April 16, 1918.

12. Wood, *1918*, 93; Stout, *The Selling of the Babe*, 39; Stout, *Fenway 1912*, 122; Jacob Pomrenke, "'Call the Game!': The 1917 Fenway Park Gamblers Riot," *Baseball* 6 (Spring 2012): 7.

13. *BG*, August 31, 1915; Pomrenke, "'Call the Game!': The 1917 Fenway Park Gamblers Riot," 8–9.

14. Wood, *1918*, 94; Asinof, *Eight Men Out*, 13–14.

15. Fountain, *The Betrayal*, 41–42; Walter Hapgood to August Herrmann, August 31, 1917, August H. Herrmann Papers, BHOF, Box 113, Folder 9.

16. Montville, *The Big Bam*, 50–51; F. C. Lane, "The Season's Sensation," *BM*, October 1918, 471; *BS*, May 8, 1917.

17. Montville, *The Big Bam*, 51.

18. *BG*, April 16, 1918.

19. *TSN*, April 18, 1918.

20. *BHJ*, April 30, 1918; Stout, *The Selling of the Babe*, 45–46.

21. Stout, *The Selling of the Babe*, 45; Wood, *1918*, 26; Creamer, *Babe*, 152–153.

22. The dialogue between Hooper and Barrow comes from Wood, *1918*, 26–27, 36–37.

23. Creamer, *Babe*, 153.

10. WELCOME TO THE SHOW

1. Miles, *History of the 308th Infantry 1917–1919*, 22–23; Laplander, *Finding the Lost Battalion*, 57–60; Gaff, *Blood in the Argonne*, 45–48.

2. Miles, *History of the 308th Infantry*, 24–25; Laplander, *Finding the Lost Battalion*, 60.

3. Rainsford, *From Upton to the Meuse*, 20–21.

4. Miles, *History of the 308th Infantry*, 24–25.

5. Miles, *History of the 308th Infantry*, 26.

6. Rainsford, *From Upton to the Meuse*, 23; Miles, *History of the 308th Infantry*, 27.

7. For the ride from Liverpool to Dover, see *PE*, November 20, 1918; Miles, *History of the 308th Infantry*, 28–30; Rainsford, *From Upton to the Meuse*, 23–24.

8. Miles, *History of the 308th Infantry*, 30.

9. *PE*, November 20, 1918; Laplander, *Finding the Lost Battalion*, 61; Gaff, *Blood in the Argonne*, 60.

10. For life near the front, see Miles, *History of the 308th Infantry*, 31–42; Gaff, *Blood in the Argonne*, 63–66; Faulkner, *Pershing's Crusaders*, 107–108, 289–291, 483–495.

11. Miles, *History of the 308th Infantry*, 33–34.

12. Rainsford, *From Upton to the Meuse*, 31–32.

13. *PE*, November 20, 1918.

14. Miles, *History of the 308th Infantry*, 40–41.

15. Miles, *History of the 308th Infantry*, 41–42; Laplander, *Finding the Lost Battalion*, 63.

11. P.O.W. 1046

1. Muck's "Prisoner of War" sheet indicates that he was interned on April 9, 1918, NA Record Group 407, Box 23, Folder "Muck, Karl." German poet Erich Posselt vividly described the process of entering Fort Oglethorpe in his camp memoir. See Posselt, "Prisoner of War No. 3598," *American Mercury*, July 1927, 313.

2. Karl Muck to Siegfried Wagner, April 25, 1919, BSO Archives; Mitchell Yockelson, "The Ghosts of Ft. Oglethorpe," *North Georgia Journal* (Summer 1997): 55.

3. Karl Muck to Anita Muck, April 11, 1918, NA Record Group 407, Box 23, Folder "Muck, Karl."

4. *BG*, April 9, 1918; *NYT*, July 7, 1918; Posselt, "Prisoner of War No. 3598," 317–318; Richard B. Goldschmidt, *In and Out of the Ivory Tower: The Autobiography of Richard B. Goldschmidt* (Seattle: University of Washington Press, 1960), 177.

5. Karl Muck to Anita Muck, May 7, 1918; Anita Muck to Karl Muck, May 15, 1918, NA Record Group 407, Box 23, Folder "Muck, Karl"; *BG*, April 10, 1918; Karl Muck to Siegfried Wagner, April 25, 1919, BSO Archives; *NYS*, April 25, 1918.

6. *BG*, April 10, 1918; *NYS*, October 27, 1918.

7. Posselt, "Prisoner of War No. 3598," 313; Yockelson, "The Ghosts of Ft. Oglethorpe," 54.

8. Gerry Depken and Julie Powell, *Fort Oglethorpe* (Chicago: Arcadia, 2009), 21–26; "Preparing for the Great War at Chickamauga Battlefield," National Park Service, www.nps.gov/articles/chickamaugawwi.htm.

9. Edmund Bowles, "Karl Muck and His Compatriots: German Conductors in America During World War I (And How They Coped)," *American Music* 25 (Winter 2007): 419–420; Gerald H. Davis, "'Orgelsdorf': A World War I Internment Camp in America," *Yearbook of German-American Studies* 26 (1991): 250–252. In July 1918, the Hot Springs camp was closed due to a typhoid outbreak and security concerns.

10. *BG*, April 8–10, 1918; Charles V. Combe, "War Prisoners," *Collier's*, September 28, 1918, 6.

11. Bowles, "Karl Muck and His Compatriots," 420; Davis, "'Orgelsdorf,'" 254; Goldschmidt, *In and Out of the Ivory Tower*, 175.

12. Davis, "'Orgelsdorf,'" 254.

13. Davis, "'Orgelsdorf,'" 254–255.

14. *NYT*, July 7, 1918; Yockelson, "The Ghosts of Ft. Oglethorpe," 55–56; Posselt, "Prisoner of War No. 3598," 316.

15. Posselt, "Prisoner of War No. 3598," 317.

16. Davis, "'Orgelsdorf,'" 256; *Chattanooga News*, news clipping, ca. July 1918; Karl Muck to Carl Huebscher, counselor of the Legation of Switzerland, July 19, 1919, NA Record Group 407, Box 23, Folder "Muck, Karl."

17. Posselt, "Prisoner of War No. 3598," 317; Muck to Wagner; A. L. Vischer, *Barbed Wire Disease: A Psychological Study of the Prisoner of War* (London, 1919).

18. Posselt, "Prisoner of War No. 3598," 319; Combe, "War Prisoners," 6, 28; Davis, "'Orgelsdorf,'" 256.

19. Combe, "War Prisoners," 5; *Chattanooga News*, news clipping, ca. July 1918.

20. Posselt, "Prisoner of War No. 3598," 321–322.

21. Baker-Carr, *Evening at Symphony*, 58; *BG*, April 28, 1918; Horowitz, *Moral Fire*, 67–68.

22. Mark Antony De Wolfe Howe, *A Great Private Citizen: Henry Lee Higginson* (Boston: The Atlantic Monthly Press, 1920), 33.

23. *BA*, May 5, 1918; *BG*, May 5, 1918.

24. Horowitz, *Moral Fire*, 70.

25. *BA*, June 22, 1918.

26. *BG*, June 25, 1918; *NYTR*, April 6, 1918; *NYT*, March 21, 1937.

27. *NYT*, April 20, 1918; *BG*, June 25, 1918.

28. *BG*, June 25, 1918.

29. "Dr. Muck Leads Orchestra Again, This Time in Internment Camp," *Musical America*, June 15, 1918; Schonberg, *The Great Conductors*, 218; Bowles, "Karl Muck and His Compatriots," 417–418.

30. Bowles, "Karl Muck and His Compatriots," 424; "Muck Again at Work," *Musical America*, June 15, 1918, 22.

31. Posselt, "Prisoner of War No. 3598," 317.

12. THE GREAT EXPERIMENT

1. *BP*, May 5, 1918; Wood, *1918*, 37–38; Stout, *The Selling of the Babe*, 48.

2. For game details, see *BA*, May, 5, 1918; *BP*, May 5, 1918.

3. Stout, *The Selling of the Babe*, 50–51.

4. Montville, *The Big Bam*, 69; *NYT*, May 7, 1918; *BG*, May 7, 1918; *BP*, May 7, 1918.

5. Ritter, *The Glory of Their Times*, 43, 57.

6. Dan Holmes, *Ty Cobb: A Biography* (Westport, CT: Greenwood Press, 2004), 32; Ritter, *The Glory of Their Times*, 87.

7. W. A. Phelon, "Johnson's Speed and Other Matters," *BM*, April 1915, 41.

8. *BP*, May 8, 1918; *BHJ*, May 8, 1918; Kerry Keene et al., *The Babe in Red Stockings: An In-Depth Chronicle of Babe Ruth with the Boston Red Sox, 1914–1919* (Urbana, IL: Sagamore Publishing, 1997), 169.

9. Nowlin, ed., *When Boston Still Had the Babe*, 7; *BP*, May 10, 1918.

10. *BA*, May 10, 1918; *TSN*, May 23, 1918; Wood, *1918*, 42.

11. *BG*, April 8, 1918; *BHJ*, May 21, 1918; Creamer, *Babe*, 155.

12. John M. Barry, *The Great Influenza: The Story of the Deadliest Pandemic in History* (New York: Penguin Books, 2005), 169–170.

13. *BHJ*, May 21, 1918; "Silver Nitrate Treatment of Tonsillitis," *American Journal of Clinical Medicine* 21 (1914): 435.

14. *BHJ*, May 22, 1918.

15. *BHJ*, May 24, 1918; Creamer, *Babe*, 159–160.

16. *BHJ* May 24, 1918; *TSN*, May 30, 1918.

17. F. C. Lane, "Editorial Comment," *BM*, July 1918, NP; *BA*, May 24, 1918.

18. *BA*, May 24, 1918; Seymour and Seymour, *Baseball: The Golden Age*, 251.

19. *BG*, May 14, 1918; *TSN*, July 25, 1918.

20. *NYT*, June 22, 1918; *CT*, June 22, 1918.

21. *BG*, May 17, 1918; *BHJ*, May 27, 1918.

22. *BG*, June 1, 1918.

23. Steven Elliott Tripp, *Ty Cobb, Baseball, and American Manhood* (Lanham, MD: Rowman and Littlefield Publishers, 2016), 1.

24. *BHJ*, June 3, 1918, June 4, 1918, June 5, 1918; *BG*, June 3, 1918, June 4, 1918, June 5, 1918; *BP*, June 3, 1918, June 4, 1918, June 5, 1918; *BA*, June 5, 1918.

25. *BA*, June 6, 1918; *BG*, June 6, 1918; *BH*, June 6, 1918; *BP*, June 6, 1918.

26. *BH*, June 5, 1918.

27. *TSN*, August 8, 1918.

28. *BS*, August 15, 1918; Stout, *The Selling of the Babe*, 62; Wood, *1918*, 146–147; *BG*, June 12, 1918.

29. *BHJ*, June 17, 1918; *BG*, June 16, 1918; Keene et al., *The Babe in Red Stockings*, 178–179.

30. Ritter, *The Glory of Their Times*, 145–146.

31. Keene et al., *The Babe in Red Stockings*, 180; Stout, *The Selling of the Babe*, 63.

32. *BA*, June 23, 1918; Creamer, *Babe*, 160–161; *BHJ*, June 26, 1918; *NYT*, June 26, 1918.

33. *BP*, June 29, 1918, June 30, 1918.

34. *BG*, July 1, 1918; *BHJ*, July 1, 1918; *BA*, July 1, 1918; *BP*, July 1, 1918; *BH*, July 1, 1918.

35. Wood, *1918*, 156.

36. Creamer, *Babe*, 162.

13. SLACKERS AND SHIPYARDS

1. *BHJ*, July 1, 1918.

2. Ritter, *The Glory of Their Times*, 145.

3. For the dugout outburst between Ruth and Barrow on July 1, 1918, see Creamer, *Babe*, 162; Wood, *1918*, 158–159.

4. *BP*, July 4, 1918; Peter T. Dalleo and J. Vincent Watchorn III, "Baltimore, the 'Babe,' and the Bethlehem Steel League, 1918," *Maryland Historical Magazine* 93 (Spring 1998): 90, 97; *BG*, July 4, 1918.

5. *BP*, July 4, 1918; *BHJ*, July 4, 1918.

6. Dalleo and Watchorn, "Baltimore, the 'Babe,' and the Bethlehem Steel League, 1918," 97; *BS*, July 4, 1918; *BG*, July 4, 1918.

7. *BS*, July 4, 1918; *BG*, July 4, 1918; Montville, *The Big Bam*, 71; Creamer, *Babe*, 163–164.

8. Dalleo and Watchorn, "Baltimore, the 'Babe,' and the Bethlehem Steel League, 1918," 96–97; Leeke, *From the Dugouts to the Trenches*, 111–112; Nowlin, ed., *When Boston Still Had the Babe*, 144; *Stars and Stripes*, July 26, 1918.

9. Robert F. Burk, *Never Just a Game: Players, Owners, and American Baseball to 1920* (Chapel Hill: University of North Carolina Press, 1994), 211–215; Charles DeMotte, "How World War I Nearly Brought Down Professional Baseball," in *The Cooperstown Symposium on Baseball and American Culture, 2009–2010*, ed. William M. Simons (Jefferson, NC: McFarland & Company, Inc., 2011), 217; Edmund F. Wehrle, *Breaking Babe Ruth: Baseball's Campaign Against Its Biggest Star* (Columbia: University of Missouri Press, 2018), 44–45.

10. *BG*, July 14, 1918.

11. *BS*, July 4, 1918.

12. Keene et al., *The Babe in Red Stockings*, 178, 191; Stout, *The Selling of the Babe*, 67.

13. Babe Ruth with Bob Considine, "My Hits—and My Errors," *Saturday Evening Post*, February 28, 1948, 28; *BG*, July 5, 1918; Creamer, *Babe*, 164; *BHJ*, July 5, 1918.

14. *BA*, July 5, 1918, July 13, 1918.

15. *BP*, July 6, 1918.

16. *BA*, July 7, 1918; *BHJ*, July 7, 1918.

17. *Boston Sunday Advertiser and American*, July 7, 1918; Wagenheim, *Babe Ruth*, 41.

18. *BG*, July 9, 1918.

19. *BG*, July 14, 1918.

20. *BA*, July 14, 1918; *BS*, July 14, 1918.

21. *BHJ*, July 13, 1918.

22. Stout, *The Selling of the Babe*, 49–50, 60–61; *BG*, May 14, 1918; *CT*, June 20, 1918.

23. *BG*, July 14, 1918.

24. *BG*, July 20, 1918.

25. *BG*, July 20, 1918, July 21, 1918; Wood, *1918*, 188–189; H. H. Frazee to August Herrmann, July 19, 1918, BHOF, BA MSS 138, National League Files: WWI & WWII, Box 1, Folder 1918, Work or Fight Order.

26. *BHJ*, July 21, 1918; *BG*, July 21, 1918.

27. *BG*, July 23, 1918; Keene et al., *The Babe in Red Stockings*, 192; *BP*, July 22, 1918.

28. Wood, *1918*, 191, 195; *BG*, July 26, 1918.

29. *NYT*, July 12, 1918; *CT*, July 12, 1918, July 13, 1918.

30. *CT*, July 27, 1918.

14. BROTHERS IN ARMS

1. Croydon Ireland, "'The Choicest of Their Kind:' How Harvard Responded to the Great War," *Harvard Gazette*, July 25, 2014, https://news.harvard.edu/gazette/story/2014/07/the-choicest-of-their-kind/.

2. (Mrs. Frank R.) Anna G. Whittlesey to Harvard Alumni Bulletin, October 1, 1918, Elisha Whittlesey, Personal Service Records, Box 121, Harvard University Archives.

3. *BG*, June 19, 1918.

4. *BG*, June 18, 1918, June 19, 1918.

5. *Harvard Class Album 1918,* 128.

6. *Harvard Class Album 1918.*

7. Rainsford, *From Upton to the Meuse*, 44.

8. Miles, *History of the 308th Infantry*, 54.

9. Miles, *History of the 308th Infantry*, 54–55.

10. Sarah Everts, "A Brief History of Chemical War," *Distillations* (Spring 2015), www.sciencehistory.org/distillations/magazine/a-brief-history-of-chemical-war.

11. Miles, *History of the 308th Infantry*, 59.

12. Miles, *History of the 308th Infantry*, 70–71; Laplander, *Finding the Lost Battalion*, 65; Adler, *History of the Seventy Seventh Division*, 40.

13. Adler, *History of the Seventy Seventh Division*, 40.

14. Gaff, *Blood in the Argonne*, 85; Rainsford, *From Upton to the Meuse*, 76.

15. Laplander, *Finding the Lost Battalion*, 65–66.

16. Edward G. Lengel and James Lacey, "Background to the Meuse-Argonne," in Edward G. Lengel, ed., *A Companion to the Meuse-Argonne Campaign* (Oxford: Wiley Blackwell, 2014), 7–8.

17. Edward G. Lengel, *To Conquer Hell: The Meuse-Argonne, 1918, the Epic Battle That Ended World War I* (New York: Holt Paperbacks, 2009), 265.

18. For Alexander's background, see Laplander, *Finding the Lost Battalion*, 69–71; Gaff, *Blood in the Argonne*, 91–92; Lengel, *To Conquer Hell*, 117–118.

19. *NYT*, May 4, 1919.

20. For transfers, see Gaff, *Blood in the Argonne*, 107–110.

21. Douglas V. Mastriano, *Thunder in the Argonne: A New History of America's Greatest Battle* (Lexington: University Press of Kentucky, 2018), 50.

22. Charles White Whittlesey, Harvard War Records Office, May 19, 1919, HUG 300, Quinquennial File, Harvard University Archives; Laplander, *Finding the Lost Battalion*, 72; Gaff, *Blood in the Argonne*, 121.

23. Gaff, *Blood in the Argonne*, 121.

24. Laplander, *Finding the Lost Battalion*, 69.

25. Frederic T. Wood, ed., *Williams College in the World War* (New York: President and Trustees of Williams College, 1926), 116.

26. Miles, *History of the 308th Infantry*, 281–282; Slotkin, *Lost Battalions*, 207–208.

27. Miles, *History of the 308th Infantry*, 115–116.

15. A DEATH IN PIG TOWN

1. *BHJ*, July 30, 1918; Creamer, *Babe*, 168–169.

2. *BHJ*, July 30, 1918; *BG*, July 30, 1918.

3. *BG*, August 4, 1918; *CT*, August 6, 1918.

4. *CT*, August 14, 1918.

5. *TSN*, August 22, 1918.

6. *TSN*, August 22, 1918.

7. *CT*, August 24, 1918; Wood, *1918*, 219.

8. *BA*, August 25, 1918; *BG*, August 25, 1918.

9. *BHJ*, August 25, 1918.

10. For the death of George Herman Ruth Sr., see *BS*, August 26, 1918; Wood, *1918*, 223–227; Creamer, *Babe*, 169–170; Montville, *The Big Bam*, 75–76.

11. Wood, *1918*, 227.

12. Creamer, *Babe*, 170; Smelser, *The Life That Ruth Built*, 100.

13. *CT*, September 1, 1918; *BS*, September 4, 1918; *BHJ*, September 4, 1918.

14. For the late-August influenza outbreak, see Barry, *The Great Influenza*, 181–186; Alfred W. Crosby, *America's Forgotten Pandemic: The Influenza of 1918*, 2nd ed. (Cambridge and New York: Cambridge University Press, 2003), 37–40.

15. L. S. Block, "The Invisible Enemy of 1918," *Yankee*, February 1982, 70.

16. Crosby, *America's Forgotten Pandemic*, 39–40.

17. *BG*, September 6, 1918.

16. THE SHADOW OF WAR

1. *BHJ*, September 3, 1918; *BA*, September 5, 1918; *BG*, September 3, 1918.

2. *BHJ*, September 4, 1918; Creamer, *Babe*, 172; *BG*, September 5, 1918.

3. *BG*, September 5, 1918; Wood, *1918*, 266.

4. *CT*, September 5, 1918; John Reed, "The Social Revolution in Court," *The Liberator*, September 1918, 21; Melvyn Dubofsky, *We Shall Be All: A History of the Industrial Workers of the World* (Chicago and Urbana: University of Illinois Press, 2000), 350–357, 407, 423–424, 433–437.

5. Harries and Harries, *The Last Days of Innocence*, 186; David Pietrusza, *Judge and Jury: The Life and Times of Judge Kenesaw Mountain Landis* (South Bend, IN: Diamond Communications, Inc., 2001), 109–112; Reed, "The Social Revolution in Court," 20.

6. Pietrusza, *Judge and Jury*, 108–112, 134; *CT*, October 7, 1917; Seymour and Seymour, *Baseball: The Golden Age*, 367–370.

7. Louise Krasniewicz, *Walt Disney: A Biography* (Santa Barbara, CA: Greenwood, 2010), 14; Neal Gabler, *Walt Disney: The Triumph of the American Imagination* (New York: Vintage, 2006), 35.

8. Gabler, *Walt Disney*, 35; *CT*, September 5, 1918; McCormick, *Hopeless Cases*, 31.

9. McCormick, *Hopeless Cases*, 31–32; Deveney, *The Original Curse*, 159.

10. *CT*, September 5, 1918.

11. *BG*, September 6, 1918.

12. *BG*, September 6, 1918; Deveney, *The Original Curse*, 160–161. In 1918, the National Commission announced that the first three games of the World Series would be played in Chicago and the remaining games in Boston due to wartime travel restrictions.

13. Stout, *The Selling of the Babe*, 65–76; *BG*, September 6, 1918.

14. Gene Fowler, *Skyline: A Reporter's Reminiscence of the 1920s* (New York: Viking, 1961), 108–109.

15. *BG*, September 6, 1918; *NYT*, September 6, 1918; Ferris, *Star-Spangled Banner*, 133.

16. *BP*, September 6, 1918; *BA*, September 6, 1918.

17. Wood, *1918*, 286; Deveney, *The Original Curse*, 172.

18. Deveney, *The Original Curse*, 175.

19. Gilbert King, "A Death at Home Plate," Smithsonian.com, May 9, 2012, www.smithsonianmag.com/history/a-death-at-home-plate-84826570/.

20. Deveney, *The Original Curse*, 177; Creamer, *Babe*, 176.

21. Creamer, *Babe*, 176–177; Stout, *The Selling of the Babe*, 82; Keene et al., *The Babe in Red Stockings*, 210.

22. Ruth as told to Considine, *The Babe Ruth Story*, 66.

23. See Creamer, *Babe*, 174–176; Seymour and Seymour, *Baseball: The Golden Age*, 254; Fountain, *The Betrayal*, 53; Deveney, *The Original Curse*, 178–179.

17. IN GOD'S HANDS

1. *NYT*, September 9, 1918.

2. When the Red Sox appeared in the World Series in 1915 and 1916, the team played its home games at Braves Field; *BG*, September 10, 1918.

3. *BHJ*, September 10, 1918.

4. *BHJ*, September 10, 1918.

5. *NYS*, September 10, 1918.

6. *BP*, September 10, 1918; *NYS*, September 10, 1918.

7. Creamer, *Babe*, 178–179; Stout and Johnson, *Red Sox Century*, 131; George M. Young, "The Players' Brief Strike," in *The Reach Official American League Base Ball Guide* (Philadelphia: A. J. Reach Company, 1919), 196; *BA*, September 10, 1918.

8. *BG*, September 10, 1918; Wood, *1918*, 321.

9. *BA*, September 10, 1918.

10. Wood, *1918*, 323–324; *BHJ*, September 11, 1918.

11. Creamer, *Babe*, 180.

12. *BHJ*, September 11, 1918.

13. Young, "The Players' Brief Strike," 198.

14. *BG*, September 11, 1918.

15. *BG*, September 11, 1918; *BP*, September 11, 1918.

16. Crosby, *America's Forgotten Pandemic*, 46; *BET*, September 10, 1918; *BP*, September 12, 1918.

17. *BHJ*, September 17, 1918; *BP*, September 17, 1918; Barry, *The Great Influenza*, 186–187; Carol Byerly, *Fever of War: The Influenza Epidemic in the U.S. Army During World War I* (New York: New York University Press, 2005), 75.

18. Barry, *The Great Influenza*, 187–190; Byerly, *Fever of War*, 75.

19. Barry, *The Great Influenza*, 232–237.

20. L. S. Block, "The Invisible Enemy of 1918," *Yankee*, February 1982, 112; *BET*, September 18, 1918; *BP*, September 18, 1918.

21. Albert Marrin, *Very, Very, Very Dreadful: The Influenza Pandemic of 1918* (New York: Knopf, 2018), 88–89; "How To Fight Spanish Influenza," *Literary Digest*, October 12, 1918, 13.

22. Edward Robb Ellis, *Echoes of Distant Thunder: Life in the United States, 1914–1918* (New York: Kodansha, 1996), 464, 467–468; *BA*, September 19, 1918; *BG*, October 2, 1918; Marrin, *Very, Very, Very Dreadful*, 95–98.

23. Block, "The Invisible Enemy of 1918," 116; *BA*, September 20, 1918.

24. Marrin, *Very, Very, Very Dreadful*, 107; Francis Russell, "A Journal of the Plague: The 1918 Influenza," *Yale Review* 47 (1957–1958): 219–235.

25. *BG*, September 26, 1918, September 27, 1918; *BP*, September 25, 1918, September 26, 1918; *BHJ*, September 27, 1918, September 28, 1918.

26. Crosby, *America's Forgotten Pandemic*, 48–49.

27. Karl Muck to Charles Ellis, October 3, 1918, NA, RG 407, Box 23, Folder "Muck, Karl"; Charles Ellis to Karl Muck, October 15, 1918, NA, RG 407, Box 23, Folder "Muck, Karl"; Posselt, "Prisoner of War No. 3598," 321; Yockelson, "The Ghosts of Ft. Oglethorpe," 56.

28. *BP*, October 5, 1918, October 6, 1918.

29. Harries and Harries, *The Last Days of Innocence*, 389; Zieger, *America's Great War*, 164; Slotkin, *Lost Battalions*, 369; *BP*, October 9, 1918; *NYS*, October 9, 1918.

30. *BG*, October 9, 1918; *BP*, October 9, 1918; *NYS*, October 9, 1918; Slotkin, *Lost Battalions*, 370.

31. *NYH*, October 3, 1918; Slotkin, *Lost Battalions*, 370; *NYTR*, October 4, 1918.

18. "WHETHER YOU'LL HEAR FROM ME AGAIN I DON'T KNOW"

1. Mastriano, *Thunder in the Argonne*, 2–5, 26–32, 173–176.

2. Edwin Lewis, "In the Argonne's Mist and Mystery," *The American Legion Weekly*, September 26, 1919, 8; Lengel, *To Conquer Hell*, 85–86.

3. Lewis, "In the Argonne's Mist and Mystery," 9, 29; Miles, *History of the 308th Infantry*, 122–123.

4. Arthur McKeogh, "The Lost Battalion," *Collier's*, November 16, 1918, 5.

5. Mastriano, *Thunder in the Argonne*, 51–58.

6. For the Foch-Pershing exchanges, see Mastriano, *Thunder in the Argonne*, 173–177.

7. Mastriano, *Thunder in the Argonne*, 167–177.

8. For the orders' path down the chain of command to Whittlesey, see Laplander, *Finding the Lost Battalion*, 149–161.

9. Lengel, *To Conquer Hell*, 224; Miles, *History of the 308th Infantry*, 148.

10. Laplander, *Finding the Lost Battalion*, 255–255.

11. Laplander, *Finding the Lost Battalion*, 256–257.

12. Charles Whittlesey, "Report of Operations [of the] Lost Battalion," 77th Division, 308th Infantry, October 9, 1918, NA Record Group 120, Box 37; Joe McCarthy, "The Lost Battalion," *American Heritage*, October 1977, 89.

13. Miles, *History of the 308th Infantry*, 148–150; Lengel, *To Conquer Hell*, 225–226.

14. Gaff, *Blood in the Argonne*, 140–142; Robert H. Ferrell, *Five Days in October: The Lost Battalion of World War I* (Columbia: University of Missouri Press, 2005), 15–16; Mastriano, *Thunder in the Argonne*, 183–187.

15. Gaff, *Blood in the Argonne*, 144.

16. Lengel, *To Conquer Hell*, 226.

17. Mastriano, *Thunder in the Argonne*, 183–187.

19. INTO THE VALLEY OF DEATH

1. Charles Whittlesey, "Report of Operations [of the] Lost Battalion," 77th Division, 308th Infantry, October 9, 1918, NA Record Group 120, Box 37; Miles, *History of the 308th Infantry*, 351.

2. Nelson M. Holderman, "Operations of the Force Known as 'The Lost Battalion,' From October 2 to October 7, 1918, Northeast of Binarville, in the Forest of Argonne, France," American Battle Monuments File, NA Record Group 117, Box 10.

3. For George McMurtry, see Laplander, *Finding the Lost Battalion*, 158–161; Gaff, *Blood in the Argonne*, 131–132.

4. Miles, *History of the 308th Infantry*, 152.

5. Mastriano, *Thunder in the Argonne*, 187–189.

6. For Nelson Holderman, see Laplander, *Finding the Lost Battalion*, 247–248; Gaff, *Blood in the Argonne*, 151.

7. Holderman, "Operations of the Force Known as 'The Lost Battalion,'" 15; Whittlesey, "Report of Operations."

8. Whittlesey, "Report of Operations"; Holderman, "The Operations of the So-Called 'Lost Battalion,' Oct. 2nd to Oct., 8th, 1918," NA Record Group 165, War College Division and War Plans Division, Box 5. The study contains the messages Whittlesey sent from the Pocket.

9. Miles, *History of the 308th Infantry*, 153–154.

10. Miles, *History of the 308th Infantry*, 154.

11. Miles, *History of the 308th Infantry*, 156.

12. Miles, *History of the 308th Infantry*, 156. Miles's chapter on the Lost Battalion is attributed to Lieutenant Colonel Whittlesey and Major McMurtry but was actually written by Captain Edwin Lewis, a member of the 308th Infantry and a journalist in civilian life.

13. Ferrell, *Five Days in October*, 26.

14. Mastriano, *Thunder in the Argonne*, 190–194.

15. Gaff, *Blood in the Argonne*, 165–166; Miles, *History of the 308th Infantry*, 157.

16. Holderman, "The Operations of the So-Called 'Lost Battalion'"; Miles, *History of the 308th Infantry*, 157.

17. Miles, *History of the 308th Infantry*, 158–159.

18. For the friendly-fire episode, see Laplander, *Finding the Lost Battalion*, 432–448; Gaff, *Blood in the Argonne*, 174–178.

19. Holderman, "Operations of the Force Known as 'The Lost Battalion,'" 24; Laplander, *Finding the Lost Battalion*, 434.

20. Laplander, *Finding the Lost Battalion*, 437–439, 443–445.

21. For the air drops, see Ferrell, *Five Days in October*, 59–61; Mastriano, *Thunder in the Argonne*, 199–200.

22. See Warren Kinston and Rachel Rosser, "Disaster: Effects on Mental and Physical State," *Journal of Psychosomatic Research* 18 (December 1974): 445–446.

23. Slotkin, *Lost Battalions*, 346–347; Thomas M. Johnson and Fletcher Pratt, *The Lost Battalion* (Lincoln: University of Nebraska Press, 1938, 2000), 131.

24. Holderman, "Operations of the Force Known as 'The Lost Battalion,'" 29; Slotkin, *Lost Battalions*, 339.

25. Slotkin, *Lost Battalions*, 340; Johnson and Pratt, *The Lost Battalion*, 130–131.

26. Johnson and Pratt, *The Lost Battalion*, 131–132.

27. Johnson and Pratt, *The Lost Battalion*, 185.

28. Holderman, "Operations of the Force Known as 'The Lost Battalion,'" 31–34; Slotkin, *Lost Battalions*, 353–354; Johnson and Pratt, *The Lost Battalion*, 222.

29. Holderman, "Operations of the Force Known as 'The Lost Battalion,'" 33.

30. For the surrender note, see Gaff, *Blood in the Argonne*, 238–244.

31. Holderman, "Operations of the Force Known as 'The Lost Battalion,'" 35.

32. Holderman, "Operations of the Force Known as 'The Lost Battalion,'" 35.

33. Mastriano, *Thunder in the Argonne*, 203.

34. Miles, *History of the 308th Infantry*, 168–187.

35. For the arrival of relief, see Johnson and Pratt, *The Lost Battalion*, 252–257.

20. "PLEASE DON'T WRITE ABOUT ME"

1. John Franklin Gilder, ed., *Americans Defending Democracy: Our Soldiers' Own Stories* (New York: World's War Stories, 1919), 335–336; for a good description of the rescue, see Gaff, *Blood in the Argonne*, 252–253, and Laplander, *Finding the Lost Battalion*, 615–616.

2. Gilder, ed., *Americans Defending Democracy*, 336.

3. Laplander, *Finding the Lost Battalion*, 617.

4. For the fullest treatment of their meeting, see Laplander, *Finding the Lost Battalion*, 617–620.

5. Gaff, *Blood in the Argonne*, 354; Laplander, *Finding the Lost Battalion*, 619.

6. Robert Alexander, "The Siege of the Lost Battalion," in Miles, *History of the 308th Infantry*, 254; Laplander, *Finding the Lost Battalion*, 620.

7. Laplander, *Finding the Lost Battalion*, 626; Robert Alexander, *Memories of the World War 1917–1918* (New York: Macmillan and Company, 1931), 230.

8. Laplander, *Finding the Lost Battalion*, 627; Alexander, *Memories of the World War*, 230; Ferrell, *Five Days in October*, 80; Gaff, *Blood in the Argonne*, 256–258; Slotkin, *Lost Battalions*, 362.

9. Johnson and Pratt, *The Lost Battalion*, 306; Laplander, *Finding the Lost Battalion*, 629–630. Johnson claims he asked the question; Laplander reports that Irwin did. We used Johnson because he was there.

10. Johnson and Pratt, *The Lost Battalion*, 306–307.

11. Damon Runyon, "Runyon Sees Return of Lost New York Battalion," in A. Scott Berg, ed., *World War I and America: Told by the Americans Who Lived It* (New York: Library of America, 2017), 609 (published in the *New York American*, October 13, 1918); Laplander, *Finding the Lost Battalion*, 631.

12. Runyon, "Runyon Sees Return of Lost New York Battalion," 608–609.

13. *NYS*, October 11, 1918.

14. *BG*, October 12, 1918.

15. Runyon, "Runyon Sees Return of Lost New York Battalion," 608; Slotkin, *Lost Battalions*, 372–373.

16. Miles, *History of the 308th Infantry*, 173–175.

17. Emmet Crozier, *American Reporters on the Western Front 1914–1918* (New York: Oxford University Press, 1959), 254–255.

18. *PE*, November 15, 1918; *NYT*, November 15, 1918; *NYEW*, November 15, 1918; *BG*, November 15, 1918.

21. ARMISTICE

1. Aram Goudsouzian, "All Gods Dead: Babe Ruth and Boston, 1918–1920," in *The Rock, The Curse, and the Hub: A Random History of Boston Sports*, ed. Randy Roberts (Cambridge, MA: Harvard University Press, 2005), 14; Stout and Johnson, *Red Sox Century*, 134.

2. *CT*, October 5, 1918; Wood, *1918*, 344.

3. Wood, *1918*, 344.

4. Stout, *The Selling of the Babe*, 93.

5. *Lebanon Daily News*, September 30, 1918, October 14, 1918; Keene et al., *The Babe in Red Stockings*, 215, 219; "Baltimore, Maryland, the American Influenza Epidemic of 1918–1919: A Digital Encyclopedia," www.influenzaarchive.org/cities/city-baltimore .html#.

6. *NYT*, October 16, 1918; *BG*, October 15, 1918, October 17, 1918, October 20, 1918, October 22, 1918.

7. *BP*, October 21, 1918.

8. *Forty-Seventh Annual Report of the Health Department of the City of Boston for the Year 1918* (Boston: City of Boston Printing Department, 1919), 44; Barry, *The Great Influenza*, 4–5, 238–239.

9. *BG*, January 20, 1918; Montville, *The Big Bam*, 60.

10. Wagenheim, *Babe Ruth*, 45–46.

11. Kennedy, *Over Here*, 231–232; John Hohenberg, *Foreign Correspondents: Great Reporters and Their Times*, 2nd ed. (Syracuse, NY: Syracuse University Press, 1995), 116.

12. *NYTR*, November 8, 1918; *NYS*, November 8, 1918.

13. Kennedy, *Over Here*, 232; *BG*, November 11, 1918.

14. Thomas Gowenlock, *Soldiers of Darkness* (New York: Doubleday, 1936), 265.

15. *BG*, November 11, 1918, November 12, 1918.

16. Russell, *A City in Terror*, 7.

17. *PE*, November 12, 1918.

18. *BG*, November 12, 1918, December 31, 1918; Edmund Bowles, "Karl Muck and His Compatriots: German Conductors in America During World War I (And How They Coped)," *American Music* 25 (Winter 2007): 440, n93.

19. Bowles, "Karl Muck and His Compatriots," 425–426; Posselt, "Prisoner of War No. 3598," 317.

20. Posselt, "Prisoner of War No. 3598," 317.

21. Anita Muck to Isabella Stewart Gardner, June 12, 1919, Isabella Stewart Gardner Museum Archives.

22. Anita Muck to Charles Ellis, June 3, 1918, BSO Archives; "Memorandum For Mr. O'Brian Relative to Dr. Karl Muck," April 16, 1919, NA Record Group 60, Box 30, Folder 9-5-542; Karl Muck to Siegfried Wagner, April 25, 1919, BSO Archives; Karl Muck to Carl Huebscher, Counselor of the Legation of Switzerland, July 19, 1919, NA Record Group 407, Box 23, Folder "Muck, Karl."

23. Karl Muck to Isabella Stewart Gardner, October 27, 1921, Isabella Stewart Gardner Museum Archives.

24. *BP*, June 25, 1919.

25. Turk, "The Case of Dr. Karl Muck," 74; *BG*, August 22, 1919.

26. *NYT*, August 22, 1919; *BG*, August 22, 1919.

22. THE REVOLUTION

1. Goudsouzian, "All Gods Dead," 17.
2. Montville, *The Big Bam*, 82.
3. Montville, *The Big Bam*, 82–83.
4. *NYT*, March 19, 1919; Creamer, *Babe*, 187.
5. *NYT*, April 19, 1919.
6. Montville, *The Big Bam*, 93–94, 97; Creamer, *Babe*, 206.
7. Creamer, *Babe*, 207; Stout, *The Selling of the Babe*, 174.
8. Goudsouzian, "All Gods Dead," 23; *NYT*, July 31, 1919; *BG*, August 26, 1919; Creamer, *Babe*, 200.
9. *BG*, September 20, 1919, September 21, 1919.
10. *NYT*, September 25, 1919.
11. Creamer, *Babe*, 205; *BG*, November 4, 1919.
12. Paul H. Douglas, "Wages and Hours of Labor in 1919," *Journal of Political Economy* 29 (January 1921): 78–80; Wehrle, *Breaking Babe Ruth*, 47.
13. Montville, *The Big Bam*, 103; Stout, *The Selling of the Babe*, 157–159, 177; Daniel R. Levitt, Mark L. Armour, and Matthew Levitt, "History Versus Harry Frazee," *The Baseball Research Journal* 37 (2008): 29–32.
14. Stout, *The Selling of the Babe*, 163, 179–180.
15. Edward Grant Barrow with James M. Kahn, *My Fifty Years in Baseball* (New York: Coward-McCann, 1951), 108; *NYT*, January 6, 1920; Creamer, *Babe*, 208; Stout, *The Selling of the Babe*, 181–182.
16. *BP*, January 6, 1920.
17. Creamer, *Babe*, 212.
18. Stout and Johnson, *Red Sox Century*, 154.
19. Seymour and Seymour, *Baseball: The Golden Age*, 356–357.
20. Bryson, *One Summer*, 128–130.
21. Seymour and Seymour, *Baseball: The Golden Age*, 427.
22. Marshall Smelser, "The Babe On Balance," *American Scholar* (Spring 1975): 301; Seymour and Seymour, *Baseball: The Golden Age*, 426–427.
23. Benjamin Rader, *Baseball: A History of America's Game*, 3rd ed. (Chicago and Urbana: University of Illinois Press, 2008), 124–128.

23. HOMECOMING

1. *BP*, May 1, 1919.
2. Gaff, *Blood in the Argonne*, 258.
3. *PE*, November 20, 1918.
4. *PE*, November 12, 1918.
5. *PE*, November 20, 1918.
6. For Whittlesey's Williams Club address, see *NYS*, November 22, 1918; *NYT*, November 22, 1918; Wood, ed., *Williams College in the World War*, 67.
7. *NYT*, January 22, 1919.
8. *BG*, December 25, 1918; *NYT*, December 25, 1918; *BP*, December 25, 1918; Wood, ed., *Williams College in the World War*, 67–68.
9. For the armory speech, see *NYS*, December 12, 1918; *NYT*, December 16, 1918; Louis Untermeyer, "A Seditious Hero," *The New Republic* (December 28, 1918), 253.
10. *NYT*, January 27, 1919, June 24, 1919.

11. *NYT*, October 12, 1920, October 26, 1920; Martin C. Langeveld, "Missing in Action: Charles W. Whittlesey's Farewell," *The Monday Evening Club*, March 9, 2009, http://mondayeveningclub.blogspot.com/2009/03/missing-in-action-charles-w-whittleseys.html.

12. For Whittlesey's health, see Laplander, *Finding the Lost Battalion*, 654–655; Langeveld, "Missing in Action."

13. *NYT*, October 2, 1919.

EPILOGUE: "A MISFIT BY NATURE AND BY TRAINING"

1. For the selection of the casket, see *NYT*, August 13, 1942; Gaff, *Blood in the Argonne*, 283; Patrick K. O'Donnell, *The Unknowns: The Untold Story of America's Unknown Soldier and WWI's Most Decorated Heroes Who Brought Him Home* (New York: Atlantic Monthly Press, 2018), 285–294; Matt Blitz, "Who Is Buried in the Tomb of the Unknown Soldier?" *Today I Found Out*, www.todayifoundout.com/index.php/2015/03/buried-tomb-unknown-soldier/.

2. Sources differ on the color and number of the roses. Later in life, Younger said he placed one red rose, but sources closer to the time of selection indicate a clutch of white or pink and white roses.

3. *NYT*, November 10, 1921.

4. *NYT*, November 12, 1921.

5. *NYT*, November 29, 1921.

6. For Harding's speech and the description of the ceremony, see *NYT*, November 12, 1921.

7. *NYT*, November 29, 1921; Slotkin, *Lost Battalions*, 478.

8. *NYT*, November 21, 1921, November 27, 1921, November 29, 1921.

9. *NYT*, November 29, 1921.

10. *NYT*, December 1, 1921. The exact order of his schedule for the Thanksgiving week is uncertain, and accounts differ in some details.

11. *NYT*, November 30, 1921.

12. *NYT*, November 29, 1921.

13. *NYT*, November 29, 1921.

14. *NYT*, November 30, 1921.

15. *NYT*, November 29, 1921, December 2, 1921.

16. *NYT*, December 1, 1921.

17. *NYT*, December 1, 1921.

18. Charles Whittlesey to Bayard Pruyn, n.d., Whittlesey Papers, Williams College Archives.

Index

Randy Roberts is the 150th Anniversary Professor and Distinguished Professor of History at Purdue University. An award-winning author, he focuses on the intersection of popular and political culture, and has written or co-written biographies of such iconic athletes and celebrities as Jack Johnson, Jack Dempsey, Joe Louis, Bear Bryant, Oscar Robertson, John Wayne, and Muhammad Ali, as well as books on the Vietnam War, the Alamo, the 1973–1974 college basketball season, and West Point football during World War II. Roberts lives in Lafayette, Indiana.

Johnny Smith is the Julius C. "Bud" Shaw Professor of Sports History and Associate Professor of History at Georgia Tech. He is the author of *A Season in the Sun: The Rise of Mickey Mantle* (with Randy Roberts), *Blood Brothers: The Fatal Friendship Between Muhammad Ali and Malcolm X* (with Randy Roberts), and *The Sons of Westwood: John Wooden, UCLA, and the Dynasty That Changed College Basketball*. Smith lives in Atlanta, Georgia.